Ingrid Schubert

Letters from Prison
1970-1977

Presented, with Comments, by Her
Family and Some Former Comrades

Translated and edited by
Gerti Wilford and Jo Tunnard

PM

HER
SPL
EBE
DEB

Ingrid Schubert: Letters from Prison 1970–1977
© Gerti Wilford
This edition © 2025 PM Press and Kersplebedeb
© Gerti Wilford and edition cimarron 2022 for the German original

ISBN: 979-8-88744-108-5 (paperback)
ISBN: 979-8-88744-117-7 (ebook)
Library of Congress Control Number: 2024943073

Translated and edited by Gerti Wilford and Jo Tunnard

Photo credits: private collection (Hedwig Schubert's photo album), Manfred Stiebel Photography Koblenz, released police images

Cover by John Yates / www.stealworks.com
Interior design by briandesign

10 9 8 7 6 5 4 3 2 1

PM Press
PO Box 23912
Oakland, CA 94623
www.pmpress.org

Printed in the USA.

Contents

"Nothing moved forward, nothing changed, the systems of oppression became clearer and clearer, starting with the family and spreading to society, the State, the ruling system, power. It was crushing, and one was still sitting there, rubbing one's fat belly while applauding those who had understood it long ago and who had taken up the struggle—against the oppression of all minorities—at the international level. And at some point, I understood that I had to be consistent in my beliefs and decisions."

—Letter from Ingrid from Lehrter Strasse Prison, Berlin, 3 November 1970

Thoughts About My Sister

My sister Ingrid Schubert was one of the first members of a revolutionary group in Germany that later called itself the Red Army Faction (RAF). The group operated mainly during the 1970s and 1980s. The letters included in this book are from the seventies, up to the death of some of the original group, including Ingrid, in 1977. Ingrid's reasons for joining the group are outlined in her second letter in the book. She was imprisoned in Berlin in 1970. After several moves between prisons, explained here in the letters and the Timeline, she died a violent death in Stadelheim Prison, Munich, on 12 November 1977.

Shortly before her death, my sister wrote her last letter to me. She was expecting that we would see each other soon, because my visit to her had been approved for 26 November. She wrote: "A few of the external conditions have changed in a way that I can breathe again without asking myself why".

During the previous weeks, Ingrid had been held in isolation, in conditions of extreme sensory deprivation: alone in an unheated, white-tiled basement cell, with constant artificial light, no external sound, one high window covered by a mesh screen, where she had contracted bronchitis. Following the lifting of a complete ban on external contacts imposed on the prisoners, a visit from her father and the intervention of the prison doctor, Dr Steirer, Ingrid was moved to a warmer cell in the main section of the prison. She could breathe more easily, and, as we learned later from her lawyer, she was thinking of applying for a transfer back to Preungesheim Prison in Frankfurt, where she had been held briefly before being moved to Stammheim Prison in Stuttgart and then Stadelheim Prison in Munich.

The transfer did not happen, nor did my planned visit. I saw her last on the evening of 12 November, laid out in a mortuary. She had been found hanging from the window of the cell she had been moved to after talking with the prison director that afternoon. Our brother was with me. Ingrid looked peaceful, but very pale and serious. It was not a farewell but something much more final.

Today, over forty years later, it is still not clear how she came to such a violent end. Every attempt to understand it has failed. Only one thing is certain to me: had she not been so totally isolated in that white cell in that empty prison unit, I would be able to ask her, because she would most probably still be here. Perhaps one day things will become clearer. In the meantime, it is important for me, and for those who knew her or knew her background, to provide some sort of testimony of her experience as a politically orientated prisoner interacting with the prevailing national and international political conditions. This is the purpose of publishing these letters.

Today is another time, and Ingrid would probably argue and act differently from the way she did then. But how differently can only be guessed, because, despite huge global change, social and political conditions remain fundamentally unchanged.

These letters indicate how an alert, intelligent and politically aware person, when confronted with extreme circumstances, must keep responding to them in order to preserve her integrity. The struggle of the political prisoners to preserve their collective identity in the face of escalating isolation and their commitment to risk their lives during several hunger strikes demonstrate the strength of their convictions.[1]

---

1   References to solitary confinement and special isolation units bear witness to how prisoners from the RAF and other political prisoners were isolated from each other and from other prisoners right from the start of their incarceration. Most prisoners from the RAF were held in different prisons from one another or held in different sections of the same prison. Many experienced solitary confinement or imprisonment in a dedicated high-security unit. The cells around theirs might be empty. They might be denied contact with others during "exercise time," when prisoners could leave their cell and walk around the prison courtyard for half an hour or an hour. Their contact with people from the outside was also limited, mainly to family and lawyers. Family visits had to take place in the presence of police officers who recorded conversations and often forbade certain topics. With each new attack by armed groups in Germany or abroad, the political prisoners were searched and deprived of their radio, newspapers and contacts.

Some prisoners, including Ulrike Meinhof, and Astrid Proll before her, were held in total isolation in an acoustically isolated section of Cologne's Ossendorf Prison.

Not everyone can understand this. The letters reveal how the struggle triggered utmost desperation and lack of understanding within our family. I heard the same from relatives of other prisoners from the RAF. These are important to note because they are the same tensions experienced by other prisoners and families in similar situations in other countries. The inhumane prison conditions that Ingrid wrote to me about were the subject of critical reports and campaigns by families and friends, as well as by Amnesty International and others.[2]

This section was a "silent wing," known in German as *Toter Trakt* (dead wing) on account of the deadly silence prevailing there. Cell walls and furniture were painted white. A bare neon light burned continuously. Meagre daylight came through a narrow slit too high up to see through. The cells were designed so that no external sound could penetrate them.

Later in the struggle, some of the political prisoners were allowed to come together at times, and for a while Ingrid joined her friends in the high-security unit of Stuttgart's Stammheim Prison, before being totally isolated again in Munich's Stadelheim Prison. Subsequently, the use of isolation was reduced, although some political prisoners continued to be kept isolated in small groups in various high-security units.

The prison conditions led the political prisoners to resort to collective hunger strikes, which they did on ten separate occasions, each lasting weeks or months. Taking control of their bodies in this way, along with specific demands to end the use of isolation and sensory deprivation, empowered them to challenge the inhumane prison regimes imposed by the authorities. The prisoners were influenced in this approach by others, particularly the Irish prisoners in the UK whose organisation of hunger strikes highlighted the importance of acting collectively, not just to gain support for their cause but also to disseminate information about their situation. The hunger strikes fuelled the growth of protest movements and calls for protecting the rights and safety of political prisoners. For example, local committees were established to challenge the use of isolation torture in prison and, later, the International Committee for the Defence of Political Prisoners in Western Europe (IVK) took evidence from the prisoners' relatives and others who were concerned about Germany's response to the prisoners' struggle. See the Endnote.

2   The isolation strategies used against political prisoners in different countries were condemned as inhumane by Amnesty International, and the strategy of total sensory deprivation was described as torture, because these were tactics devised to break the prisoners' collective identity and make them renounce their political stance. In relation to the situation of political prisoners in Germany, Gerti had contacted Amnesty in London, and Paul Oestreicher, then Chair of Amnesty's British Section, agreed to investigate. For some time, beginning in mid-1973, he was in regular contact with the Federal Prosecutor's Office and the Stuttgart High Court's State Security Chamber trying to mediate on behalf of the prisoners over their demands for an end to solitary confinement and other isolating practices. Over time, the prisoners from the RAF grew disillusioned with Oestreicher's apparent closeness to the authorities.

Amnesty's work in Germany continued, prompted by people involved in its German section and others campaigning in their local communities. In its 1974 report on prison conditions, Amnesty appealed to the authorities to cease their use of isolation. In 1977, at the end of the period covered by Ingrid's letters, its annual

The letters included here represent only part of Ingrid's corre-spondence. I have focused almost exclusively on her letters to me because I didn't want to include those to other family members with-out their consent, and some relatives—including our parents—are no longer alive. The letters don't constitute a real exchange either, as almost all my letters to Ingrid no longer exist, but I hope that my occasional footnotes will help clarify the conversation we were having.

I also hope that the letters will prompt further questions and discussion. For me, they offer insights into a young woman's life at a particular time in history and in a particular place in the world. She looked to the future positively, with courage and confidence, but had no illusions about the uncompromising power structures in our society. She experienced these in prison, and she wrote about the importance of staying alive to their consequences and of understanding the dividing line between the prisoners and the guards in authority over them. Her letters are, above all, lively, self-critical and humorous, much like herself.

I can hear her voice as I write.

Who Was Ingrid?
Ingrid was the youngest of four children. When she was born on 7 November 1944, I was seven, our sister Helke five and our brother Klaus two and a half.

Earlier that year, in spring 1944, we had fled from the Saarland, in the west of Germany, where we had lived until then. The Allied Forces were closing in, and my parents decided it would be best to wait out the end of the war further to the east, in Unterfranken, living with our father's older brother and his wife in our grandfather's house in the village of Maroldsweisach, near Bamberg. Our grandfather was then in his eighties, our uncle and aunt had no children and were willing to share their relatively spacious house with us. In the village, we were considered "Saarländer" and "city people" and were treated as strangers,

---

international report on prisoners and human rights included a critical analysis of the prevailing conditions in both parts of Germany. In relation to the RAF, Amnesty expressed its concerns "about some aspects of prison conditions in the Federal Republic of Germany, particularly regarding solitary confinement and isolation practices". Amnesty's 1977 report was also critical of special legislation limiting the right to legal representation in court proceedings. See *Amnesty International Report 1977* (London: Amnesty International Publications, 1978, 249–53; available at https://socialhistoryportal.org/sites/default/files/raf/0019770900_02_0.pdf).

which was difficult for us older children. A few miles further east was what later became the border between East and West Germany, and we children were warned not to stray too far into the woods. We never knew what might happen if we did, and we harboured wild fantasies about the "Russians", who seemed to be the new enemy. Ingrid, of course, was too young to notice any of that.

Our father was rarely there. He had been a member of the National Socialist Party and had risen in their ranks as an administrator and loyal party member. He had been the mayor of several towns, most recently Metz, in Alsace-Lorraine, which was occupied territory. During the last months of the war, he and other men from the village were ordered "to defend the Reich to the last man". I remember this as an odd phrase, because there seemed so very few men about anyway. We saw little of him, because he still had work in Metz and the Saarland. And then one day he wasn't there at all; we learnt that he and other men had been taken prisoners of war. As a result, we were surrounded mainly by women, older children and people from Poland who, as I found out much later, had been forced to come and work as labourers on the farms and in local industries. Our uncle, for instance, had two or three men who helped with his wholesale grocery business.

This was a very confusing and unsettling time for us children, especially when it was announced, early in 1945, that the Americans, as victors in the war, were coming our way. White sheets were hung out of windows, but the villagers fled to their vaulted storerooms built into the surrounding hills, and there we stayed for some nights until we dared emerge again. It was a long walk along the road back to the village, and we were a straggling column of women, children and a few older people. Ingrid sat in her pram, looking around with curiosity, and we walked alongside her and our mother, fascinated by the army tanks and the generally young soldiers in khaki uniforms who smiled down at us from their high vehicles in the middle of the road, some of them men with black skin. We had never seen people of colour before, nor people with such wide smiles and white teeth. Were we supposed to respond to their greetings? Should we take the chocolate they offered us? Were they not our enemies? Quite a dilemma, that none of the adults seemed to notice. We got back to the village, where more white sheets had been hung from windows and door frames. Everybody was very quiet. How should we children behave towards this friendly enemy?

During the following weeks and months, we found solutions, each in our own way. I don't have many detailed recollections of this time, either of Ingrid or my other siblings, nor of my mother, except that she was always there for us. Sometimes she took Ingrid or another of us by train to her parents in the Saarland where, thanks to the French occupation, one could buy luxury goods—nylon stockings, real coffee, cigarettes—which could then be bartered for essentials. Illegal practices, including smuggling, were common, but people also cared for one another and stuck together. Although I trusted our mother, I was always happy once we had crossed the border without a problem. Today, I know that we owe much of our current inner sense of security to our mother and the family surrounding us, because even when she was away from us we knew that she was always thinking of us and cared about what was happening to us.

I don't know exactly when our father was released from the prisoner-of-war camp. He and Ingrid didn't know each other, and we had all become a bit estranged. He developed a progressive and debilitating skin disease, and things got more complicated in ways I did not understand but that were probably related to his illness and his emerging depression. I remember how life in the village protected us from the worst effects of the defeat in war. We always had enough food, and slowly our father found work again. Klaus, Helke and Ingrid went to the local primary school, where each class filled one or two rows, as portrayed in the photo in this book, where Ingrid sits in the second row and Klaus in the back one. As the eldest, I was sent to boarding school. I travelled by train at the start and end of each term until 1948, when the devaluation of our currency meant that the family's funds were running out, and I had to leave.

Many years later, after Ingrid's death, I visited her friend Brigitte Mohnhaupt several times in different prisons. She told me that once when they were together in Stammheim Prison in Stuttgart they had exchanged childhood stories, and that Ingrid remembered her father selling fish from a wooden cart. That's exactly how it was: after his release and once he felt better, he and some friends from the village managed to get hold of fish, which they smoked and sold. They also somehow reproduced the famous "rollmops" which were made with pickled herring. I still remember the smell of that fish.

We moved to Wiesbaden in 1951, and two years later to Koblenz, where we lived above the factory that our father had helped establish. Here they produced the washing powder Rei, famous at the time for its slogan "use the detergent in the morning, have the afternoon free" (*morgens rei, mittags frei!*). This became a family joke; it was our first lesson in the power of advertising. Our father was director of the factory until it was taken over by Procter & Gamble.

For Ingrid and our brother, the best years of their youth started at that time, as Klaus told me later. They attended their respective high schools, had a large circle of friends and went to the many parties and dancing lessons that had just picked up again. Ingrid experienced less parental control than we older sisters had at the same age. She had her brother as protector and "guardian", although, as we learnt subsequently, Ingrid became distanced from Klaus after she met and fell in love with Larry. Ingrid refers to some conflict around this time (see her letter of 3 November 1970).

My memories of these first few years in Koblenz, as "normal life" developed again, are not the happiest. Financially, it was very hard, because everything was in short supply. The mutual help and cama-raderie and the foraging and planning that mothers and fathers had been so good at during the chaotic years after the war were now less evident: people withdrew into their private worlds, and the losses from the war and the urgent need to rebuild lives took priority.

During the 1950s, the smug German middle-class mentality against which Ingrid reacted so strongly, the effects of which she pointed out in the letter to her brother mentioned above, was establishing itself again. I felt a growing wish to change my life and get away from it all. I followed a friend to London, where I met my future husband, whom I married in 1959.

When Ingrid visited us in London with a friend in 1962, I noticed in her the first signs of a similar rebellion and dissatisfaction with post-war German society. As with teenagers generally, the dissatisfaction was vague, but it was perceptible and quite strong at times. During later visits and meetings in the 1960s, her political views were influenced by world events, particularly those in the USA, and we often discussed—but never for long enough—her and our growing awareness of the impact of the last war: of its consequences, including the initial partition of

Germany and the subsequent erection of the Berlin Wall.[3] There was almost total silence in society about the war crimes and the Holocaust. There was also silence within our family about what had happened, for which increasing evidence was becoming available. But we didn't challenge our parents, and we avoided asking questions. Was this out of respect for them? Or was it our unease about the truths that we suspected and that remained largely unspoken? Or that were ridden with guilt and shame? Whatever the reason, pressing practical needs always came first.

Ingrid had chosen to study medicine at the University of Bonn. It was during her practical internship at a psychiatric clinic that I first heard her sharp criticism of the German health system and of what she described as its unfair class system. We met Larry, by then her boyfriend, who was also studying medicine and who seemed to have influenced her, especially politically, or so we assumed within the family. He later denied this, saying that Ingrid was by then well able to form her own opinions. After her first diploma, she moved to Düsseldorf, and later joined Larry at the University in Berlin, where both became active in the community, trying to help those who had become addicted to drugs. Ingrid and Larry lived together in several shared apartments, and they participated in discussions and activities of the Left, in which Germany's role in the Vietnam War was hotly debated. The worldwide revolt against this war, against colonialism and against persistent and ongoing racism actively engaged her and the many others who wanted fundamental change. Some became increasingly militant, believing this to be the only effective way of gaining recognition for their cause.

Ingrid was an energetic person with an abundance of humour, sensitivity and a thirst for action. She describes in her letters how fed up she was with endless discussions and inactivity. She met Ulrike Meinhof, at the time an influential and respected journalist whose

---

3   World War II left Germany divided in two. The western half was the Federal Republic of Germany (FRG), shaped by the Western allied forces of France, the UK and the USA. The eastern half was the German Democratic Republic (GDR), shaped by the Russian occupying forces. In 1961, the East German government built the Wall that divided East and West Berlin. It was built to prevent large numbers of the workforce from leaving East Germany. The Wall was symbolic of the Cold War that now split the world into two systems: capitalist and communist. The Wall and border posts throughout Germany remained in place until 1989. See Eric Hobsbawm, *The Age of Extremes* (London: Abacus, 1994), 225f.

far-reaching criticism of West Germany's socio-political system in the early 1960s had been well received by the Left, old and young alike. Ingrid started to work with Ulrike and several other activists, all of whom wanted to bring about real and radical change. There were plenty of precedents for arguments to attack the powers in place by armed struggle, but none of us had the slightest idea that Ingrid was beginning to get involved in this form of action.

After Ingrid's final State examination in medicine, which she passed with a good grade, we shared our last time together in Koblenz. It was Easter 1970. As we walked in the local woods, she mentioned to me her plan of delaying work as a doctor, because she wanted to settle some more important things first. She hinted at the possibility of going underground, which frightened me. I didn't really believe her, and I tried to argue that this could turn out to be highly dangerous and self-destructive. But Ingrid was a person with strong inner convictions; she could distance herself emotionally if it seemed necessary, and she did so without giving up her love for people, friends and her family in particular. As mentioned earlier, her first letter from prison, to our brother and his wife (3 November 1970), explains her thinking and the beliefs that made her act the way she did. Despite the doubts she struggled with, which she never denied, she remained consistent in her beliefs.

My prison visits to Ingrid were always an uneasy mix of total joy, much laughter, uncertainty and discussion, infused with infinite sadness, pain and anger. Despite the constant presence of guards, the short time we spent together was always precious. From her and the other prisoners I learnt about the unsparing, inexorable circumstances of the situation they faced, and about the absolute necessity for prisoners to preserve their own personal integrity. One mustn't surrender to the system; rather, one must be conscious at all times of the dividing line between oneself as an individual and the machinery of surveillance and control. As Ingrid wrote:

> In the attempt here to create an artificial unity between prisoners and guards—who are dependent on each other and, therefore, need to work with each other—the entire project shows its limitation, the fact that some people are prisoners and some are guards and there's nothing in between. It is the front, and that's what

they try to obscure in every way possible + they succeed in so far as the prisoners don't see through it. That makes sense. The result is totally broken people who comply to the utmost degree. (Letter from prison in Frankfurt, early May 1976)

I was terrified, scared for her, as were so many others, particularly our mother. In her way, she tried to help improve things but was met only with Ingrid's angry reactions: she could not stand these "bourgeois" methods of securing improvements in conditions and engaging with the authorities through mediation or by being "friendly". To Ingrid, it was about us choosing a side.

The letters show how important the children in the family were to her—the nieces and nephews she wrote to and who she wanted to see. Our elder son visited her once with me in the prison in Berlin. And my brother and I visited her in Stammheim Prison in 1976 with four of the six children in the family, an occasion when nobody really knew what to say to each other. After that, she and I saw each other one or two more times before her transfer to Munich in August 1977. As far as I remember, the visits took place with a glass partition between us. It was terrible. Neither of us wanted this kind of contact and our correspondence grew more complicated. I found or kept fewer letters from her during that time, but I remember several requests for money and a lot of frustration between us. Her voice sounded less familiar, a bit more distant. At the time, I ascribed this to her new environment in Stammheim Prison. I concluded that this was important for her, because this was now her world.

Stammheim was an impossible environment,[4] a completely alien experience, hard for us to process or understand in any way. In retrospect, I should perhaps have tried harder to reach her, but I didn't know how to do that without running the danger of alienating her completely.

Throughout all these years, we remained close but also at times infinitely far apart. To me, and to most of the families, the time of the hunger strikes and the absolute determination with which they were conducted was the most difficult thing to comprehend. The prisoners'

---

4   Stammheim Prison: At this prison in Stuttgart, a special isolated section to hold the political prisoners was constructed inside the prison building. See sketches of this section, page 225. In addition, a special courtroom for hearing the trials against the prisoners was built on the prison site. See the Endnote.

relatives met frequently,[5] and our mother went to those meetings to gain a better understanding. She, who always lent a helping hand, who always had ideas for resolving bad situations, now felt stunned and helpless in the face of people—including her daughter—who harmed themselves by denying themselves food.

Ingrid understood these feelings; she knew how she and others affected their families. Soon after her arrest, she wrote to our grandmother and our parents: "The sorrow I'm causing you all is certainly unforgivable but think of prison as not being the end… in here you grow very strong, in here you find the substance in yourself that allows you to remain alive."

Her closest friends during these years in prison were her comrades: they knew each other best, and they shared their experiences, as well as their thinking and strategies, through their information system (the *info*) of letters and messages,[6] facilitated by their lawyers and friends. As the prisoners affirmed repeatedly, their common experience of being imprisoned, locked up and powerless, left them inwardly free and collectively supported.

---

5   The relatives' group was an important source of comfort for the parents and siblings of individual prisoners and a means of sharing solidarity as the prisoners struggled against the conditions imposed on them. Over time, the group and those associated with it met with greater frequency to exchange information and for mutual support. They often had a public presence, increasingly so after the first prisoners' hunger strikes in 1973. For example, they led demonstrations calling for the release of the prisoners, or association time for them, and they occupied the offices of the United Nations in Geneva and of the International Committee of the Red Cross in Geneva and Brussels. They also organised sit-ins and demonstrations in media offices and other venues. See the Endnote.

6   The *info* became the platform for discussion between the prisoners from the RAF. Letters were photocopied and circulated to the prisoners by lawyers' mail. In her witness statement of 3 August 1976 at the Stammheim trial, Ingrid defined the *info* as follows: "Information as a weapon—used like this because information creates consciousness, and because in isolation it's a struggle for consciousness. The *info* as a surrogate for communication and as a survival programme for totally isolated prisoners—continuity of the collective learning process". The *info* was also used as an exchange forum to prepare for the trials and for discussion with other political prisoners. It was subsequently banned, and some lawyers were charged and imprisoned for helping to distribute it. A book with excerpts from the *info* reveals the strength of the prisoners' collective approach: Pieter Herman Bakker Schut (ed.), *das info, briefe von gefangenen aus der raf aus der diskussion 1973–1977* [The *info*: Letters by Prisoners from the RAF, from the Discussion 1973–1977] (Kiel: Neuer Malik Verlag, 1987). See the Endnote.

My decision to make Ingrid's letters available to her family and friends is the result of many talks with relatives, friends and those young people who knew her background and wanted to know more. I hope the letters clarify some things but also lead to new questions and thoughts.

I thank my brother and sister, my other relatives and Ingrid's friends who are still alive, for their contributions, their support and their collaboration in collecting and checking the letters. Without their advice and positive criticism, I would never have come this far. Any inaccuracies or mistakes remain, of course, my own responsibility.

Gerti Wilford, September 2015

Postscript December 2023

Since the first (private) publication of Ingrid's letters in 2015, a second German edition has been published, and I have now translated Ingrid's letters and reports for this edition. I could not have done so without the invaluable help of my co-editor Jo Tunnard. Jo lived in Nicaragua in the mid-1970s, in the run-up to the overthrow of President Anastasio Somoza's regime by the Sandinista National Liberation Front. For this book, she corrected my somewhat idiosyncratic language and helped me preserve the tone of Ingrid's thoughts and words. Exploring the nuances of my German and her English brought home to us the challenge of translation: understanding all the possible meanings of words and expressions in one language and selecting the best fit available from the other. Our aim throughout has been to stay true to the sense and spirit of Ingrid's letters, while also finding the right words and sentence style to bring to life for English readers the passionate principles, the keen wit and the sisterly friendship that marked our seven-year prison conversation.

We would both like to thank Janet Allbeson for her very constructive scrutiny of our manuscript. Janet lived in Berlin during the 1970s, and she remembers the witch hunts in the media and the "wanted" posters in town. Her detailed comments and astute questions helped us improve our understanding of some key issues.

In addition, the editors of the German original have been happy to discuss the text and provide valuable suggestions throughout. They wrote an endnote for the German edition that has been included here.

Its authors knew Ingrid and, like her, spent time in prison, including long periods in isolation. Their contribution is based on their own experiences and brought a new dimension to our work.

The response to the private publication had indicated that a broader readership might be interested in these experiences from a particular period of European, and German, history. One valued friend, Professor Dr Eia Asen, who had been a medical student in Berlin at the same time as Ingrid but had not known her wrote, "I can imagine Ingrid through her letters, high-spirited and almost alive… maybe we even met throwing tomatoes at the Shah of Persia during the demonstration against him. I believe your book could give much to a larger circle of readers, and you should think seriously about how it could be published more widely in Germany. It is part of our history too".

This edition also includes memories and reflections from Ingrid's niece Susanna Wilford, throwing some light on the role that Ingrid played in the family and the importance of knowing more about her. From the English side of the family and our friends, it was mainly the younger generation who had encouraged the translation of the letters, as by then they knew about the period of decolonisation, the Vietnam War and the post-war conflicts that involved and affected people everywhere. The RAF had formed itself in ways similar to other organisations opposing existing systems, often with the use of force and the threat of loss of lives. It is instructive to see the ways in which the movement was influenced by other political conflicts in Europe and elsewhere and the different ways in which political prisoners were treated.

My sister would now be close to eighty, and I think she would not be surprised by the current conflicts throughout the world. We would still be able to understand each other, perhaps even better than before. She was deeply upset by the loss of her closest friends in prison, but she was planning to organise her future, and she was fighting to rebuild her sense of integrity. Her last words to me spoke of hope, not despair. She did not want to die, as her lawyer and the prison doctor testified. Both had seen her during those last days, and they had found her to be positive and looking towards her future. She wanted a transfer so she could continue her studies. Nothing indicated that she might want to take her life. I cannot believe in this so-called suicide.

One might try to find other meanings for this loss of life. Ingrid and her companions wanted to bring about changes in society by using revolutionary means, which failed to bring the results they hoped for. But they did succeed in raising questions and calling institutions to account in their specific context. They challenged the legitimacy of State power, and they were crushed (or attempts were made to crush them), as Ingrid and others described in their reports of what was happening while they were in prison. Their deaths are not that surprising, really, but their lives are, as was their persistence in continuing with their struggle for survival. The struggle is now carried on by others in different ways in Europe and across the world.

We have had to live with the fact that Ingrid is no longer here, is no longer alive, except in her letters and in our memories.

Ingrid's Letters and Reports

Note: The letters benefit from being read in conjunction with later sections of the book: Remembering Ingrid, the Timeline of events during the period she writes about, and the Endnote by the editors of the German edition.

Letters 1970

Ingrid is arrested in October with four others when a Red Army Faction safe house is raided by police. While two of those arrested (Monika Berberich and Brigitte Asdonk) are sent to different prisons in West Germany, Horst Mahler is incarcerated in Berlin. Ingrid and Irene Goergens are also held in Berlin, in the Lehrter Strasse Prison for women. Their arrest confronts them with the reality of being locked up for twenty-three-and-a-half hours a day, with very few or no opportunities to socialise with each other or with other prisoners. In these early letters, Ingrid explains why she is part of the group and how its members can maintain their collective identity while held in different places.

29 October 1970

Dear Gerti,

COME, when you have time, but not immediately, as our mother was here yesterday.

Ingrid

P.S. Would be best on a weekday, it's easier then because of the visit permit. Take a taxi straight to the Moabit Criminal Court in Turmstrasse and ask for Judge Weiss. Ask him for a permit for a longer visiting time, and I'll do the same from here.

Love to all!

3 November 1970

Dear Klaus, dear Moni,[1]

The DM 50 that arrived today reminded me that I might perhaps be able to describe to you how a relatively sheltered daughter of the bourgeoisie could become a jailbird.[2]

You asked me if I could hate, and I can assure you that I hate the bourgeoisie. For now, let's leave this sentence as it stands. I can tell you that this hate began rather early, so early that you yourself experienced it without understanding it.

It started early in my development, and you witnessed it. But you didn't realise that it was not merely the attack of an adolescent against parental and fraternal authority (to me you were the epitome of a petit bourgeois), although it may have looked like that. No, for me it was an outpouring of tremendous rage against the false and phoney morals and the set of rules for proper conduct laid down by the middle class.

It seemed no more than youthful anti-authoritarian protest, manifesting itself in my nonconformity while remaining very much part of the Establishment. Being a bourgeois, I managed to take many liberties, and there were lots of them, but I took them secretly, always. And although I began to hate the lie, the game played out according to middle-class rules, I still carried on doing what I wanted, thinking that this was part of the process of emancipating myself from the shackles of my class. But I *only* procured advantages for myself. And the anger I felt when I realised that the rules of the bourgeoisie require lies and secrecy—something I never identified precisely—meant that I became convinced that I had to reject my middle-class background completely.

I realised that it wasn't enough to detach myself as an individual from the rotten morals of the exploitative middle class. I had to do something proactive against their focus on material things; their obsessive dedication to acquiring and increasing their assets; their craving for law and order; their prying, snubbing and destroying; their attitude of "I will only give you something if you give me something in

---

1   Ingrid's brother and his wife Monika.
2   Deutsche Mark, the German currency at the time (1DM equivalent to approximately 0.50 pounds/dollars).

return"; their dull and contented "I'm alright Jack"; and their jostling and pushing for the best place. Pages could be written about all this.

The apparent liberality in our society—it is, of course, possible to emigrate—is a relevant detail of the machinery of oppression used by those in power, but I understood this only when I grasped the relationship of the bourgeoisie to the working class. Oppression, which up to this point I saw only in the context of the individual, I now began to understand in the wider context of the proletariat. I understood that this damned rubbish (outlined above) had been stamped onto the working class for centuries and presented consistently as the only goal worth striving for. It's no wonder that this has led to the complete "degeneration" we have today.

But wait, I'm still talking about the phase of my passive resistance. This began when the protests got underway for everyone. The resistance had kicked off earlier, but initially I'd played my part by attending demonstrations and teach-ins, trying to find my voice by zealous shouting. I remained passive because I continued my life as a private person, securing myself a good standard of living, now based on shared housing. I was a mixture of active and silent collaborator, plagued by a permanent guilty conscience, because the loathing for those in power that grew within me only ever manifested itself verbally or by my acting as a "bogey of the middle classes".

My study of medicine,[3] which I'd started with such nebulous ideas, became useful when I provided medical assistance in the underground movement.[4] In the meantime, I'd become quite certain that I didn't want to practise this noble profession in a hospital or private clinic, even if I could act there in a humanitarian way. The string of frustrations, inevitable in an environment of fussy and painstakingly detailed and reformist work, could only undermine my personal position, not to mention the problems I would encounter with the existing and dominant system. So life went by in fantastic surroundings which afforded every liberty, with cool people and all the comforts the underground offered, up to a time when everything seemed to degenerate into neurosis: we emptied the flat and waited for it to fill up again, and the

---

3   Ingrid finished her medical studies at the Free University of Berlin in 1970.
4   In this case, the "underground" refers to West Berlin's counterculture scene during the 1960s.

dissatisfied and "we-don't-know-what-to-do" people increased steadily, and they repeated the same petty-mindedness and complacency that I so hated.

The uninspired political scene wore itself out in pompous words and discussion spectacles, and its rigidity pissed me off in a big way. Nothing moved forward, nothing changed, the systems of oppression became clearer and clearer, starting with the family and spreading to society, the State, the ruling system, power. It was crushing, and one was still sitting there, rubbing one's fat belly while applauding those who had understood it long ago and who had taken up the struggle— against the oppression of all minorities—at the international level. And at some point, I understood that I had to be consistent in my beliefs and decisions.

To come back to your question. I don't hate the middle class as individuals, not at all. I love human beings, but I hate the system which forces the individual to live by these basic rules. Still, hatred is the wrong word.

The second question is: "What will come of it?" I guess I can only answer that when I'm out of here; we can't ignore that there's something like censorship over here.

I'm not sure why I'm sending this outpouring to you of all people. If you think it's appropriate, send the whole thing to Koblenz,[5] and from there to England,[6] so I don't have to write so much again. And I'm not sure whether this has made anything clearer.

Greetings to your little family.

Ingrid

12 November 1970

Dearest Sister, it always takes a while until the letters get through, and then it takes time for me to get the urge to write again. In here, I'm constantly busy, but life passes in different and contradictory phases. And at the moment I'm again finding it rather difficult to say something

---

5   The hometown of Ingrid's parents.
6   Where the Wilford family lived: Ingrid's sister Gerti, her husband Michael and their
    children Marcus (ten), Christopher (seven) and Susanna (five).

right or of any importance. A letter I wrote to Klaus the other day flowed much more easily. I hope he'll let you read it.

It's difficult to bridge the worlds between us and help you grasp what is incomprehensible. Words! Dear me, how much has been said and written, and what has really been achieved? How little has really been done. Yes, everybody says that something must be done, and then immediately shrugs their shoulders, asking "but how?", resigned in the face of the monster that is capitalism. Shackled by the system, constantly oppressed, and yet, believing themselves to be free, they carry on because they don't know any other way.

Of course, life is good, one can enjoy everything, one is young, it's possible to help here and there—and so what? What do you change by doing this? Everything is aimed at personal satisfaction. Everyone can call my bluff by asking me for a clear answer. That leaves me apprehensive and on my guard. Clearly, I must think about all this much, much more.

Do me a favour, all of you. Don't say you're thinking of me all the time. I know you can't help it; it is after all very frightening, too terrifying and new, but it honestly makes me feel really uncomfortable. I am doing splendidly. I don't feel like a martyr or anything of the sort. I would rather you see yourselves as my friends, not family in the sense of having to fulfil obligations, because that for me has negative undertones. I'm less than ever prepared to make compromises, which, of course, results in an uncomfortable life.

Dearest, the last few sentences are not directed at you so much as those in Koblenz. Please come if you have time. You can bring *nothing* except books and clothes, and I have plenty of the latter, so make it just books. Or money, not for myself but for the fund set up for all political prisoners who are in prison without money, and there are many of them.

Shower your family with kisses.

Your Ingrid

9 December 1970

Dearest,

Opened my eyes again at last and decided it's time to write. Must say that half the time I'm sitting in this hellhole with my eyes closed, mainly because I don't want to see the same image before my eyes, also because I can concentrate better with my eyes shut.

When I'm sitting on the chair with my feet on the table next to the radiator and facing my window, I can see the reflection of the upper floor window bars in the two large windows of the wall in front. When I'm sitting at the head of the bed underneath my window, I look at the door, which is now quite colourful but still indescribably ugly. The spyhole is an act of sheer impudence, so I painted over it.

I'm still waiting for the typewriter to come, as I can't bear my own messy handwriting any longer. But I really want to write to you now to explain the calamity with the hack lawyer.[7] You couldn't have known what sort of lawyer he really is, and I didn't recognise it either. Besides, he wasn't really necessary at all. In short, he's not only one of those underhanded scoundrels but is also a hack; even the other lawyers refused to work with him because of his arrogant manner. I'm jolly glad to have escaped the fiasco of working with him. I've concluded that I don't have to rely on recommendations at fourth, fifth or even sixth hand and that I should never ever work again with lawyers who conform to the system. I do hope he'll send your money back without deductions. I'm certain all of this was well meant, but the whole affair was completely pointless. Please trust us to turn the matter around.[8] Over and done with.

More substantial thoughts fit for publication haven't come to mind so far. Inspiration from books is still lacking too. I study some medicine every so often and paint a little, and, apart from that, I get enraged to the core with the way I get churned by this perfidious prison machinery. There's a difference between understanding something intellectually and experiencing it directly. The more direct the experience, the more direct one's reaction. What used to be an accumulation

---

7   A lawyer in Berlin whom the family in England engaged for Ingrid, not knowing that an early decision by the prisoners from the RAF was to work only with trusted lawyers.

8   A reference to Kristine Sudhölter, Ingrid's chosen lawyer.

of knowledge about things, an intellectual structure, now sort of fills itself with substance. Not that what one sees here wouldn't be "that bad after all", but, on the contrary, now I can see how bad it really is. Incomprehensible? I refrain from more detailed comment on the subject.

A frequently quoted sentence from Cleaver:[9] "It's time for each and everyone to decide whether they want to be part of the problem or part of the solution." Such phrases aren't gospel truths, of course, but this one does provide food for thought about what the problem is and what's the solution, and eventually a decision must be reached. "Modern" human beings show a certain sense of pride when believing, without giving it much thought, that they are part of the solution; after all, they are well-respected and responsible citizens. But what would they say if you asked them where, in their opinion, the problem actually lies? Ostentatious displays of political colours and emblems are indeed hideous and don't contribute at all to a solution—they only fog and befuddle you from concentrating on relevant issues.

Damn, I do need a typewriter. I'm using my knees as a writing desk at the moment—not very comfortable.

I imagine you'd actually benefit from four weeks in a cell, away from your domestic chores and your gaggle of children. There's an easy way to get inside. You approach this project with the mentality of a down-and-out looking for a place to stay in the winter, and you get to know a suspicious person, maybe a lawyer or a columnist, and you wreck their car. Then you become a suspect, ready to be locked up. Endless chains of suspects can be produced in this way, given that staying in unsavoury living conditions is a suspicious activity, with every dwelling with mattresses on the floor deemed to be a "commune". The bourgeoisie's abhorrence must be nourished constantly. Berlin is a strange city, even more so from the perspective of a prison, and especially a prison like this, with a marble entrance.

I just came back from my evening small talk with the comrade who lives two storeys above, so my hands are stiff from the cold. I really don't want to imagine summer in the clink.

---

9   Eldridge Cleaver, a member of the Black Panther Party leadership in the 1960s and
early 1970s.

Now for something from literature. Brecht said, "It's better to rob a bank than to own one". This maxim won't feature on the wall above my bed, but still…

We have a priest here who is ill with asthma and has snow-white hair. He's an old social democrat and thinks he knows Marx. He always wants to know who the spiritual leaders are, the current Jesus prophets, and where they stand. I can only shrug my shoulders, but apart from that the old man is okay.

My lack of concentration allows me to weave only fragments of sentences. Blame it on the lack of protein. It's the same problem with hair loss, both typical conditions of prisoner ill health. I'd love to wolf down a two-pound steak, British of course. The grub here gets on my nerves. At first it was quite exciting to have a warm meal every day— never mind what it was—but now that excitement has gone. We have a wonderful shopping facility here, we call it Neckermann.[10] We can buy eggs, but it's totally impossible to make them edible as there are no cooking appliances. Oh well, enough of this drivel, it's getting a bit boring.

Irene was taken to a different prison by the henchmen of justice (note the rage in my tone of voice!), where they are giving her a really bad time.[11] With the intention of implementing "educational proce-dures", they keep her in isolation, to be "soft-boiled" and forced into submission (cleverly capitalising on the fact that she's only nineteen). And because we are not the kind of people who say, "Oh well, things are what they are, and we can't do anything anyway". We will do some-thing… hush, Allah have mercy on my door.

I hope the opportunity will arise to write something more serious. Before then I'd like to congratulate you on Christmas. Well, that's the wrong thing to say, it's nothing to do with congratulations. Have a great hop around the purple tree in the company of all your little frogs and super toad. You know *I* don't care about having to spend this cookie-and-cake feast in the clink. Of course, at home there will be a more critical tone, but they've assured me that I'm in safe hands here. Cool

---

10 A popular mail order company. The prisoners used its name for their shopping in prison because they had to tick items off a list, like ordering from the Neckermann catalogue.

11 Irene Goergens was arrested with Ingrid. Ulrike Meinhof had made a film with her called *Bambule* (Mutiny) about her experience of institutional care.

or what? (Sentences like this have always made my hair stand on end, even if you understand their point of view, whatever that might be.)

Must stop. I don't know what to do with myself right now, so I won't be able to write anything much of significance. There won't be any Christmas presents from me, but what's new? Nothing much came from my side anyway. I could send a little piece of my blue-and-white prison bedcover to Susanna as my contribution to pop art, but maybe I'll be able to think of something more appropriate for her tender age.

Heavens, I've got galloping madness. Now get real, throw yourself into your messed-up bed, lights out.

👄 👄 👄 👄 👄—these are kisses, one for each of you.

Ingrid

12 December 1970

Indeed, my dear sister, you got the wrong end of the stick completely. But don't worry, you can't help it. (Sorry, I still have no typewriter and my biros are all used up.)

The three points you emphasised in your last letter have been partly answered and I want to stress that:

1. In no way is Irene in a better situation than I am (you all are so quick to judge everything, without a clue about how things really are).

2. I need an experienced but really *neutral* lawyer (I'm not even convinced of that, would just like to know what their allegations are really based on, so certainly not this "slimebag", whom I only heard about later).

3. That's what Kristine will be doing.

So hopefully that's now clear. And the whole thing shows that you can't do anything else for me other than send books and letters. Okay?

A word about Irene: she has known the whole system of repression and oppression better than any of us, so she's very clear on where she stands; she doesn't "make" enemies, she just reveals them as such. And we won't feel treated "unjustly"—we are submitted to a class system of justice, a judiciary that is determined by the ruling class. We don't judge by moral or ethical standards but think in a political way; we don't, for instance, consider help as something that serves our own interests only. First, there are no "our own" interests, and, thus, second, help can only be what doesn't contradict the common interest. Help is a completely ugly word because it presupposes helplessness and pity for the "victim". These are completely false categories for people who define themselves politically and would never pity themselves. Being alone is something of the past (at one time it sometimes drove me half crazy). Angela Davis, some two thousand miles away in a New York prison,[12] is as close to me as my neighbour in the next cell or as comrades in Berlin, Munich or elsewhere. Letters, parcels and money, that's not "help". I don't know, goes without saying, maybe not. It's a kind of help at least.

This shit biro has stopped writing; it's done for today.

More another time.

Kiss,

Ingrid

16 December 1970

16 December in the year of the clink. Hello to the whole sparrow family. Christmas can be red or green or yellow. Perhaps even white. Where you are, it's probably grey but beautiful. Be happy and have fun, and I'll do the same.

Your books arrived only yesterday, and then I spent the evening lying on the floor, a real gag. When you fold your legs in such a way that they are crossed and you bend down to achieve the desired result, meaning the nose touching the knee, you suddenly no longer know what to do next, should you breathe in or out? You suddenly have to stop, to check your book for how to continue. Thank God I spent most of the past years on the floor in similar positions and can, therefore, be proud of the fact that I am not quite so Western in my decadence. I also seem to have had some early foresight about the healing effects of headstands, which was really clever on my part: Do you remember

---

12   Angela Davis, an academic and political activist in the United States, was accused of helping Jonathan Jackson try to free his brother George Jackson and other prisoners from the Soledad Prison by taking hostages in a court. See Ingrid's letter of late September 1971. Davis was held in prison for over a year before being acquitted of all charges. See also the reissue of her 1974 autobiography edited by Toni Morrison, with a new introduction by the author about its relevance today: Angela Y. Davis, *An Autobiography* (London: Penguin Books/Hamish Hamilton, 2022).

how in Wiesbaden the entire family soon began to stand around upside down and how we began to somersault all over the place? I wanted to join the circus then.

As far as childhood memories go, it was my happiest time, I think, having recently tried to reflect on those years.[13] There wasn't much, although everyone surely tried their best, but my main memory about education, for instance, was an unconditional belief in authority, be it teacher, priest, chef or anyone else with a Dr title. But let it be.

Can only type with my left hand; the right wrist is a right mess for now. Refused to take my break unless my comrade gets her shopping allowance and open-air break and unless they take off the shameless wire netting in front of her window. Two pigs were there in an instant, twisting my arms and wrists. Running battle here—am hearing from the corridor "come, come, show me, you aren't allowed to pass anything on, give it to me… oh, okay, it's a Catholic newspaper, you can pass that one on".

As to the books, Sweezy is indeed a difficult chapter.[14] Once you see the numerous x y z u v squares you begin to feel quite weak, but they really are for economists only. And because all my life I've read books in a very unfocused manner, I stick to the well-known underlining to get certain fixed points. You can't say all of that isn't new. Maybe it is, but the issue isn't settled like that, because what's important isn't what's new but the consistent understanding of each individual step. For instance, "The production produces the consumption: 1) by providing its material, 2) by determining the manner of consumption, and 3) by arousing in the consumer the need for the products already produced as objects. Thus, the production produces the object of consumption, the manner of consumption and the urge for consumption." It means that the demand isn't determined by the consumer but by the income relations, which in turn reflect the production relations. So the big advantage of the

---

13 The family lived in Wiesbaden for two years, after moving there from the country-side. Living in a town, with Gerti attending a larger elementary school, was a new beginning for the whole family after years of change. They stayed there, in an airy and light basement flat with direct access to the surrounding garden, before moving to Koblenz.

14 Paul Sweezy, economist, co-founder of the Marxist journal *Monthly Review*. Ingrid's copy of his *Theory of Capitalist Development* (German edition *Theorie der kapitalistischen Entwicklung* [Frankfurt: Suhrkamp, 1970]) is held in the Stammheim Library at the International Institute of Social History in Amsterdam.

"free" capitalist market economy, the interplay of supply and demand, is mere pretence because the consumer doesn't determine anything but is, in fact, being determined.

One shouldn't forget that Marx's works constitute an analysis and not an instruction manual for practical action, something one would so dearly like to have, so we could at last be able to participate in the solution to the problem. Read something else, for instance *Seize the Time* by Bobby Seale and the books by Frantz Fanon, like *The Wretched of the Earth* about the Third World. And Marcuse, *One-Dimensional Man*. He provides very good analysis, though somewhat literary. I'd also read Cleaver, *Post-Prison Writings*. I'd like to read these too but so far nothing has arrived, not even Lukács. Maybe those out there are on holiday.

Larry arrives punctually every fortnight,[15] looking like a well-worn corpse. He works as much as ever, like a madman, compensation for frustration, but still in the belief that he is quite happy. (This machine is really quirky.)[16]

The Christmas parcel from our parents has just arrived, I'm drowning in cookies. But as soon as the stuff arrives one loses all appetite, having previously licked all ten fingers in anticipation. I'll have to write back immediately, it's a really wonderful parcel. I've already tried sending them a Christmas letter, but truly, it's not easy. My hand is now okay. So a temporary goodbye until we write again.

Ringa Ringa Roses. Bye bye.

Ingrid

29 December 1970

Hellooooo. Except for the fact that no Christmas songs can be heard from downstairs, nothing much has changed. I mean that it doesn't matter whether it's a holiday or not. What has changed is my position. I'm breathing high-altitude air, if breathing is the right word. Am now on the fourth floor, with a better view over the sports stadium and rooftops. We no longer see the world striped by bars. The view is now checkered instead, thanks to some fine wire netting.

---

15   Larry, Ingrid's partner during the 1960s, who had also studied medicine.
16   A reference to sticky typewriter keys.

Collective punishment for expressions of anger. Which had no effect, of course. So all fourteen of us political prisoners awaiting trial started a hunger strike, though the men, cowards that they are, stopped after six days (had they known in advance how tough the Christmas chicken was, they'd certainly have continued).

Why? We demand the reinstatement of our basic democratic rights. Sounds good, no? And says nothing about the anger about the load of letters, books and newspapers that are not coming through, the non-existence of free choice of visitors, the fact that some of us have been subjected to forced gynaecological checks after visits from our lawyers, etc., etc. Nothing worked, naturally. The status quo remains, and we are as fed up as before, up to the hilt. The alarming thing is the sense of progressive stupefaction, which is certainly perceptible. Aware of the danger of such a condition, one tries to subvert the monotony of time in here by increasing the number of distractions: getting up late, refusing breakfast, refusing to do what is asked, making unusual requests, etc. The function of such irregularities is clear. We need to find ways of increasing our capacity to concentrate. You might assume that it would be easy in here, but that's fiddlesticks. Reading three pages makes you fidgety; you have to jump up, but in the knowledge that this is totally useless, because eventually you will have to sit down again.

Hey, this isn't a lament. I'm fine, as before: no breakdown, no sadness, no hopelessness, only a quivering impatience or something similar, the feeling that something should happen.

By the way, yoga is quite good in this situation. Have become a perfect master, without book or trick, although the complete state of bliss to be attained like this remains doubtful. Ooff, somehow my wit is lacking today, have lost that little touch, the sparkling spark. Huxley, well, yes.

I was outside just now—with a bit of snow even the barbed wire looks passable. It was probably installed so that we don't leap across it, from our standing position, just like that: the wall on the wall, a Berlin of walls and barbed wire.

I'm hungry, damn it. The entire Christmas parcel has already been wolfed down, without me gaining even an ounce. In here, a comfortable sense of hunger in the morning develops into the most voracious gluttony by night (what luck there's nothing left). Pure hunger as compensation for lack of love. It doesn't mean you can't make love fantastically in the morning too. But here, never—not mornings, not evenings, nor ever any time. Simply never. This too is part of basic rights.

As for books, send me what you think will be suitable. I'll order the ones I want, as it's quicker and better from here. Yet nobody can speak of speed; it's always an eternity before anything I order arrives. Ah, here comes the meatloaf, or baked breadcrumbs more like. A brief interval—horrid. These frustrating attempts to compensate quality with quantity.

The thoughts don't flow. I could bore you with all sorts of stuff, of course, but it would be like the food, quality abolished. So I turn to the books with a nod towards the bed.

Also, should you talk to Koblenz, please try and point out gently but firmly that the basic contradiction starts with the clothes they send. In a word, they shouldn't send me anything to *wear* again; it just takes up space. I'm telling you this because I've just written to them and forgot to mention it. (I simply *cannot* put those pullovers on.) Full stop.

Eva[17]

Oh sorry, I forgot, it's your birthday. Or should we not mention it? No matter how old, the bones still fit together (you should try some yoga, you'll notice how stiff you are). Flowers and kisses to you separately.

---

17 Ingrid's middle name, and the one she was known by in Berlin. In prison, her friends also called her Eve or Nina, as is the case in some of their testimonies in the Remembering Ingrid section of this book (p. 187).

Picture for the children in England, late 1970 or early 1971

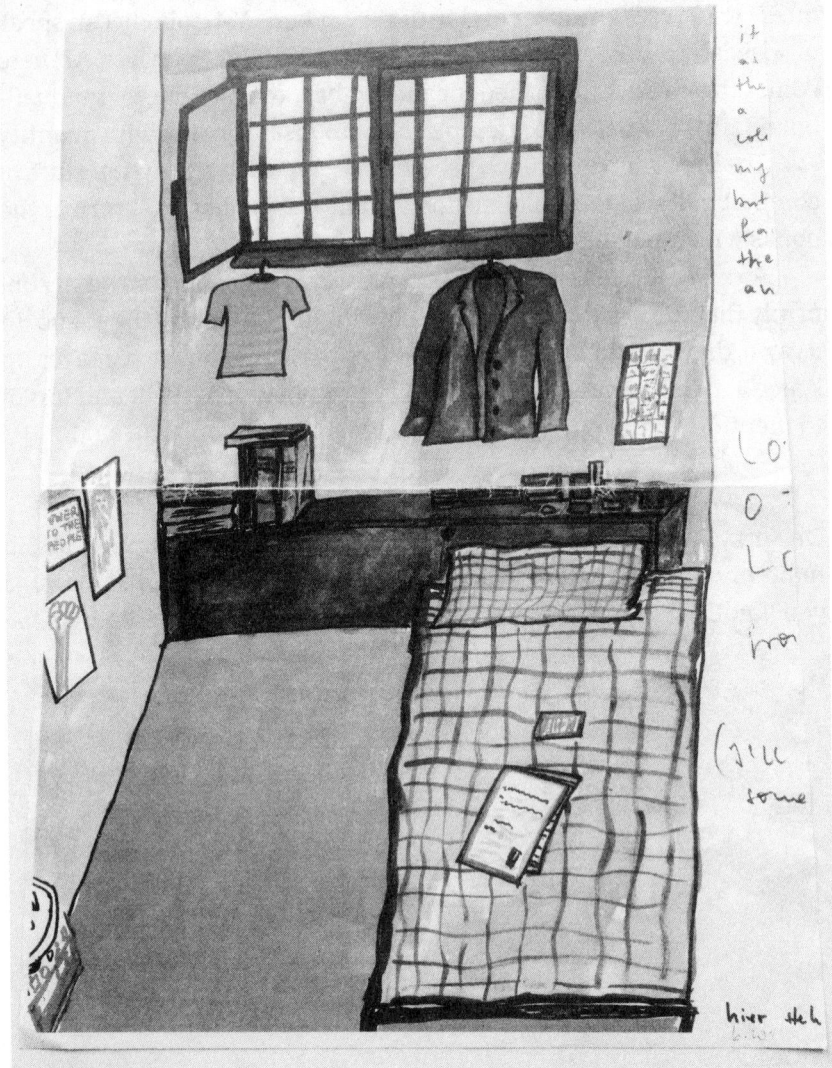

Ingrid's original drawing was a bright combination of pink, blue, orange, purple and green ink.

Text in the margin

It seems like there's lots of colour in my cell but, in fact, there isn't any. Lots of love from Ingrid.

Letters to Her Niece Susanna

... AND READ ... AND READ....

AND READ.....

UNTIL

UUUGH!

... SO I DECIDED TO WRITE
TO MISS "BROKEN-LEG"
AND HERE WE ARE
WITH MANY KISSES TO THE MISSES.

Dear. Susanna !

the whole world   a big
colour pot. And a lot of
love. Don't you think so? Many
thanks. for the easter-pictures. I got
them (→ 🐰 🐰 🐰 🐰 ,, – the whole lot
of them) in my room now at the
wall. I never found out where all
these bunnies come from. And to which
place they go. — so I guessed, they do not
exist. — What about your hair? Is it
as long that you can sit on it? Mine doesn't

die Banane hab ich mal gemalt. laß sie dir schmecken

ALL ALL ALL LOVE TO THE BOYS ♡

grow any more, doesn't get enough fresh air.
All day in this tiny room, you know.
I would really like to see you all again,
you and the boys and Daddy. Mummy I saw
a fortnight before. I think, I won't see you
before you are all grown up. You must
send me some new pictures of you all and
your friends ! Will you ?
What about school ? chrrrrchch. silly
question. And teachers are half as clever
as they try to seem to be. Uff. — I send the
letter to England, because I think you are home
again.   Many many thousand million
              KISSES   from Ingrid

DEAR SUSANNA, [drawing] told me, that you are soooo clever

so sure you know, that ⭕ is round and that △ has 3 corners, but can you solve this problem:

What did one wall say to the other wall? *

I dou... ...

If you find the answer, you will get

6 000 000 000 kisses. Can you count that with your [hand drawing]? I would like more, to send

you a [camel drawing], but this animal is extremely seldom in Germany. Same

...ble with [elephant drawing] So I hope you have

a very very big birthday party with

[drawing of children]

and a ... of Opa's wine

and a big kiss

from Ingrid Uschi

LOTS OF LOVE
FROM DOOPY
my little
man-in-the ear
friend

* Meet you at the corner!

Letters 1971

Early in the year, Ingrid is moved to the prison for men in Moabit (West Berlin), to be closer to where the trial against her (and others) will be held. The regime here is more punitive, with most of the day spent in solitary confinement. She writes about not allowing herself to be defeated and about turning the instinct for self-preservation into a positive force. She is transferred twice more during the year, first returning to Lehrter Strasse Prison from March to May, and then back again to Moabit Prison in October.

5 January 1971

Dear Sister, when in prison, never write a letter when you're in a bad mood. I must have disregarded this maxim when I wrote last time, so my letter must have been a terrible piece of work. I believe I did mention your birthday, but apart from that I spoke only about food. No hard feelings, I hope. Just now I'm in a more cheerful mood, no obvious reason why, but that can change from second to second, and it's probably caused by the fact that I register everything with a magnitude that's often overwhelming. I don't wait for letters, but, nevertheless, I'm happy when some arrive, and they do sometimes contain hilarious things. Tell me, what does Larry write to you? This is an amazingly difficult topic, and it took me a week to wrestle with it. It also prevented me from having a look at the lovely books. Now I've got a few steps further with our relationship, and that's good for him as well.

I thought I'd explained the "Studier" thing well enough by my hints,[1] but it looks like I must try again. First, if a lawyer comes and suggests it's best to make a confession (of what, actually?) without having had a look at the files, even if his argument for failing to do this is his wish to remain objective, he already violates the principles of his profession and shows he's susceptible to media reports and the waffle of judges. Next, it's a well-known fact that behind his clients' back he communicates in an over-friendly manner with his "colleagues" the public prosecutors. You can imagine the outcome of such behaviour. And, finally, he hasn't a clue about political procedures, as he admits. So he is in every way unqualified to represent me. Do you finally understand?

In a moment of positively brilliant clarity of thought, you dash off the comment that it's downright criminal to keep us here without a reason. How true! There are twenty more cases like ours—which borders on mass criminality that endangers the community. That's why we went on strike, with serious intent. We were totally unsuccessful, but that was to be expected, because failure is inherent in the system.

But the sum of these experiences doesn't lead to resignation. On the contrary, if you allow me this sweeping remark, it increases the determination to be stronger in our resistance. The justice system exists everywhere, but that doesn't justify the way it works.

By the way, my letters will have even less content from now on, because the other day one of them was confiscated. Nobody should speak to me about the right to freedom of expression. No problem if I want to talk freely and without inhibition for three days about my big toe. But beware! Beware! The same doesn't apply when writing about head stuff!

When you've time, I recommend reading the tome by Ernest Mandel, *Marxist Economic Theory*. It's a lot more readable than Sweezy, and it gives you a lot of interesting historical material.

I don't need any books to relax, am relaxed already. But I lack concentration. I'm alright for the moment, I've stuffed myself with fruit and eggs and imagine myself to be really fit. A nice Swiss guy who claims to know me sent me an incredibly nice parcel, though full of useless stuff. For example, there was a huge pot of butter, but not the real thing, the sort you can only use for roasting. It tastes horrible on

---

[1]   Refers to the lawyer found by the family and rejected by Ingrid.

bread, like coffee without caffeine, really laughable. However, he also sent a rum cake, and I'm quite tipsy with this unusual treat.

Meanwhile, Susanna is cooing happily again. Pa writes something about measles (it's a really heart-warming letter). He's coming in January.

Now I must start on the books; I've been starved for too long. You can't complain about too few letters. It's not my fault if they take so long.

The dangers of solidarity[2]—I must think about that one.

So long, bye bye,

Ingrid

1 March 1971

You poor strikers, or, rather, victims of strikes. In view of the massive onslaught of letters from you I must answer them, despite lack of inclination and the postal strike. I tried several times to let you know about my disinclination to write, but this doesn't seem to have got through to you, otherwise you wouldn't wait for post with this slight touch of hysteria. We didn't write to each other for months at a time in the past, and I don't consider this current situation so extraordinarily different that we should change fundamentally now. It's natural that one assumes "outside" that the frustration (in here) creates an insatiable need to communicate; it does indeed periodically, especially in the beginning, and then, at some point, collecting senseless facts loses its value.

Oh well, but there are some things to talk about that have happened in the meantime. For instance, a few days ago, Irene and I were moved to the men's prison, which is directly connected to the criminal court. For security and other such similarly ridiculous reasons. In fact, it's rather fun to be finally rid of those fussing women and the stench of the placenta-like dependency and come into the roaring din that we're still being "protected" from (haha) in every way, but I guess that will pass.

It means you can converse with over fifty different people by shouting through the window, and there are more than a few old friends amongst them. Friends in the sense that you know of each other one way or another and from various times, including "fixer" times, when

---

2   Gerti had asked Ingrid about this.

I was engaged with them with devastating lack of success, in a Release sort of structure.[3] Larry and I ran a sort of mini-version of the model and Larry still slogs his guts out with it. It's hopeless, as everyone knows, but one can't give up trying, especially when you understand only too well from your own experience what it is to be high.

Oh, nearly forgot, the trial started today. Quite a coup by the lawyers, who'd applied to the court for the jury to be dismissed for being prejudiced because of this crazy press campaign that you've probably heard little about. As it's virtually impossible to find a single impartial judge or juror, putting at risk the most elementary basis for a fair trial, it should be abandoned. So they need to consider this application first before they can proceed. It will continue on Thursday, and beyond. It may last forever. It's a pity, really, that you can't see the Springer press every day, but *Der Spiegel* is almost no better. Did you read the article?[4] What rubbish.

Haha, a choir outside shouts "Freedom for Micky" (that's me). Unfortunately, I can't reply, or the guards will come again with their immense show of power. They really are threatening, their fists permanently in front of your nose, no space for rational thinking. "I have the keys so I have the power". I don't demand humanitarian pity from them, but consciousness, yes. But that's missing.

You'll be surprised—your books arrived some time ago and have been read, especially *The Liberation of Guiné*,[5] which was good. I knew *The Hobbit*, but it was still good to read it again, real relaxation. I am, however, at a loss to understand what this miserable animal book was doing with the rest.[6] Never mind. Otherwise, I've got terrible aggro with books; the orders are constantly misplaced, and nothing that I want arrives. By the way, I've now had enough of Salinger, after a while his

3 The "Release" network emerged during the late 1960s as a self-help movement against the criminalisation of people addicted to drugs and in favour of establishing an appropriate structure of medical and legal support.

4 *Der Spiegel*, at the time one of the most-read German news magazines, published a ten-page article in February 1971 about the police raids in Berlin. The "Springer press" refers to Germany's largest newspaper publisher, the Axel Springer Corporation, which included daily papers such as *Die Welt*, *Bild* and *Berliner Zeitung*.

5 *The Liberation of Guiné*, by Basil Davidson, with a preface by Amilcar Cabral (London: Penguin Books, 1969), was the most complete description of the liberation struggle in Guinea-Bissau towards the end of the 1960s. Ingrid's copy can still be found in the Stammheim Library at the International Institute of Social History in Amsterdam.

6 Gerald Durrell, *My Family and Other Animals* (London: Penguin Books, 1959).

literary waterfalls begin to bore the eyes. Literature in general becomes tiresome. Beautiful words for the sake of their beauty might be a feast, but as soon as there's no direct relevance I feel dissatisfied. I'd rather leave it then.

I recently sent a very sharp letter to our parents. I had to—it was necessary again—it's wrong to be considerate when it's not appropriate. I must be able to rely on her to be able to reduce her role as mother to a reasonable distance, otherwise I'll always have to defend myself against it to avoid being overwhelmed.[7] The other option is to break off the contact, which shouldn't be necessary. Pa, as always, is much more sensible, and his visit demonstrated that. I now have a female lawyer—she has a good reputation and I like her, hopefully she's efficient, which she seems to be. I can't form a judgement yet, but she's not like that "Studier" type.[8]

I must stop, as the lights go out soon. I cannot and do not want to give theoretical explanations to you, in response to questions about solidarity, etc., which are only possible here in truncated form. Thank Michael, he doesn't have to struggle to write to me, I understand him completely.

Greetings to your stable, inclusive of cats, and as many kisses.

[signature]

Today I received your letters of 15 and 17 January. To answer your question, the delay was due to the strike. Here the post is faster now: new judge, new rules.

30 March 1971

Dear Sister,

Yes, I'm still sitting here, more than ever but also better. A few days ago, the new warrant blew into this hole, its contents a paragraph like

---

7 A reference to her mother's repeated attempts to try and get better conditions for Ingrid, including by talking to the authorities.
8 See Ingrid's letter of 5 January 1971 and the reference to a "hack lawyer" in her letter of 9 December 1970.

chewing gum "par excellence", protecting all participants from pursuing high-flying plans.

The current trial proceedings reveal to the gentlemen for the prosecution their stinking air bubble, making it necessary for them to present the next one.[9] And I am sitting more comfortably, for obvious reasons.

Back to you saying I'm being stupid: your misunderstanding, unclouded by any real knowledge of the different prison situations, in no way entitles you to such hackneyed remarks as "true emancipation". So I don't take that or your ignorance (based on your chosen career) at all seriously. More worrying are the high waves of fame.[10] It seems to me that you imagine I don't register these. Not only do they make us sick, they are also most unwelcome even though they've diminished recently, since we deny the press any opportunity to play their famous game of twisting words. Certain newspapers are angry about that. While the Berlin Left flounders helplessly in its homespun cloaks of factory-like group work and analysis and tries to compensate for its hollow words with promises of money and care parcels. Even that doesn't work. And doesn't even surprise the thirty or so poor victims of the State, by now in prison for almost a year. Those internal squabbles can hardly be conveyed; it's just that they're almost as sickening as the filth in the press.

In case you're really interested in coming here, please prepare yourself for a different form of prison experience from the fireside atmosphere and fussing around in the Lehrter Strasse. That's missing here. You sit in a room that's barer than bare, with three men as guards, who can be guaranteed to savour every syllable that might be passed on to colleagues as entertaining stories at every suitable opportunity. Their faces, where you can usually see a good part of their psyche, seem to come out of a textbook. And you won't get a whole hour anyway. Just as it's impossible for us to access the legally prescribed exercise yard, which, according to regulations, "is distinguished by plants and green areas that promote relaxation". The reason given is that we'd have to pass right along the building where all these sexually frustrated men

---

9   The first trial against Ingrid and her co-defendants Irene Goergens and Horst Mahler, from 1 March to 21 May 1971.

10 A reference to the distortions published in the press. The prisoners kept their distance from journalists, to avoid feeding false stories about themselves.

are—just imagine the consequences—so instead we walk around the yard where the dustbins and rubbish are.

Well, more reading than ever, as well as all sorts of other trivialities and unmentionables. Picking your nose, for instance. Suggestions for books are difficult. At the moment, I'm with the classics, godfather Marx and similar ghostly figures. And I can't think of any English titles. One has to be careful about the choice of books, so as not to become too scattered and thrown wildly in all directions. It's a complete nonsense to ask you for German books, as I can get them here within a week (unless they forget the order again, as is often the case and which, to put it mildly, makes me mad, because having to wait for something in particular gets on your nerves). Perhaps you'll find a more recent book about the British Labour movement, preferably by neither a bourgeois nor a conservative scribbler, though I can't think who. But I'd like to recommend a book about the little-known story of China's last fifty years: Edgar Snow's *Red Star Over China*.[11] It looks rather thick, but it's an exciting page turner, well written and easy to read. It seems the most authentic, as the author is the only Western journalist allowed to enter that little country. I hope the victory in Laos fills you with, let's say, joy. Or you are my sister not, ha.[12]

Well, here for once we have a nice lady guard who brings me hot water for coffee after lunch. Irene is sitting diagonally opposite me in the cell and we can chat at length about such interesting things as lust for cake and press-ups. She comes under the juvenile law here, but that seems no reason to separate her trial from ours. What luck that we're still together.

Well, that's it. See you later, maybe. Try and find good weather when you come. Greet your brood and your betrothed and thank him for his numerous little cards. I hope he doesn't wait for answers.

Ingrid

---

11 Published in 1937 and updated by the author in 1968 (New York: Grove Press, 1994).
12 In January 1971, US troops invaded Laos with the aim of stopping Vietnamese guerrilla transports over the so-called Ho Chi Minh Trail. Within three months, the invasion was beaten back by the liberation armies of Vietnam and Laos.

10 May 1971

Dear Sister, you've no idea how lazy I am when it comes to writing letters, so please note the honour bestowed on you by my letter today. Though nothing's in it.

The trial, difficult to believe, is nearing its questionable end, unless the crazy prosecutor conjures from up his sleeve a few more gags, like some "V-men".[13] This man plays for high stakes, to put it mildly, a professional cheat. I'm much more preoccupied by the temperature of 24° Celsius outside this hole, while I, clad only in hot pants in this cell, have (what craziness) absolved myself of my thirty nightly squats, twenty press-ups and thirty back bends (yoga's a bit too passive for me) and washed myself obediently, and now look forward to a thrilling evening with Lord Knut's hit songs. Pffft.

Masses of books, a bad thing really, as they distract you too much. Many are just skimmed, with the intention of returning later for a more thorough read, but then one is overwhelmed again. Your stuff here, especially Russell, hasn't been read yet.

But I'll now give you a list to read in the order below. Some of it is sticky reading but worth it.

The Development of Socialism from Utopia to Science (Friedrich Engels)

The Origin of the Family, Private Property and the State (Engels)
The Breakthrough in Sexual Morality (Wilhelm Reich)
Dialectical Materialism and Psychoanalysis
The Function of the Orgasm
What is Class Consciousness?
Sexuality in the Battle of Cultures

All these are by Reich. They are important because he uncovers the important mental structures that the grandfathers weren't aware of: "The structure of a character is the frozen sociological process of a particular era".

Wage Labour and Capital (Karl Marx)
The Communist Manifesto
State and Revolution (Lenin)

---

13   Secret agents of the Verfassungsschutz (VS), the federal and regional intelligence agencies for domestic security.

Red Star over China (Edgar Snow)

The Mass Psychology of Fascism (Reich)

As background to Reich: Frantz Fanon, *The Wretched of the Earth*.

Well, that will give a foundation. Added to this will be the countless documents about the freedom struggles in the Third World, analysis of class struggles here, study of Mao's writings (most important), etc., etc. To list it ALL might overstretch your reading capacity. Even if you had time. And I should have ample time to give you more hints. Quite a few other people have been convinced, in advanced years, of the necessity of communism! Nothing against your age!

Your feeling of alienation in Larry's flat is easy to imagine,[14] as I know this peculiar atmosphere well and would probably feel similar in the circumstances. It's more likely, though, that I'd break into unstoppable attacks of rage about the extent of the lascivious melancholia and resignation of him and his circle of friends. Everyone has eyes and ears to see and hear, and what do they do? They sink into deplorable depression, helpless shrugging of shoulders and guilty conscience, elitist and submissive at the same time.

I've also written to our parents; presumably you heard that. A difficult subject, and the prospect of a possible transfer to the prison in Koblenz (!) doesn't make it easier. I don't know what the final sentence will be,[15] everyone can add it up on their ten fingers. As the prosecutor is furious at his lack of success, he will probably demand the same sentence for each of us. That's it, writing brings nothing.

Warm kisses to you all.

7 June 1971

Hello, all of you. For some time now, I thought that something in writing might be necessary, knowing that the longer one waits the more difficult it will be to get down to it again.

First, something to clarify our situation here: so far absolutely nothing has changed, not a jot, and nothing will change in the near future, as the by now well-known wheels of justice for appeals, or for rejection or

---

14   At Ingrid's request, Gerti visited Larry, Ingrid's former long-term partner.

15   Ingrid's two trials resulted in a total sentence of thirteen years.

acceptance of an application for an appeal, grind on dreadfully slowly. It probably means waiting two years for a new trial, if the application is accepted, and staying in remand detention during that time. I don't expect it will be accepted, simply because I know I can't expect anything at all from their side. (How could I hold a shred of hope? It would be absurd.) So that means a change into prison garb a few months from now.

I'm less bothered about that. The subjective conditions will be a few degrees less palatable, but the principle will be the same, except that you don't sit for twenty-three-and-a-half hours in your cell; you can whizz around a bit more. What's really frightening is the length of time—and that some people agree with it. The mere fact that not a shred of further evidence was presented on the last day of the trial than on the first day is as indicative as the grotesquely feeble reasoning behind the judgment and the dirty tricks during the trial, such as secret service agents, perjury, psychopaths as credible witnesses and more.

The press is aware of all this and is silent, because the prominent one (and he really suffers under the length of our sentences) was acquitted.[16] A totally new type of justice (ha, the word itself is a joke)— the pig who murders a small-time car thief by shooting him in the neck is excused with the label of suffering "psychological confusion". One knows how these poor officers are constantly under stress, yes! Clearly, nothing can be said about feeling bitter or any other kind of nonsense—different processes are at work here. In "bleak hours" of doubt or self-criticism you arrive repeatedly at the same result. This gives me strength, has a sort of cleansing effect. White in, grey out.

I'm not sure if our mother's visit helped her. The two hours under supervision were torture, though the last hour less so from my point of view. I tried to take away some of her fear, but how can I achieve that properly if fundamental positions cannot be shifted to a shared understanding? Although this wouldn't help anyone either. For the individual, there is no relevance in the one-and-only truth. Everyone has to follow the truth that seems the only one possible after examining all the evidence—plus one is constantly subjected to change, critique and revision. Some sentences by Che Guevara, Mao or Cleaver would appear as total and absolute nonsense to the bookkeeper, the doctor, the housewife round the corner, and rightly so in their situation. But ask a

---

16　Horst Mahler, acquitted at this trial, though convicted at a later stage.

Black Panther, a Vietcong or me, for instance, and these sentences are true. And it's exactly the essence of these three examples, their justification, which is truth. Because all have a common enemy and a common aim, each in their own way using their own means of getting there.

An important step is to find a way out of existing limiting dimensions, no matter how finely meshed, diverse and complex they might be, and into new dimensions that negate individualistic aspects yet value you highly as an individual. This, incidentally, is less linked to purism or asceticism or similar "Prussian" concepts—probably never before has there been such an urge to develop all sorts of silly and crazy joys of life. It also means, I think, that only then can one develop properly, taking a step beyond mere consumerism.

Which reminds me: you either failed or passed your exam for a place at university. It's really strange to ponder exam anxieties. Either way, my heartfelt congratulations. What will you do with this? Have you overcome your winter dysphoria? Are new aims in sight? The next winter arrives without fail but will be different, do you think?

A thousand warm kisses for the children. I'm looking forward to their pictures; the Scape Bubble Car (not sure who drew that) hangs above my private loo, very decorative. Once I'm a "convict" (official term) I can take books and the like with me, but there's still ample time for that. Until the appeal is over, a transfer to Cologne or elsewhere, where prison conditions will be much stricter than here, won't happen.

So off to the next letter; I'm in the mood today and that needs to be put to good use.

If you eventually go on holiday: freak out!

Ingrid

For Michael, of course, a big kiss too.

20 July 1971

Dear Sister,

Your letter has finally caused the collapse of the pyramid of unanswered letters. This should be a definite call to put an end to the frustration of not being able to write. It's not that I don't know what to say. It's more that the vegetation in the brain succumbs to a sheer

insurmountable "clumsiness" as soon as you try to formulate something. I can't think of it as anything other than a sign of the onset of
decay (perhaps a bit too strong a word) that I'm only just becoming
aware of—the result of a lack of lively debates and the confrontation
with reality. Values shift, retain only relative meaning—one slips into
defensive self-accusations, such as "who will be interested in this?" and
one is subject to the pleasure principle which isn't the worst thing, as
long as it's productive. Exceptionally, you're allowed to guess correctly
that I'm not in a good place emotionally. The reason is obvious and is
in the newspapers, but maybe not in England.

A girl was shot in Hamburg, someone I loved with revolutionary
love.[17] The media's lies about how it happened: you can't do much
about that, they're part of the set-up. And I really cannot talk about it
anyway, as I haven't come to terms with her death, perhaps never will.
My reaction hasn't been all that clear, at least not as clear as I'd expect
of myself. The senselessness, the obsession, the inevitable, the necessary—all visions of her last minutes and much, much more.

The legal, sanctioned, consistently brutal force on the other side.
What is meant by legal murder? What distinguishes the screw who
kills three Black prisoners from the prisoner who throws a guard down
the stairs (*Soledad Brother*, I already have the book) before the law that
claims to be able to judge them both?[18] This isn't the kind of violence
we're dealing with over here, but differences of scale mustn't obscure
the view of the same principle. It's only a matter of time before the USA's
already accepted fascism will remove the last inhibitions on Germany's
latent fascism, accompanied clearly, of course, by lots of "woe and alas".

There, I've slithered into the wrong gear again. This is a much more
complex process, not clearly understood by me. I'm fighting resignation,
despite the sunshine outside and our obvious well-being here: we can
move around a lot, can run, practice sports, watch TV—repression in a
honey pot, we have adjoining cells, exercise time together, there's our

---

17   Petra Schelm, shot in Hamburg on 15 July 1971 during "Operation Kora", a major
     dragnet operation against the RAF.
18   In January 1969, three prisoners in the Soledad Prison, near Los Angeles, were accused
     of murdering a prison guard after another guard had shot three Black prisoners. The
     accused, George Jackson, Fleeta Drumgo and John Clutchette, became known as the
     Soledad Brothers. See George Jackson, *Soledad Brother: The Prison Letters of George
     Jackson* (London: Penguin Books, 1970). See also Ingrid's next letter.

constant laughter, which, prior to the deadly shot, was really genuine. Now it's hollow, filled with a kind of melancholia that's quite wrong in this situation, and I know this will change again. Our constant mood swings don't count; there's sufficient strength within us, and we shall be able to talk to each other again.

What do you mean by "personal words" to our parents? What else do I write except just that? It's not much, but I've never been able to talk with them as with others on my wavelength. This cannot be fundamentally changed now. Besides, their visit wasn't so long ago that we can talk about a complete breakdown in communication. As far as the money's concerned, where should I conjure up an account number? As far as I know, there's an account that our parents opened. I'll ask Kristine, my lawyer, who should have reached you by now; she wanted to visit you during her stay in England. I've got a chessboard and played with it a lot when Brigitte was still here.[19] She's been transferred to Essen, into a freezing, damp hole in the cellar, where her fingers freeze, with the outside temperature 28° Celsius!

Sister, I'm determined to conquer this mountain today and will tap my fingers until they bleed. This letter is not to be read as weighty evidence of the start of a depression, but as the expression of a new step, which will lead I know not where, but certainly not backwards.

Much love, etc. Thank the children again. I've sent them something too. Their pictures decorate the corner around my loo (a very practical installation—everything in one room!).

Bye,
Ingrid

September 1971

Late September. Hi, please don't ask how long I've wanted to reply to your glowing sun-drenched letter with its descriptions of ruins. If it's not done at once, it's no longer possible to do, just as it's impossible to respond in a discussion after three hours (though I can almost imagine

---

19 Brigitte Asdonk, arrested with Ingrid. See her testimony in the *Remembering Ingrid* section of this book, pp. 193–94.

this in my case, and with the current lack of language and discussion, especially when I think that discussion has always been my weak point).

Your letter today taught me to grin again, because it demonstrates the misconceptions about those inside by those who live outside the prison walls, necessarily taking the direction of resigned apathy, etc., because the NOTHING (of life) cannot be imagined in over-stimulated heads. Sure, and if you're not strong enough to get these stimuli by yourself, you will rot like a bag of rubbish.

Other prisoners here exemplify this: they can't imagine what we do all day in our cells—they don't know what they could do themselves and are dependent on the most monotonous work for diversion, be it only through the same repetitive movements. Evening in the cells is terrible for them. They read rubbish and will never get the chance to reach a higher level of consciousness as long as they live. It's absurd to claim that everyone has the same educational opportunity—none of that is true, except on paper, cloaked in the mantle of democracy, and the selection begins at birth, determined by class alone, by money. Terrible, but the reality is so well known that even *Der Spiegel* thinks it's worth putting on record. Believe me, I'm glad to have extricated myself in time—yet still too late—from my petit bourgeois privileges. This doesn't mean it's worthless to study medicine or whatever; it all depends on the background and your intentions. What you can't root out is the pattern of dominant moral and ethical concepts, and this must be fought.

Shortened like this, it all sounds rubbish. Why not come again? But announce your visit in good time, as we now have strict rules, fortnightly visits only.

Bring one of your children, or will it be too shocking for them? I really want them to recognise early on how privileged they are. I wondered whether to write to Marcus, but I really have no idea what he's interested in, what he thinks about at his age, what to him is a matter of fact. I often think of the whole riff-raff of children in our family (a direct expression of this is the crocheted thing for Susanna—did it arrive? please send me the measurements of all the children every now and then, that would be good), and I reflect on how they are fully formed and developing in predetermined ways—unless they jump off at a later stage, which may then be the subject of incomprehension and head shaking. But I must admit that I wouldn't know what I'd do under the present conditions in society. That's why I let it be at present, erm, under duress, so to speak, expressed in nocturnal orgasms.

Anyway, there are plenty of activities here, all half-started, nothing completed. I've got a guitar and am waiting to be taught. Greetings to Chris. Let's see who can play first. I bet it will be him. He should strive to be like Mick Jagger—have a lot of fun! I started learning Spanish, using a book published during Nazi times: "Today is the Führer's birthday" and other such pleasantries. It looks easy because I can still remember bits of Latin but don't really want to learn the words; it's no longer my thing. Send me some French books if you like, but not too difficult please. I'm doing yoga again, this time with Irene, who is stiff as a plank and completely bent (encourage your kids to do lots of sport). I often revisit the holy medicine and teach anatomy to anyone who wants to listen. I'm surprised at people's ignorance of the layout of their inner organs.

About the psychology of the guards, there's no difference between them and German housewives. They are beginning to recognise through their interactions with us how absurd their ridiculous power is, based on a key and their civil service status, which doesn't mean that they would change. We also have a pastor creeping around, totally rotten. After being here a year now, the conditions haven't changed in any way. Damn it, just imagine this going on for ten years!

By the way, I was as shocked by the brutal murder of George Jackson (remember the book)[20] as by the murder of Petra in Hamburg—hardly different. If one looks to the US one can only wonder with what lethargy the fascist process over there is regarded here. "It's far away, not our problem". That the same elements are working over here is ignored even more. It's true, Sister, believe me.

Why don't you want to study political science? If it's confusing, it will be clearer if you study it. Or are you afraid that it enables you to understand *too much*, to be swallowed by the communist monster? Don't worry, the usual presentations in these universities tend to make inveterate anti-communists out of people. Heaven help us.

---

20 George Jackson became politically conscious in prison. He joined the Black Panther Party and became an example for many. He was shot dead on 21 August 1971 during an alleged attempt to escape from prison. See previous letter.

I agree with what you said in your last letter about Kristine,[21] but she's still learning. I'm confident that I won't draw the short straw before the next trial, which I don't think I got anyway; it just seemed that way. Her frequent visits touch me, as does her solidarity. Other visits are from old and new friends. The scene in Berlin is as dead as an old dishcloth; they know little or have nothing to say, and they are all at bitter loggerheads with one another about the question of who might be teaching the real true truth. It follows that during demonstrations they fight with each other, if they hadn't already done so. It elicits tired smiles here, and I continue to munch my carrots, which is another fad: green food, raw, meaning I had to organise half a kitchen here. Mad how one arranges oneself; it borders on resignation, but it isn't. Would it be best to throw all this away and start again at point zero?

Off to our "free time" now to play football. If I do become a convicted prisoner here, there will be a monster of a show because there's nothing, absolutely nothing, for female prisoners by way of sport or any chance to move about in fun ways. Stupid excuses are cited, using the argument that women don't want anything else, according to questionnaires and research. It's the same with those miserable TV programmes they put together—nothing but manipulation, I tell you.

So bye, don't forget the measurements of all your creatures. The hat for Susanna is much too big; maybe you'll put your head under it next time you go skiing.

Hugs for you all,

Eva

Oh yeah, if I want to hug someone, a human being, I have Irene, even though at times I'd like to chase her through the brambles (as my only object of aggression). There are four trees in the yard plus a patch of grass—the day outside wouldn't be necessary, but I could use it for something else.

---

21 Gerti and the family wondered whether Ingrid's chosen lawyer was sufficiently experienced.

28 October 1971

Your dear whopping big kisses that you all painted for me are winking at me from the wall, giving me immense pleasure.

I've ended my interminable avoidance of the typewriter over the last few weeks by tying myself to the chair armed with coffee. After contemplating for four hours the fascinating emergence of a candle out of palmin,[22] I thought to myself, "Schubert, this cannot go on". All because of this damned sheet of metal in front of the window, behind which we landed as innocent victims of a malicious intrigue: a few ladders against the wall of the Lehrter Strasse in full daylight,[23] and in next to no time we were seized and carted off here without any explanation. This wobbling dumpling of a prison director made three crosses behind us,[24] even though we had displayed exemplary behaviour, which, nevertheless, still prevented other prisoners from being allowed to talk with us "radicals".

During the all-too-short journey here, one of the lovely guards said that with us "Hitler had missed something", and here in Moabit the young prisoners are told that we threw a bomb at a man that tore him apart in front of his wife. Hate propaganda *comme il faut*, born out of incorrigible ignorance and conditioning towards an inability to make judgements through schools, the education system and the mass media, particularly Caesar Springer and his B.Z.[25] It's too bad you can't see these newspapers. Oh well, in any case, and I don't know why, the day seems three times as long here as in the Lehrter Strasse and, proportionally, my head feels much larger at night because of the lack of natural light (a dim lamp is on all day) and air. No sign of even a tree. I would call this torture if I wanted to capitalise on these conditions.

At the moment I don't want to let it affect me, and I try to do what I can to avoid it. One of the first things you learn here is to never ever

---

22 Palmin, made from coconut oil, was a substitute for frying with grease and margarine.
23 Ingrid and Irene were sent to Moabit Prison on 14 October 1971, immediately after a failed attempt to free them from Lehrter Strasse. See Anne Reiche's testimony in the *Remembering Ingrid* section of this book, pp. 195–96.
24 Three crosses: in Germany, an expression of relief.
25 *Berliner Zeitung*, a Berlin tabloid published by newspaper publisher Springer.

let them get you down under any circumstances and to always use your instincts for self-preservation as a driver to re-energise yourself.

No doubt this could also be learnt outside prison, but here— where the contradictions are displayed so openly—you probably come closest to the existential minimum. The biggest (no, hardly the biggest) problem here is to not allow yourself to be eaten up by the trivialities imposed by the prison bureaucracy, with the result that you're halfway to becoming beholden to the pompous rituals of "security and order" (affecting simply *everything* in here). Quite apart from the fact that this nonsense destroys all sense of reality about life beyond the walls. Take the inevitable use of bundles of keys and, thus, weapons of power used by women who are otherwise smitten with blindness that makes you doubt whether you can ever speak of emancipated women en masse, as a whole—it unnerves you over time.

It would be good to write to Marcus, but right now I'm not in the proper frame of mind, like I was a while ago. And, anyway, he or anyone like him wouldn't be admitted; nobody under fourteen is. The authority for visits is still or once again Mr Pahl—strictly once a fortnight, apart from exceptions for those coming from afar. Our good old father is coming next week.

What on earth did you ask in your last bunch of letters that all ended up in the shredder? I can't read the Tolkien now, despite starting it, because you can only have eight books in your cell here, and every exchange of books means a mass of paperwork to complete, full of misunderstandings and lots of aggravation. These types interpret every justified request as a personal affront.

I've no wool right now, or I'd make something for you too, but I doubt whether a bigger version would look as funny. Susanna just has to lose a bit of weight, now or never!

Obviously, "doing good is essentially selfish": it's the principle of Christian charity under whose banner more harm than good was done over the centuries, and not only in the area of individual deeds. The whole of Africa became a victim of white imperialism—and was still expected to show gratitude. Heavens!

You shouldn't be the only one to delight in my letters when I'm in the mood to write. So goodbye, and don't send anything to this address, as nothing will reach me. If you want to send me wool or similar, address it to Kristine, as she's got the permit needed to bring it to me.

A thousand kisses to the people.

Ingrid

26 December 1971, to Her Niece Susanna

Written in English

Dear Susanna,

Do you think this is too much colour?[26] My fingers and mind nearly drove [me] crazy with all those different needles, wools and so on. It was first meant to be a jumper for Monika (Klaus' wife), but it became smaller and smaller—so this is the result. Hope it fits in spite of your belly! If not, maybe it fits Chris as a jumper. Ugh!

Everything else is okay with me, lots of eating during Christmas, gosh, I put [on] 10 pounds I'm sure. Did you have fun in Koblenz? And have you been skiing afterwards?

Give my love and 100000000000000000 hot kisses to Mummy, Daddy, Marcus, Chris, cat, dog, mouse and rat and everybody you meet!

Bye bye,

Ingrid

Many thanks for your picture you sent me as birthday present. It's hanging on my wall.

---

26 A reference to a garment Ingrid had knitted and that ended up as a jumper for Susanna's favourite teddy.

26.12.91

DEAR SUSANNA,

DO YOU THINK THIS IS TOO
MUCH COLOUR? MY FINGERS AND
MIND NEARLY DROVE CRAZY WITH
ALL THOSE DIFFERENT NEEDLES, WOOLS
AND SO ON. IT WAS FIRST MEANT TO
BE A JUMPER FOR MONIKA (GLAUS
WIFE), BUT IT BECAME SMALLER AND
SMALLER — SO THIS IS THE RESULT. HOPE
IT FITS IN SPITE OF YOUR BELLY!
IF NOT, MAYBE IT FITS CHRIS AS
A JUMPER. HUGH!

EVERYTHING ELSE IS OKAY WITH ME,
LOTS OF EATING DURING CHRISTMAS,
GOSH, I TOOK 10 POUNDS I'M SURE.
DID YOU HAVE FUN IN WOLLEKA?
AND HAVE YOU BEEN SKYING AFTER-
WARDS?
GIVE MY LOVE AND   100 000 000000 000 000

HOT KISSES TO mummy daddy
Marcus, Chris, cat, dog, mouse
and rat and everybody you
meet!

BYE BYE

Ingrid

Many thanks for your picture you
send me as birthday present. It's
hanging on my wall.

Letters 1972

This year, more RAF members and sympathisers are arrested. In Berlin, Brigitte Mohnhaupt, Katharina Hammerschmidt, Anne Reiche, Verena Becker and Inge Viett end up in Lehrter Strasse Prison. Almost all the male prisoners from the RAF are held in prisons in West Germany. The trial in connection with the 1970 bank robberies begins in October. For the trial, Ingrid and Irene are joined in Moabit Prison by Brigitte Asdonk and Monika Berberich. In December, Ingrid and Irene are transferred back to Lehrter Strasse for a while, because their cells in Moabit are needed for Gudrun Ensslin and Ulrike Meinhof, who have been transferred to this prison because it is closer to the Berlin court where the trial is being held and where they will give their testimony.

24 January 1972

Oh, Sister, okay, let's try one of those courses.[1] To stabilise my uncoordinated thought processes, I'll give it a go. It would be useful to regain a more focused way of working—to be more goal-orientated. Perhaps it will also help me convey to Irene something like general knowledge, as I always seem to miss contextual information, a sort of framework of facts, for instance, about history and all that other stuff learnt at school, which people like me have either forgotten or repressed yet which seems an important part of our so-called knowledge base.

---

1   A correspondence course that Ingrid wanted to do, and started, but decided not to complete.

Okay, so what happens next? Will you write to them and order everything? The only course I'd consider is "social psychology". But the crunch question is this: Where do I get a radio? Seriously, as far as I understand, radio and TV are the most important part of the course and the written part merely supplementary. I also read somewhere that one can manage it without a radio. Well, ask them, check this, and if it sounds okay then order it.

As far as foreign newspapers are concerned, I've wanted to order *Le Monde* for ages but have been wary of the complications this would create as I can't order it here through the prison. I don't know which English newspapers might be moderately progressive—maybe you can enlighten me. But too many papers are a pain, because, in the end, you even read the latest marriage announcements.

Your books (from November) have disappeared, and the judges and their lackeys sift through mountains of dust to find them. What a mess! After a long battle, my cosmetics weren't returned. They seem to think—and this after a year—that something sinister might be hidden in them. God knows what! Oh hell!

No, I don't feel like writing. There are no questions of burning importance. At present, the wagon rattles along with endless monotony. So long, my greetings to everyone.

Ingrid

17 February 1972

Hello,

Am sitting here in loose sleeves and shaven head (someone praised this method as guarantee against hair loss) and am waiting for Larry, who hasn't arrived, so I'm writing this still filled with anger and sadness about the strange and sudden disappearance of my other half: Irene was transferred to another institution last week, without reason and, of course, without any warning. It's the very place that had been thought insecure and, therefore, unsuitable for us, dangerous females that we're deemed to be. I'm left here sitting like the proverbial cow in front of the mountain, confronted by this silence, incapable of any initiative, gliding downwards into introspection. What else is there to do? The endless repetitive chats with any of the ladies outside my door (who suffer the same loneliness) about people in their household, knitting, problems in the prison system, yield nothing but mush in your brain, meaning you have to try really hard not to go crazy.

So where's the course?[2] It would be good to do some translating, though I'm not sure if it would be the right thing for me, as I've never done it before. The German language is reputedly not the easiest, and there are enough people who master this better than I can, me with my constant bad marks in school (even now I wonder how I survived that culture of torture and force). Clearly, I'll also survive the rubbish here without too much damage, especially as there's an end in sight, because sometime soon (autumn at the latest) our show will be staged and all four of us united again.[3]

All this stuff in *Der Spiegel*, these serialised fairy tales[4]—take heed, Sister, as I keep saying, don't get tricked. That's their very purpose. They read like a horrific crime story, with convincing details from live eyewitnesses (some true, but based on a totally incorrect premise). And Horst's stinking allegories aren't much better,[5] even apart from the despicable opportunism of his writing for the select intellectual circles that *Der Spiegel*'s readership represents.

You misconstrued his sentence about revolutionary criminality. Not (for heaven's sake, no) that being criminal is revolutionary, but that working in a revolutionary way involves breaking the law, because the law in force is that of the ruling class, and it would be absurd to believe that one could attack this class without touching their legal system. It is, so to speak, a necessary concomitant, to which the "enemy" attaches this ridiculous importance only to use it as a hook for their hate campaigns.

---

2   See previous letter.
3   The second trial against Ingrid, Irene and the others was planned to start in autumn 1972.
4   A series of articles in *Der Spiegel* reported statements by Karl-Heinz Ruhland, who had turned crown witness for the prosecution in trials against members of the RAF.
5   In a contribution to *Der Spiegel*, former lawyer Horst Mahler, who had been arrested with Ingrid and three others, stated that the revolutionary Left "must be criminal by definition". Mahler's penchant for making statements and issuing documents without consultation with the others, as well as his rapprochement with the orthodox Marxist-Leninist Left, would lead to his public expulsion from the group in his second trial in September 1974. See André Moncourt and J. Smith, *The Red Army Faction: A Documentary History, Volume 1: Projectiles for the People* (Oakland/Montréal: PM Press/ Kersplebedeb, 2009), 255–57, 288–91.

This isn't at all new; it's been applied since time immemorial against all communists. In this case, it's done with special refinement and provides an idea of the strength of the system. It is absolutely not seen as a brainless power machine—otherwise, why all the effort? On the contrary, the precise impression of its complexity, its perfection, sits on your neck—if you think of it in the short term. But there's also the "tirelessly grubbing mole of the revolution",[6] however foolish it may sound.

I haven't seen or found any trace of Anouilh and origami paper folding. It's possible they got lost in the pile of books; I'll have another look. Me make paper boats and planes! I hardly dare touch my never-ending knitwear. It should have been a pair of trousers, and maybe it will get finished when I regain my freedom.

The appeals procedure goes on and on without getting anywhere, but I'm sure the application will be refused, not so much because of the Ruhland thing but also because a repetition of the whole case is too tiresome for them,[7] and they don't care anyway how long we remain in here, "just give them more". The next trial has now been allocated to here, as you may know. There won't be any advantage either way, except that we stay in this blessed land, meaning jail. I'm debating whether I'd rather scrub floors or wash dirty clothes and how I could reduce my coffee consumption to an amount compatible with my income (eighty cents a day, try living on that).

To think about prisons for women only gives you gall stones, because strangely enough prisons for men have long had the necessary small change for the oh-so-lovely reforms, which, by the time they come into force, are long out of date. There are, apparently, too few women here to create the necessary pressure: not worth it, no interest, etc.—all these favourite excuses, yet the small number should in fact make it easier, damn it. One could write books, but I go on about it every day, so let's leave it for now.

Whew, probably had too much coffee, am constantly flitting between window and typewriter as if I might miss something outside. But all I see are countless pigeons and seagulls flying around, quarrelling about crumbs of bread and full of the excitement of spring. To look

---

6   The "tirelessly grubbing mole" refers to a quote from Shakespeare's *Hamlet*, borrowed several times by Karl Marx, famously in *The Eighteenth Brumaire of Louis Bonaparte* (New York: International Publishers, 1963), 69.

7   See footnote 4 above.

out of the window I must first drag the chair there. That's how you create work for yourself, but doing these gymnastics all the time is boring and only gives you jelly bones.

Do I have anything of importance to say? Lots, but not here—as usual. What do you have to say about what's happening in Ireland?[8] The British youth can't be as unpolitical as you once thought. That alone should make it possible to get some things moving unless one assumes fundamental passivity. (Newspapers still not here, holy forgetfulness!) Should I send you candles, home-made? (Unfortunately, mine were taken from my cell during a raid the other day.) What do people think can solve the permanent British crisis? Back to Labour? = back to new crises. February's *Le Monde* has been paid for, but I've not seen a single copy so far. I'd need a whole day to read it anyway.

Dear people, this is the end for today and, oh, I forgot our dear Chris. Has he survived his birthday without my expressly conveyed special wishes? (Mother's calendar doesn't quite seem to do its trick.)

Humpeline will soon lose her plaster cast and be proud of a thinner leg (which I wish I had too!).[9]

A thousand kisses,

Ingrid

No idea about books for the moment, just ordered a list of psychology titles.

13 April 1972

Oh dear, I seem to have shocked you again with a letter about stuff long out of date, because I'm now as happy as ever. The two weeks of solitude did me good, and meanwhile I've been blessed with a new neighbour next door: Moni flew in from Mainz.[10] Besides, it's wonderfully crazy

---

8   A reference to the demonstration against the British Army in Derry on 30 January 1972, when British soldiers shot dead thirteen demonstrators and wounded seventeen others. The subsequent official inquiry confirmed that the demonstrators were unarmed. The event became known as Bloody Sunday.
9   Humpeline: Susanna had broken her leg.
10   Monika Berberich, who was charged with bank robbery along with Ingrid, Irene Goergens and Brigitte Asdonk.

weather outside, which should make me sad but, instead, energises me, creates a high for today at least, so I'm writing endlessly, until my fingers are sore, because this energy must be used.

There are no signs of distraction at all. It was very good to have some work to do that needed concentration, like the translations for Larry, which also earned me a creaky back. The sociology course has arrived, but I've not started yet, apart from a cursory read while waiting for the tutor, who came for the first time today. She said she couldn't comment on the books until she'd talked to some of those doing the third trimester. So I'll start doing it on my own and try and get some of the more urgent books from here. I hope I won't lose interest, unless something happens that distracts me from it, which is likely if—as expected—there will be more people up here.

There's a rumour we'll soon be back in the Lehrter, once their special little surveillance towers or similar security bits are in place. There's also talk of a new trial date in May, which seems illusory, as we've not even been charged yet. No doubt it will be a farce, just like in Düsseldorf,[11] where they sweet-talked the accused and would almost have decorated him with the Federal Cross of Merit for his services to the State. It's really laughable to keep referring to the State and the rule of law in this context—as happens constantly and ceaselessly—without any reference to the complete lack of truth in these assertions. One will simply be branded a liar. The execution of Tommy in Augsburg came as a shock[12]—there are clearly people trained to shoot accurately, which for them means shoot to kill.

I'm searching and searching for your last letter, which I can't find, even though that seems hardly possible in these eight square metres. Right now, I'm reading *The Loyal Subject* by Heinrich Mann.[13] It's repulsive, really disgusting, because this loyal subject is everywhere, on every street corner, that's what's frightening.

---

11   A reference to the ongoing trial against Karl-Heinz Ruhland.
12   Thomas Weisbecker was shot dead on 2 March 1972 by a Regional Criminal Investigation Bureau squad.
13   The younger brother of Thomas Mann, also a writer, but more radically inclined and critical of the rising Nazi regime in Germany. He criticised the tendency of the German people to conform to the new Party's ideology and objectives for the sake of alleged greater security.

And now I've lost my nerve and must run to the window and breathe in more of that velvety air outside. I embrace your whole clan of people. Marcus is flying to Koblenz at Easter, and our mother has indicated gently that, however welcome the children are at any time, she finds it all a bit much right now, especially as Oliver wants to come too.[14] But when anyone asks her about it, she protests vehemently because, naturally, she cannot conquer the temptation to sacrifice her own interests for her family.

Have a good time. Until whenever.

Eva

Don't send the *Guardian*, as *Le Monde* is meant to arrive any time soon.

13 April 1972, to Gerti's children

Written in English

HELLLOOOO Susanna Marcus Chris cat dog elephant pig and all!!!! Did I forget somebody?

This minute I finally received all your lovely pictures and poems, ships and little men—weeks after they actually arrived here. This happens often, because all presents sent to me (a lot) first wander into the cellar, where they are piled—nothing else!

Please tell Gerti that I got only two of the announced books, Sartre and Simenon remained somewhere, maybe flying through the universe (as space-bubbles!) but as I'm swimming in books, it's not too bad.

I MUST say—I am ashamed, because my head never produced such poems or pictures. The one and only poem I ever produced was one with a cow sitting on the bottom of the sea saying wow—or something like that. Not very visionary, is it? And the only pictures ever done were in school, themes like "father in front of the mirror shaving"! but thanks to many friends outside and inside prison I'm far away being a modern hermit (and the poet himself neither, I should say), though twenty-four hours a day kept in this room with proportions of a better lavatory.

---

14   The first son of Ingrid's brother Klaus and his wife Monika.

Most of the time I'm sitting at the window, at the moment talking to the other two girlfriends wall-to-wall to me or to the boys by whom we are surrounded. Most of them are between seventeen and twenty years old and highly damaged by society. Putting them in a cage like mad animals means to perpetuate the evil which has been done to them from childhood on. Imagine that you *never*—I really say never—in your life had the chance to be accepted as a real human being with needs, wants, love and proudness. What would you do? Rebel of course, which for *them* means stealing this and that, a short-circuit leading to prison again and again. Michael can tell you a lot about these things, I think, which you never get to see as long as you're bound to such a lovely home as yours. But I don't want to terrify you, some of it will come to your mind again when confronted with it.

In some weeks I will go back to the other prison, which is only for women, and will start to work there. I don't know how much I will like this, because it is the most stupid work one can imagine, but I can watch TV again, talk to many others and rush around.

tell Mummy that I will write her some day!!

to all of you smashing kisses

the NOT Hermit,

Ingrid

18 April 1972

At least the post arrives more quickly now. So far, dear Sister, this is the only perceptible sign of a change in my status.[15] From now on it will be read only here, and everything else will also be decided by the institution here, causing us considerable difficulties until they decide that they have managed to install sufficient security devices at the Lehrter.

I hope you're clear that in no way am I shocked, angry, fearful or whatever I might be after such a laughable decision. It was clear from the start what the outcome would be. The joke is not that they rejected our appeal but that they allowed the prosecution's appeal against Horst.

---

15 The appeal against Ingrid and Irene's sentences (six and four years respectively) was rejected. As a result, their status changed from remand prisoner to convicted prisoner.

The purpose behind all this is crystal clear and not in the least surprising for us—they beat us with all possible harshness, and an insistence that RIGHTS cannot be our thing, when it's clear that these methods are but repressive instruments of the class that needs to be fought. It's almost amusing to see their open and unguarded behaviour, casting aside the famous rule of law as a mere useless burden.

Soon we'll be climbing into the blue overalls without batting an eye—I'm almost anticipating it with excitement, maybe because it's a change. However, I wouldn't mind the current conditions continuing for some time. The three of us close to each other and surrounded by a lot of people is bearable, so much so that one can't get to do anything else, nor would I want to. My pitiful failure to continue with the course needs to be confessed—the mistake was to agree to it in the first place. I *should* have known that the slightest interruption would rob me of any wish to marshal the concentration or willpower to stick with it. School-like studying is hell, on top of my doubts about the method, which is purely positivist rather than critical. Marxism is a sociological method too, but seems to me much more precise because critical. I'm not excluding the possibility of another attempt later, just that this is impossible now and for the near future. I can recommend the course to you, though, as you aren't in the process of learning another method and, therefore, wouldn't feel disturbed by it. The question is whether you will persist with reading the books, which you really should, as the subjects are very interesting. Have you ordered the books for me? It wouldn't be lost money—my time is rather limited at present, but it might be possible again in the future when I've thought about it more. I'm not sure yet what to write to the tutor.

If the letter to the children has arrived (it went off about a week ago), you'll know that only two of the books you sent reached me. I don't know where the rest have gone. The pictures are fantastic, as ever—I'll soon need an extra cell for my picture gallery.

Meanwhile *Le Monde* does arrive, but it comes with terrible irregularity because of some payment issues at their end. It will probably sort itself out. And if I reach the dubious pleasure of a daily work routine, I'll have to organise nightshifts to deal with the newspapers.

Give my love to old mummy Wilford.[16] Death is one way of living.

---

16   Michael's mother, who was diagnosed with cancer and died five years later.

Thanks to the State's selfless generosity I no longer need money or clothes from outside, so please don't send anything.

19 April. What did I say? You've barely started writing when you have to hop into a bathtub with the obligatory chat to follow. This is what removes any pressure to communicate in writing, and, luckily, I'm not the only one experiencing this. The other two here were in total isolation previously, writing endlessly, but now they write less and less. It's understandable: both have been waiting for their trial date for a year and a half and are still waiting. It will presumably now come in September at the earliest, for six people, including Irene and myself. Horst, as "the head", will be led to the gallows separately—and now I must go for my daily courtyard walk with the three others. I embrace you all.

Ingrid

13 June 1972

Hey Sister,

I'm giving the machine a rest and talking with my hand, as it's still very early morning, and I don't want to disturb the sleep of my three co-fighters. There was a bang in an apartment and, for the umpteenth time, some mysterious bits of paper with alleged plans have driven us back here into the "tower" at Moabit Prison,[17] after just one month of hard labour as convicted prisoners in the Lehrter Strasse. It meant a holiday from the arduous existence, a holiday that, in fact, we didn't want at all. The initial reaction of anger (against being transferred here again) gave way to total weariness and twenty-four-hour head banging.

Your last letter (ages ago) had to remain unanswered, as I was busy with potatoes in the basement for twelve hours a day, after which I wanted nothing but to rabbit on with someone *not* about potatoes, and then sleep and... Then there was lots of "free time", i.e., occupational and wellness therapy for the women, who need the exact opposite of that in terms of minimal conditioning for what awaits them on the outside.

---

17   On 1 June 1972, some explosive powder went up in smoke in a Berlin apartment, leading to police raids of the prisoners' cells and "bits of papers" being seized. Female political prisoners were held in solitary confinement in a special section of Moabit Prison for men, nicknamed the "tower". See the Endnote.

We witnessed a month of concentrated misery, seeing these products of a broken society, their hatred, their resignation directed against nothing other than themselves, and those others who are meant to reproduce in here the "sane" world outside using all the tricks that in here cost you dearly, being harsher and more blatant than they are on the outside. The superficial impression for occasional visitors is of a peaceful coffee and cake party, the big prison family. But everywhere there's a jealous and envious watchfulness, like who sits with whom, who gives who a piece of cake, how someone got hold of knee socks (forbidden in here)... etc.! And with us there was an even more difficult relationship, most likely a matter of class, and our confronting them with a kind of solidarity that is unknown to them though real for us. To make this clear for everyone is a task for which the expression "long-term" is too short.

Hey, please hold off with your visit until they've packed us back to the Lehrter, which *must* happen at some point, because the conditions here are so impossible. Besides, they can feel secure now that they hold all the trump cards in their hands.

I guess you'll be off into the sun sometime soon—take my restless mind with you, so that at least it will be refreshed.

A million greetings to your commune.

Ingrid

24 June 1972

Dear Sister,

I really have to admire my patience—I thought it was clear that everything about me and our defence isn't a family affair but is as much part of political action as everything so far. I can understand your urge to "help me", but it's neither necessary nor even possible because of fundamental differences in understanding about what such a trial and everything around it means. It is NOT about the length of the sentence, a few years here or there. The fact that you believe that the help of an unprejudiced top lawyer could change anything shows that you still believe in a State founded on the rule of law—but we know, and always have, that this illusion isn't quite enough to have us survive this thing. You and everyone else may find it completely crazy, dumb, stupid or whatever, but please understand that we do not beg for mercy. Absurd. Our respective choice of lawyer is a collective decision—and we now have the opportunity to discuss this—and not something determined by what each one's relatives would be able to cough up for specialists. In the context I now live in, I am not the sister, not the daughter, not a needy person. The approaching court cases will be vile, but this should in no way tempt us to seek services from those who, with their liberalism and neutrality, only stabilise the system.

Alas, Sister, you can really only shake your head when confronted with such a lot of stubbornness, or call it stupidity, if you like. You're just as much a victim of headlines and dirty lies as everybody else. I can understand you all so well. To hell with the tied hands here, who cannot tell you what the truth is. The need to be massively critical of what has happened so far is no doubt a matter of course, not as a negation but as a starting point to the next step. To talk about the past is perhaps justified to some extent with regard to the Red Army Faction, i.e., this group only, but not for the "movement" (terrible word, but there's nothing better) since the revolutionary potential which *does* exist doesn't diminish with the arrest of a few people.[18]

Sure, for the past few weeks, I too have felt like stretching out all four limbs, wishing for total resignation, but I get caught again by the burning question that keeps the four of us here busy, of how to do things differently and what to do in the future. Getting away from individual "downers" is the first thing, diverting ourselves with translating texts and noting down our experiences so far, to be passed on to those who still have to face them. I flip out from time to time because of my own inadequacies, barely able to hold two thoughts together, hollow, and yet my head overfull. When I tell you this, I trust you won't turn it around and say, "You see, you can't hack it".

I was astonished by the card from Michael, and not a little amused. Why does he think he needs to feel badly because he hasn't written to me? If only he could see the box of unanswered post here! Fifteen hours' worth! The short intermezzo as a convicted prisoner, inclusive of all privileges—ha, work—relieved me of all obligations to write, as there really was no time at all. I stood between potatoes and cooking pots until five in the evening, and then we had free time: television,

---

18   Several RAF members were arrested that month. See the Endnote and Timeline.

groups, guitar lessons, whatever. Our combined efforts to return to the other prison have quickly been curtailed; nothing can beat the security hysteria, and, as usual, one is powerless. They are turning out the lights now. I hope I'll feel energetic enough to carry on tomorrow morning. Sleep well. It's still light outside, and they try to force us into bed! So we sit by the window.

Hmm, I slept badly—during one of the last cell searches they confiscated Susanna's giant elephant as a threat to order and security.[19] Somewhere the word "pig" was mentioned. That's the way of thinking here.

I've finally got the clothes, which feel comfortable and make me look like a bride in a Soviet commune, anno 1945. Big training trousers and a vest, oh God.

But back to the beginning: I shall not accept and couldn't understand it if you all take my refusal of your help as an affront. Is that clear? And now I'm going to translate some French news items.

Marcus's letter was a surprise. I'd like to send you (but don't have a copy) a newspaper photo report of a giant festival for children in Kreuzberg, taken over by the Left and youngsters from the area. It includes a hospital that's been empty for a year. I'd have loved to be there, as would we all.[20]

Hey, delay your planned visit until we eventually return to the Lehrter Strasse. It should be decided by the end of the month.

Any number of big kisses for you all, and I won't write to Michael separately—Does he read these letters?

Hugs,

Ingrid

---

19 A drawing by Ingrid's niece Susanna.
20 A reference to a festival in Berlin the previous month. After the shooting of Georg von Rauch on 4 December 1971, an empty hospital building in Kreuzberg had been occupied by young people and renamed the Georg von Rauch House. A few days after the children's festival, the whole area was raided by the police in search of members of the 2nd of June Movement (an urban guerrilla group active mainly in West Berlin from 1972 until it joined the RAF in 1980).

20 September 1972

After a visit from Gerti

Hello Sister. Sorry to confront you with my handwriting, and worse: in red, except for the black pen smudges.

There's so much, I don't know where to begin, so starting with the most recent: our next trial begins on 24 November and Schily will most likely be there.[21] We applied for it, and he's already been accepted for Horst's (starting 9 October), albeit contrary to a recommendation by the Federal High Court. The final decision should come anytime, and if Schily isn't allowed to represent us, we're thinking of Heinrich Hannover, who's even more liberal and well-respected. I must impress upon you that none of this will change anything in any way, except perhaps the way the trial will unfold. I'm saying this now to keep you all from disappointments and to suggest that you let go of all illusions. No matter what we would, could or should want to say, the result is already written on the wall. And something else, an urgent request: don't pounce on him, leave him *in peace*.

If you want to find out regularly what's going on, best to order the *Süddeutsche Zeitung*. I don't have *Le Monde* yet. As we don't have written confirmation of whether we're staying here, best to wait for that first. In reality the decision has been taken, we're staying put, and we continue to be annoyed over confiscations. Here you write until your fingers bleed, and then the fruit of your thoughts lands in your personal file instead of the hands of the intended recipient.

Your visit obviously left a rather discontented and unresolved tension on both sides. You seemed to arrive in that state, and I found myself feeling restless and, because of one of these phases of repression here, not really in the mood to convey this in this unconveyable prison situation.

The "show" one puts on is necessary, precisely because you get nowhere with normal, rational, simple, logical, human thinking. ("In here you will get nowhere with logical thinking"—literal quote). You always land at the eternally bureaucratic barriers that have taken hold

---

21   Otto Schily was one of the defence lawyers involved in the trials. In later years, he
     became Germany's minister of the interior.

in the subalterns' brains, and which (almost inevitably) are believed to be their "own" ideas and actions, so you are forced to confront them again and again with their own absurdity. How well or badly you succeed is another question, and how it works on people from outside, who don't understand this whole Kafka, is yet a third question.

At the moment, however, it's rather quiet, nothing but the usual total blackout of information (letters + newspapers), hampering defence preparations and twenty-three-and-a-half hours in the cell, so same as ever. That's how the levels shift. Up here, there's quite a different atmosphere anyway (mostly), more akin to the Lehrter Strasse, so more relaxed, except at moments when you're once again not in sync with yourself. And that's really nothing unusual, a typical prison thing.

What does it mean to lose your sense of reality? The prison has its own reality, where values are defined differently, and that affects you. The assessment of, and with it the relation to, the outside, the "true" reality, remains a very concrete one, for as long as those who have the upper hand in this high house don't stop you being informed. They are the ones who try to destroy this, deliberately and brutally, so this is where the real "enemy" sits, because what's this other than hostile?

I'm not hanging myself over that, but one has to see it, though it doesn't affect my capacity to continue considering myself as an active subject. We don't make sacrifices, and we aren't victims; we're in a context where everyone is important—for oneself and for those with whom we continue to live, even if they are outside these walls. The importance of this is small but relevant. If this dynamic is interpreted wrongly it leads to questions like: What does all this mean? What's the sense of it? Questions that use standards and values that make no sense in the prison reality. So it's not us who have lost our sense of reality but all of you, who see only the number of years and the window bars, not what meaning this has for all of us here.

Small interim check: in eleven days, nine of seventeen letters and postcards have been confiscated.

It's not important to throw around brilliant slogans—that's the privilege of politicians and factions of all shades. What's important is to adopt in each situation the particular function that's possible and necessary. No idea what that has to do with fanaticism, but it's certainly about the unconditional resolve you find so hard to understand. Without a doubt, I've got a completely different view of Munich than you, all of you, the whole outraged "civilised" world that accepts all other killing without batting an eyelid and even supports it energetically. Israel is the sanctioned aggressor, however much the liberals and critics of the world may "regret" its retaliatory strikes[22]—and what do they do but excuse them anyway? And this from the safe position of neutrality, believing that they never do anything wrong and, thus, sanction "peace as the peace of the graveyard". Taking sides with those who resist is dismissed as "stubbornness". Really? On what basis?

It *is* cruel, the whole world is cruel, and that cannot be met with pious hopes.

The words of the guerrillas are mentioned only in passing. The loudest and most revered words are those of the "civilised", who for centuries have elevated themselves to masters of the entire world. The deception with which the group had been lured into the trap and the natural hypothesis used to justify the trap speak for themselves. I know, I know, terror is not the means. But for those in power, it is *the* means, only more sublimely so.

Enlightenment—the magic word that is elevated to being the only possible means; wonderful, only the system is *so* strong that it can obstruct this means with all its might. The militarisation began on their side and is being expanded rapidly. The use of military might against strikers, youths and families looking for a home has gone on for years, ever since there's been a movement that resists, that doesn't keep still. Everything that is changing in the current evolutionary process, women's emancipation, the education sector, youth self-determination, etc., is the expression of a growing consciousness, but it doesn't attack the existing power relations. On the contrary, these are being stabilised by them; they absorb them (for example, anti-racism: advertising children's clothing using non-white children, advertising as an opinion-building factor. Progress? No, exploitation of existing class conflicts to maximise profit).

---

22 A reference to the 1972 Olympics, when Israeli athletes were taken hostage by the Palestinian Black September organisation, demanding in exchange the liberation of 234 Palestinian prisoners. A diversion was orchestrated at Munich's Fürstenfeldbruck airfield, and the hostages and a police officer died in the ensuing shootout. Three of the eight Black September members survived and were released following a plane hijacking the following month. The Israeli air force "retaliated" with air strikes against ten Palestinian refugee camps in Jordan. The RAF issued a document addressing these events (*The Black September Action in Munich: Regarding the Strategy for Anti-Imperialist Struggle*). See Moncourt and Smith, 205–36 (see p. 57, footnote 5).

I'm *not* saying what the RAF did was right in every detail. Huge mistakes with huge consequences, one of which being the current impression (by inmates, for instance) of what the RAF is. One question here was: How old does one have to be to join the group? Symptomatic, sure, but it doesn't contradict the initial concept, which can be criticised only for its application, and this—"to learn from mistakes"—is happening!

Dear me, now I've given you and everyone else food for further upsets and fears about my being stubborn and intransigent, fanatical, losing perspective, etc. But that doesn't worry me. I can't avoid it. I can only say this: my head is still in the right place. The biggest regrets are those of the censor, in his position on high, for stealing my typewriter. Haha.

No other news from the jail front, sitting and writing and, as the latest luxury, a radio. Real luxury—but these are the standards by which prison is measured: behind walls, everything ordinary is a luxury, a gift from God.

Have the prisoners at your end come down from the roofs yet? A lovely image, and a good one.[23]

Don't gag on your breakfast, Sister, and greet your large family with lots of kisses. I'll now write a few more letters and have them confiscated again.

Greetings,

Ingrid

Oh yes: for my birthday please send a *small parcel* with your fabulous English-type biscuits.[24] I've always nibbled those with pleasure, but *nothing* with ginger, liquorice or peppermint. There's time, though, I suppose.

---

23 Riots occurred throughout British prisons between 1969 and 1972, as prisoners organised coordinated acts of resistance. In summer 1972, inmates at Pankhurst Prison climbed onto the roof to proclaim their solidarity with other prisoners and demand improvements in prison conditions.

24 Ingrid was twenty-eight on 7 November 1972.

10 November 1972

Hello Sister, I started a letter the other day after your excellent parcel arrived (you can do that more often!), but then my wish to write faded away, and now I can't find your latest letter again. Seems some method here.

I heard wonders about your mania for seeking self-improvement—sorry, no offence intended. I really didn't think you were so serious about this. Wonder where you want to get to with it, once you realise that all this self-improvement and gaining insight only results in the dreary isolation of indeed being able to explain and understand everything but, from now, with even less possibility of applying what's been learnt. Oof. Doesn't mean what you're doing is wrong, as long as you don't do it as *"l'art pour l'art"*, as an end in itself.

The second part of the birthday greetings have just arrived. I'll answer the children separately, and I'm frantically searching and searching for the Turkish satires, but they're not in there. Will have to extend the search to Pontius and Pilatus.[25]

Ma and Helke were here,[26] and during the second of their two visits I lost my usual calm and an unnecessary dispute arose that exasperated Ma totally. My fault, as nothing can be explained or resolved in this way. Though I've rarely seen such a fragile person. It's like touching porcelain, and doing that now, when I'm used to handling granite and speaking the language of those around me. That's become my language, which alienates me completely from a "refined" way of speaking—which has become foreign to me.

Helke has also remained unchanged, running along well-trodden paths. I'm always a bit stumped by how this is possible, without questioning oneself and one's surroundings. All contradictions are smoothed over with the ever-comforting homily that "things will get better" and "so much is changing already, patience". Patience, yes, but not with the wrong side.

Everyone thinks we're up to our ears preparing for the trial; not a bit of it! There's hardly anything to prepare. We have no part in the legal wrangling, there are only small details to discuss, and only time will

---

25 "From Pontius to Pilatus": German expression for "running from pillar to post".
26 Helke, Ingrid's second eldest sister, lived in Koblenz with her photographer husband Manfred, their daughter Nicole and Manfred's parents. After the parents died, Helke and Manfred took over their well-established photography studio in central Koblenz.

tell what we'll do apart from that, and we do have sufficient time. The conditions change so quickly, so we want to remain flexible. Horst's trial proceedings are already mapping out the route. The only interesting thing for us will be to study the different faces in court. No, it will be a bit more than that, but whatever we do, it will always be wrong.

I liked the way the SPK[27] in Heidelberg sabotaged their whole trial by passive (later active) resistance to appearing in court. They did it as the only possible way of showing that we have nothing to do with this justice system. Important, however, that at the same time a counter-tribunal was held at the university, accusing the State of systematically destroying collectives like this. Similar tribunals will be set up in other European countries. They serve a purpose, when organised properly. Am curious how it will develop. Here, similar things aren't possible, because the necessary active people are missing.

Hey, are you sad when you realise that the kids are starting to withdraw from your influence? Please don't be! It's the start of your dependence and, thus, for the kids an unconscious form of blackmail. In any event, Marcus is reaching the stage of development when his old parents don't understand anything anymore, regardless of how you act. Or are you so good that he can accept you as partners? What a joke, me talking to you about bringing up children, but I'm thinking about myself and about the young people I talk to here, some of them only sixteen, so not so far from him in age.

I'm tired now; I wrote deep into the night yesterday, after a long break. There are always two to three weeks in between, when nothing moves, the brain stands still or rather moves backwards. And my hand becomes an instrument from hell, my writing driving me crazy, because it reveals so much about me that I really do not like.

Tell Susanna never to cut her lovely hair! And I kiss you all and say thanks to the children for their work. I'll reply as soon as I feel ready to write to them.

Until whenever. You will certainly be able to come some time.
Greetings,
Ingrid

---

27 The Socialist Patients' Collective (SPK) was an initiative in 1970–1971 by patients with mental health disorders and medical staff, whose catchphrase was to "turn illness into a weapon". See Moncourt and Smith, 109 (see p. 57, footnote 5).

3 December 1972

Well Sister, everything has arrived; heartfelt thanks for it all. The books have to pass by the judge as usual. The blouse—lady, I'm not as old as this colour! But it will be useful, even if not with the trousers you had in mind—I no longer fit into them, sad but true. Briefly, with reference to my last message, your planned visit: the prospect of spending three days talking to you in the presence of four strange ears is frustrating, but please be assured that you are always welcome in my modest dwelling here. That goes without saying. The dates depend on what suits you best (I'm always at home). Are you going on to Koblenz for Christmas? Isn't that going to be a bit hectic? I shall probably be incredibly ill then, due to overeating.

So do whatever's best for you—come when there's a good opportunity.

The family must be under the false impression that I've become a fanatical knitter. I can hardly move for all the wool here, and I've put this well-intentioned occupational therapy tool into my cardboard box for safe keeping. Remember, be careful what you ask for!

Dearest, a thick book awaits me, and I want to conquer it once and for all. Still, or again (for the third time), *Das Kapital*.

Ten thousand hugs to the whole people. Until soon!

Ingrid

Letters 1973

There is a month-long hunger strike early in the year. Some forty political prisoners demand an end to being held in solitary confinement, which for most of them means total isolation from each other and from other prisoners. This hunger strike ends when Ulrike Meinhof, who for eight months had been subject to acoustic isolation in a high-security wing of Cologne Prison, is transferred temporarily to a cell in a different section of the prison. As nothing else changes, three months later approximately eighty political prisoners join a second collective hunger strike, which lasts for seven weeks. Ingrid describes and reflects on these events and, in response to an earlier request from Gerti, she describes the normal daily prison regime. Towards the end of the year, she is moved back to Moabit Prison for two months.

8 January 1973

Dear Sister, hoho, late—but it's coming, the warm birthday kiss, together with all the good wishes, hopes, ideas… that you can imagine for yourself.

The gap in correspondence has an easy explanation: the four weeks in the Lehrter Strasse (they couldn't tolerate us any longer last time either; that seems to be the extreme limit) was one single huge dream of PEOPLE. That's what it is there, and it was good. And since we had to be on guard every minute in case we were snapped up and returned to this place, we concentrated on being prepared until, though still suspicious, we finally felt secure in the knowledge that we could stay and so began to unpack our stuff. Then, "thwack", we were grabbed by the scruffs of our necks, for the fourth time, and this time it was really nasty, because only two days earlier we had received reassurances from the prison director and the judge that we could stay.

That's the story of the newest lie. Lies are the basic principle here. Full stop.

The annual "oil paintings" (+ scarf!) have arrived. My collective thanks to all the artists, even though I don't yet have the super cell that would allow for such an art exhibition. Apart from the fact that, due to the frequent transfers, my possessions have been reduced to one box—which, as I'm finding out, is quite sufficient. However, I've decided to start painting, if I can get some paint in here, which will mean more hard labour, like Sisyphus.

Back in the Lehrter Strasse a smile would get you your stuff. We played guitar, sang, performed war dances, all of which resurrected some prison corpses back to life up to the point that they found themselves amongst a mad circle of stamping dancers. Easy living and, at the same time, the whole prison problem highlighted, because living together with people shows all the more clearly that prison must be abolished. Just like that. Never and under no circumstances can prison have a function—sure, this society needs this pinnacle of absurdity. You know, this is becoming increasingly clear.

I'll now start to do more reading—concentration's going to the dogs. One needs to find the right balance, so as not to rot intellectually but also not to distance oneself too much from other people and become too abstract. That's the huge danger of this isolation, which only differs in small measures from the isolation in the Cologne and Mainz Prisons, etc. The physical liquidation takes a bit longer, and, if they'd had the space and opportunity, they would have reached that stage long ago. The concentration camp of the future is very close.

The trial[1]—a farce! Horrifically boring, some action every now and then, and then more yawning boredom—the setting has nothing to offer, nor do the bystanders. We use it as leverage for our demand to be taken back to the Lehrter Strasse. This is where you can expose such lies, but, of course, nobody is interested, and the corrupt scribblers of the press

---

1   The second trial against Horst Mahler lasted from October 1972 to February 1973. At the end of 1972, the trial for bank robbery and "membership in a criminal organisa-tion" began against Ingrid and five others.

don't think it necessary to publicise even one word of the context that we explain—everything is turned into shrill noise (naturally, because we are women!) and a racket.

The press reports about the appearance of Ulrike and Gudrun, etc. at Horst's trial were also openly defamatory and full of lies, but obvious only to those who were there. In their scribblings they cannot admit that they were fascinated (as they admitted verbally) and had understood some of it—but their jobs, their nicely secured existence, would be on the line. So they'd rather sell themselves...

What are you doing, all of you? Still so busy? The holy Christmas (which I'd totally forgotten) must have been a bit exhausting, or was it calm and peaceful? Prison Christmas was characterised by outsize cakes all over the place, and I attracted a lot of public anger for my minimalist parcel (and, of course, the reduced calories have had no effect so far; I simply cannot stop).

I'm just listening to East German beat; they're catching up. Music is such an important factor.

What else can one say about Vietnam? The whole world has understood by now that Nixon is a murderer,[2] but they aren't interested, so he can get away with it, smirking coldly. And Vietnam is only the beginning (and the end). Yes Sister—this is our thing.

For the children, again twelve big kisses (four each) for their paintings. I'll return the favour with more colour but doubt it will mean much to them.

For you and Mike, warm embraces and kisses.

Ingrid

19 March 1973

Hi, dear Sister, you have challenged me with a pretty task here. These last few days I've had to recover from the four-week strike.[3] What's

---

2   Richard Nixon, US president from 1969 to 1974. In this letter, the "x" in "Nixon" was drawn as a swastika, as in many leftist publications of the era.

3   The first collective hunger strike of the prisoners from the RAF took place from 17 January to 16 February 1973, demanding the end of solitary confinement and the abolition of the special isolation unit in Cologne Prison, where Ulrike Meinhof was subjected to total sensory deprivation. See Ingrid's letter of 6 March 1974. In an

not to understand in the logic of a hunger strike? They need your body in order to execute their punishment, so they *must* preserve it—you threaten to withdraw it from them and, thus, unsettle the whole system. Ghoulish, but those are the plain facts. You also demonstrate that you are prepared to risk everything in order to alert the public. Apparently, the hunger strike was systematically suppressed from all media and false reports disseminated, spearheaded by the Springer press. We gained a few things, but whether they will last remains to be seen.

(By the way, why is this logic so hard to understand, while Gandhi is praised as the big hero of passive resistance? I have memories of this man being upheld by our mother as exemplary and worthy of praise. Holy non-logic. As soon as your own skin is involved, everything is suddenly wrong? You're on the wrong track!)

Then, the Egg![4] I really don't expect that you or even more so our parents would understand. That would mean understanding almost everything! It's not about an egg (unfortunately nothing better was available). That was merely the material expression of an idea or, in other words, part of the conclusion we reached when analysing these trials. A trial is not a forum, not anymore. That was still possible when the courtroom conveyed an atmosphere of "neutrality". Would you kindly ask the court, these six judges and two prosecutors, to understand why they are at the pinnacle of the repressive system? There's nobody else there with whom you can have a confrontation. The press plays the villainous game of the paid scribblers, who write what they *must* write. In the meantime, the audience knows that the system cannot be attacked in the courtroom—not with words. Discussion? With whom? About what? Horst tried it, Margrit tried it—they had to fail because, in doing so, they were denying their own practice.[5] Ulrike and Andreas tried it as witnesses—they were sucked in by the force of circumstances.[6]

---

attempt to break the strike, Andreas Baader was deprived of drinking water for five days. The prisoners ended the strike after Ulrike Meinhof was transferred temporarily from the Cologne special unit. As nothing else changed, a second collective hunger strike was called, lasting from 8 May to 29 June 1973. This time Andreas Baader was deprived of drinking water for ten days. See the Endnote.

4   An egg filled with ink was thrown at the judge during the hearing but missed him.
5   The trial against Margrit Schiller in Hamburg for "membership in a criminal organisation" lasted from November 1972 to January 1973.
6   Ulrike Meinhof and Andreas Baader were briefly summoned as witnesses at the trials in West Berlin.

Absurd to have to act as a witness; like any other role in this spectacle, it is no longer acceptable, and everything one does in there can only make sense if it shows the judiciary in all its naked ugliness. Clearly, an egg is rather banal, I agree. If it had hit its target, it wouldn't have been.

It's truly strange to hear that I should consider how each of my incomprehensible stupidities causes increasing pain to our parents. My whole being hurts them a thousand times! And my being is that of everyone whose suffering is so great that nothing can stop them from attacking the murderous logic of what's happening. And it *is* murderous. It hurts, of course. It's bound to. To prevent that isn't the point.

In this sense, I'm not just an individual—I cannot be separated from what I do. When I do something, I am identical with it. If not, I cannot do it—I would be lying. Political identity means unity of being and necessity. Existing society functions according to the exact opposite principle: do everything that you must but don't want to in order to exist.

Listen, when I describe more precisely what you want to know about prison it might turn into half a book. I'm sending you this short version. If you have more detailed questions, ask me. What will you do with this?

I had a letter from Donald Churchill, I think it was. I cannot remember him. Tell him I'll answer sometime, when the mountain of letters that grew here while I had no energy for four weeks has been reduced. I was pleased that he thought of something like that.[7]

What do you mean by "getting on with people"? That they should be integrated smoothly into the existing ossified relationships in society? That leaves open the basic question of why people become "disturbed" and what the progressive moment of this "disturbance" would be. Explanations based on some environmental influences are lame; they diminish and falsify the total violence of social influences. Nobody is born "disturbed" (unless there is some organic damage, something that makes them so). Violence takes different forms and begins in the family (family as the seedbed of every State). When seen as a product, the disturbed don't fit into the standardised image. They aren't disturbed, but disturb—disturb the rest, disrupting the stereotype. The progressive, active moment in this is when, as a product of their environment and

---

7   A family friend in England who was interested in events in Germany.

influences, they take their disturbance as an opportunity to uncover and attack its causes.

You want to integrate them and, in doing so, you obscure the very contradiction that they reveal—securely, superficially, to make it all more pleasant. I assume you're referring to the juvenile delinquents. Precisely, this is the enormous hook that Michael hangs onto: reintegrating them into a society that will do nothing other than destroy them again.[8]

I'm stopping now, as it's nearly 2:00 in the morning. Surely not an answer to your question, especially not the last point, but perhaps a small push to consider things differently. The massive question remains: What can you really do in your situation if you want to achieve any change at all?

Greeting you all,
Ingrid

Attachment to the 19 March 1973 Letter

Gerti had asked Ingrid about the daily prison routine and about any differences in the treatment of political and other prisoners.

Moabit (approx. 1,300 male prisoners)

1)

Daily routine:

6:00	Door bolt unlocked (thunderous noise), lights on
6:30	Knife thrown into cell
7:00	Breakfast
	Bread, 30g margarine, prison broth
	Wednesday: 50g marmalade
	Sunday: 30g butter, 50g artificial honey or cabbage salad

---

8   Michael had been a magistrate at the juvenile court for several years, where he realised that the legal representation of children and their parents was pitifully inadequate, especially in cases where parental responsibility was at risk of being taken away by court order. He set up a specialist legal practice and helped promote independent representation for children and parents involved in these cases brought to court by local authorities.

7:30–11:30 Exercise time (walking around the courtyard)
           Half of each floor: 15–30 people walk for half an hour, in circles, in pairs, behind each other
           Forbidden to exercise in any way: run, smoke, call up to windows
12:00   Lunch + fruit twice a week
           Saturday: 200g fruit quark
           Sunday: tinned fruit or pudding
15:30   Evening meal: bread, 30g margarine, sausage or cheese
17:00   Lock up = knife taken out, finished, no door opened after this
22:00   Lights out (from outside)

Tuesday/Wednesday: 3-minute shower, in groups

Monday to Friday morning: visits, 20 minutes every two weeks, with GP, dentist, nurse

Saturday morning: cell cleaning

Sunday: church (only for those without an accomplice)

Youth education groups for those under 21 and without an accomplice: one hour a week, table tennis, chess or TV

Adults: every two weeks, a movie (Heinz Rühmann[9] or similar)

Library: once a week, exchange of up to five books, mainly trivial literature but specialist too (foreign languages, professional textbooks)

Radio: centrally controlled, 6:00–7:30, 10:00–10:30 (for educational programmes), 15:30–22:30

2)

That's the external framework, dominated and interrupted by meal times and exercise time. In between, the prisoners' main occupation is: SLEEPING and reading Western stories and porn.

Communication is only possible through conversations at the window and during courtyard walks, initiated by bartering (tobacco, Western pulp stories, porn). Those who never learnt to communicate in this way are totally dependent on their four walls for twenty-three-and-a-half hours a day. The "educational groups" consist of four to six people each at most, thus twenty people out of the *total* of two hundred youths (or more, not sure). "Recreational" possibilities, *nil*. No sport, no discussion groups or similar, no television, etc., no nothing.

---

9   A popular film actor.

Rules: all is forbidden but much is "tolerated", i.e., it remains forbidden and, thus, everybody is permanently punishable, and that's the way it's handled, arbitrarily. For instance, it's forbidden to stand by the window. *Everybody* stands by the window, day-in, day-out. Every evening, some are picked on and their chair and table (on which they stand) are removed. Those who resist are moved to the bunker (an empty cell in the basement with no bed or just a plank bed). Longer bunker punishments must be ordered by a judge. The scale of punishments is broad: from cutting down food (only dry bread and prison broth) to the curtailment of shopping and an empty cell or bunker for up to ten days (or more, not sure exactly).

Privileges for the clever ones who know the ropes. Either through official channels or because they know how and who to suck up to. Privileges are *the* poison, because people are played off against one another. "I can't do this or that because I got permission to do such and such". Privileges include your own typewriter, transistor radio, books, more frequent visits and the like. These are official and can be withdrawn at any time for "misuse". Unofficial ones: preferential allocation of work (for instance, as "trusties"[10] = a popular job, because it allows much freedom of movement on the floor and throughout the prison; also an exploiter's job, enabling many business transactions). Getting out of the cell using a thousand excuses (having to go to the doctor, to the clothes store and the like). Getting things to people (cigarettes, etc. for the workers).

Work: far too little for 1,300 people.

Older ones are favoured: locksmiths, car mechanics, joinery, gardening, kitchen, laundry, courtyard orderlies, section orderlies, clothes store, etc.

For the younger ones: industrial work—painting boxes, assembling electrical equipment, etc. Wages between 0.80 DM and 1.80 DM (more or less, don't know the exact "salaries" here).

Can say little or nothing about the kind of working environment and the special conditions. Naturally, the system of privileges and favouritism is much more pronounced here. As already said: ask me questions about particular things for more precise answers.

---

10   A prisoner used by the authorities to distribute the food and perform other tasks outside the cells, a role that brings with it certain privileges.

3)

Our average daily routine here:

Fundamental difference: our section (four cells + one cell for guards) is completely separate from the main prison. We get our food in big pots at the usual times, but they leave it here so we can help ourselves when we want.

Mornings: get up when we wake up, for me mostly around 9:00, but it depends. Faffing about, breakfast 10:00–11:30, yard time, forty-five minutes (Moni + Brigitte,[11] Irene and me, remand prisoners and convicted prisoners separately!). Newspaper reading until lunch.

Afternoons: gymnastics, writing letters or reading books, some-times chatting at the window.

15:30 supper, then together with Irene in one of our cells until 17:30.

18:00 doors closed: knives collected, water fetched, silly stuff.

After that, it's work time: letters; theory; discussion at the window of certain problems; talk with the guys about their problems; more exercises; fiddling around (wash, tidy up or move things around—if not in the mood for anything else); sitting still for long periods and thinking (never boring!); working on certain texts (though the material is very restricted, as nothing comes through).

24:00 lights out (that late for us, to prepare for trial). After that, listen to music, dream, heavenly peace, best part of the day.

We're "privileged", of course: we have money and enough people who look out for us. A privilege we reject, wanting to be integrated into the normal prison routine. That way, material privileges could be shared.

4)

The difference from the time when we worked in Lehrter Strasse Prison is clear: here, total concentration on ourselves and theoretical reviewing of the prison situation, its meaning in the process as a whole. Enough time to recognise connections, learning through books, news-papers and by talking about it. Theoretical participation in the prison situation of the young ones, i.e., not being able to act together, not having the same conditions, not being exposed to the same influences, not experiencing the same (real) oppression.

In the Lehrter Strasse: there, at the workplace, there are perma-nent contradictions between the supervisors and the workers. On the

---

11   Monika Berberich and Brigitte Asdonk.

one hand, sharing the same conditions, undergoing the same sensory experiences, means reducing the distrust towards me/us and, on the other hand, the possibility of making them conscious of their position in concrete situations, of what developing self-confidence means, the meaning of oppression of women and oppression in the workplace. That happens through very small "banal" personal stories, because, of course, their own problems are enormous, determining everything. Destroyed. By participating in all "leisure time" activities (groups, TV), getting to know each other, gaining mutual trust, understanding → criticism → reshaping → criticism → constant process.[12] We were there for much too short a time (one month), which is no time to say anything.

28 October 1973

Hello, what wonderful news that you are coming. I hope not out of fury that no letters arrive anymore, you as living postman, so to speak. No, it's great, we can speak then. But the permanent attendant is, of course, a disturbing factor, because I can't be as I'd like; it will be more wooden and VERY incomplete. And the difficulty with Sundays is that the gentlemen will be at soccer then. So you'll have to check with them whether it might be possible without them. Will be a busy month, parents coming too.

But something else (in a hurry again, of course—not just saying that, it's true!): yesterday I ordered a journal from England: *New Left Review*, 7 Carlisle Street, London W1. I'm not sure if they are sufficiently progressive to send it free to people in prison (many leftist newspapers do that here). Could you call them and also ask them to send it as fast as possible? And if it costs something, could you pay for it? Hmm. Would be nice.

The *Sunday Times* arrives now. It's okay so far, can't evaluate yet whether it's worth it or not—depends mainly on the economic section. So let's leave it as is for now. Apart from that, I need nothing right now. Fully covered. What it's about, now and in the future, is to work on an accurate analysis of imperialism. That's a constant and damn difficult learning process, because it implies that Marxism must be heard and learnt and really drummed in. It's fun once you have grasped a piece

---

12   An acknowledged Marxist principle.

of it, how to apply it, what it can be used for, what Marx had already found, precisely because he developed this correct method. Which isn't about idolising Marx but about applying the right method. The war in the Near East or Watergate can't be explained and understood without it. And, as said earlier, the secret reveals itself bit by bit.

Okay, until soon—and bring yourself, completely. Yes.

For all children and men, big kisses and hugs,

Ingrid

4 November 1973

Hello, as far as the visit's concerned, I've realised that the decision about whether a visit is possible without police surveillance is not up to the prison management, who only do as they are told, but lies with the Justice Department. But this month would be a bit too much anyway. So come when you can and when Michael can free himself from the dreams of his youth. (Also a kind of nostalgia—don't you think? But good too: freedom to think what you like again, even though the restrictions of Cambridge University thinking are a given. Or is it Oxford?)[13]

Analysing what you're suggesting or, rather, what you think might be required, I get the impression that we're lost idiots who, by denying this, only confirm our idiocy. A bit blunt of me—but that's what it looks like. And because liberality and humanitarianism are your chief guidelines for life, you think you're helping me by taking me off this "treadmill". Your need, your urge, to "help" me turns into helplessness; it has to, because *in* this need you are imprisoned in *your* cage, your bourgeois ways of thinking that exist objectively, based on your whole history, yes, on your class position. You're desperately running up against it, like an errant bird wanting to flee its cage because it's getting too constricted. And the thing that's becoming too constricted, i.e., what's annoying, is the contradiction between the growing realisation that this society is a prison in every respect, utterly so, pushing for a solution that must be a socialist one, versus your objective class position, which prevents you from turning this realisation into action

---

13   Michael had taken a break from his legal work to take a Masters in Criminology at Cambridge University.

and keeps even mere thinking within certain boundaries. Thinking determined by the relations of production, which, in turn, typically, are perceived as natural and unchangeable.

Your class position forces you to think like that, i.e., defensively, passively—because, if you were to think in a Marxist class-conscious way you would already be walking the path of revolutionary thinking. The barriers to this are powerful. If by extension one applies this to those who have capital—themselves using ad absurdum the application of Marxist analysis—they wouldn't be what they are any longer, because they would have to throw away their stuff; they'd understand what havoc they cause. No wonder, therefore, that Marxism and, above all, those who actively advance it are being pursued with such bitter hatred from that quarter. As for *how* and to what extent and with what perfection that happens—for that you need only read the newspapers carefully every day.

You sigh again... "totally obstinate, this sister of mine, this one-sidedness"... well, that doesn't upset me in the slightest, because I am biased, of course, that is the only thing that allows me to be alive, and more than that: it's what produces joy and fulfilment in the first place. To be a member of the bourgeoisie doesn't mean you have to remain a prisoner to it. The decisive factor is where you seek and find your identity, what you identify with, whose immediate human rights you want to uphold. We're a long way from revolution, it's true. And the tendency for ever-growing evolution is wrong. The money managers and their government cronies realise that socialism is unavoidable—that's why they want it *top down*, planned capitalism, with an evolutionary transition, of course, because it's still capitalist. It's clear that won't make a scrap of difference for the individual worker and will mean as little for the masses over here as for the masses in the Third World[14] (except that they'll be bombarded with even more rubbish and useless consumer goods, which they'll have been compelled to produce themselves).

On the contrary: as the contradictions become ever sharper, the *revolutionary* tendency will become clearer too, pushing things forward,

---

14   The term Third World (*Tiers Monde*) was coined in the early 1950s by the French sociologists Claude Bourdet and Alfred Sauvy to indicate the emerging Non-Aligned Movement while referencing the *Tiers Etat* of the French Revolution. Liberation movements in the Third World adopted the term as a rallying cry in their fight for self-determination.

even though it may take—must take—decades, because capital has an enormous power and isn't stupid. Once the division of the entire world is concluded at every level (economically, militarily, culturally) and the insatiable expansion of imperialist capital can't be satisfied any further, it will all be about self-preservation. Because with the expansion will come resistance against it, which they will be compelled to *destroy* if they want to survive.

Look at Vietnam. It didn't work out there, because the people's urge for freedom was stronger, and this resistance is now spreading across all parts of the Third World. Capitalism sees this very clearly. And because obvious genocide like that in Vietnam creates problems in their own camp, they resort to all means possible, from capital investment to development aid to direct support with money and weapons to rightist movements (see Chile, Greece).

All this analysis of these methods fills books and is *outrageously* clear. If unaware of these facts, one can't determine the extent of it or be certain about how to evaluate the methods—but reading newspapers with a critical eye opens up the brain beautifully.

It's clear that it can't be the socialism of the Soviet Union, because that's also State capitalism. But for the period that interests us now it's no big deal, because the real issue confronting us is imperialism—a terrible, horrific fact surpassing everything so far. Take, for example, the politics of raw materials: it revolves only and exclusively around the needs of the imperialist centres—the USA, the European Union, Japan, and some satellites. That's only a third of the world population. When the other two-thirds, the already hungry and starving masses of the Third World, start to assert their right to *live*—and they will—there will be a genocide of unknown proportions. That's started here already by letting them starve, by leaving the *superfluous* (superfluous to capital, because they don't generate profit) to destroy themselves. Those laughable donations of grain and bread, the sweetener, the beautiful gesture, cynicism in the extreme, while at the same time arms and military means of destruction are brought into the very same countries for the suppression of freedom fighters.

Of course, it's all more complicated than that. It takes a while to get an overview of the entire sophisticated system. Once you find the thread you never stop pulling at it. Not out of some stupid fascination, but because that's the reality we're dealing with and that everyone is part of—much as you'd like to stay out of it and no matter how much you try to repress it.

And good old Charlie was no clairvoyant or prophet,[15] but he did manage to work out intellectually what all life is based on and how it develops, and he created the scientific method of Marxism. No superman or whatever, just a very clever human being. And because Marxism is a method based on applying the contradictions in nature and all forms of life, what Marx did had nothing to do with foresight. He developed his thesis from the circumstances that existed objectively. *Without contradictions there would be no universe* (that's from Mao, by the way). And that's as valid today as it was a hundred years ago—in its *general* form. And the essence of Marxism is that the *specifics* of every situation must be analysed and determined afresh. That's the task whatever we're working on: determine the main contradictions of today, analyse them comprehensively, develop revolutionary theory. I'm busy with this, but mostly as someone constantly having to trace the roots, meaning I must work incredibly hard to understand everything, to work independently. I can't analyse—not yet (a bit like your problem: wanting to express something clearly but not quite getting there).

Well, I've taken some time and don't know what I might have failed to answer, but I hope for now this is sufficient stuff for explosive debate. By the way, Brecht was almost as good a dialectical thinker as Marx, but says it in poetry, with each poem or play needing to be seen in its historical context.

Until sometime, and warm kisses to all the kids.

Hugs,

Ingrid

4 December 1973

Hello all of you. First, a collective thanks for the collective works of the collective of artists. A big kiss for each of you.

Next, I was shown your letter announcing that you'd be over here from Saturday to Tuesday, and that you want to come and visit. I think I told you in a previous letter that Saturday and Sunday don't work as

---

15   Karl Marx.

visiting days unless, of course, the Political Police will forgo their presence.[16] An inquiry by the prison authorities confirmed that they aren't prepared to do that, so you won't be able to come Saturday/Sunday, only Monday/Tuesday. Shit, but perhaps you'll be able to get two hours— you should, otherwise the whole enterprise is hardly worthwhile. And Berlin in winter isn't pleasant either, but I know you'll explore the National Gallery, where it's warm, and where taxis work on Sundays. Maybe you could look at the jail from the outside; it might almost be worth it. Just a thought.

Then: what to bring. Please, nothing. I don't need cosmetics, and I've more than enough books. But I need some money for a pair of boots I can only buy via the social service here. If you feel like donating a little sum towards that, it would be more practical, though perhaps not as loving from your point of view. But better no frozen toes than horrid paste all over your face. The other thing you could do is look for catalogues or even book titles about the IRA and Ireland in some leftist or liberal or just normal bookshops and send them to Brigitte Mohnhaupt, same address here, as she's working on Ireland.[17] I'm on South Africa, still collecting references, as before. And finding it hard to make head or tail of it. It's a jumble.

I have terrible toothache, a wisdom tooth—just wanted to tell you. Until soon. Have a good journey. And hugs,
Ingrid

---

16 All visits to prisoners from the RAF, except visits from their lawyers, took place in the presence of police officers from the State Security departments of the Federal Criminal Investigation Bureau (BKA) or Regional Criminal Investigation Bureaus (LKA). In West Berlin, at that time, the State Security department was called the Political Police (*Politische Polizei* or PoPo); it was successor to the Nazis' Security Police (*Sicherheitspolizei* or SiPo).

17 In May 1972, the struggle by prisoners from the IRA (Irish Republican Army) for recognition as prisoners of war entered a decisive phase. Following a hunger strike, British Secretary of State for Northern Ireland William Whitelaw granted the prisoners "Special Category" status (POW status in all but name). In January 1973, most were moved into the compounds of the Long Kesh detention centre, which until then had only held internees, and not anyone convicted of an offence. Long Kesh held 1,874 nationalists from 1971 until internment was abolished in 1975. See Ingrid's letter of 6 March 1974.

Letters 1974

The political prisoners hold a third collective hunger strike, lasting twenty-one weeks. Part way through, the female prisoners in Berlin are taken to the Moabit Prison hospital, eventually to be force fed. The death of a prisoner on hunger strike, Holger Meins, prompts widespread demonstrations. In the run-up to the hunger strike, the prisoners from the RAF intensify their internal discussions and are working on various political analyses, as reflected in Ingrid's letters of this period.

Ingrid talks about the prison system and describes its impact on both political and other prisoners. She also describes what it means to be part of a collective, with its learning processes and strong sense of responsibility to the group.

11 January 1974

No, I need to contradict you and tell you that we got quite a different impression of Oestreicher.[1] Exactly the same impression as the *Guardian* newspaper, comparable to Heinemann,[2] which will then be

---

1   Anglican priest Paul Oestreicher was chair of Amnesty International's British Section. For more about Amnesty International's work about political prisoners in Germany and other countries, see p. 3–4, footnote 2.
2   Gustav Heinemann was president of West Germany from 1969 to 1974. He was known for soothing the conscience of his supporters by making humane gestures, e.g., appealing to students after the assassination attempt against their spokesperson Rudi Dutschke in 1968 and pardoning repentant witness Karl-Heinz Ruhland. See footnote about Ruhland with Ingrid's letter of 17 February 1972, p. 57n3.

used as propaganda against us. Oestreicher is practically saying that the demands have been fulfilled—and that there is no isolation. He has very close contacts with the State Security agencies.[3] Well, enough. Don't expect too much from him—stay critical. It also looks like he's trying to get quite a bit out of it for *himself*. But you needn't do anything further about this for the moment, such as getting in touch with him or anything.

Here are the book titles I mentioned:

Mao—*On Guerrilla Warfare* (Cassell 1962)

Ian Craig—*Assault on the West* (Foreign Affairs Publication House 1969)

Maurice Zeitlin, Robert Scheer—*Cuba: An American Tragedy* (Penguin)

Philip Agee[4]—don't know the title yet but about the CIA (presumably this title) and being published by Penguin in January. See if it's out already.

Nothing else for the time being. The *Economist* continues to arrive. If they continue sending it without any subscription, you'd better cancel it properly.

The children's artworks arrived too, the Jumping Jack hangs on my wall. Let's see when I can write to them, when less tired than today. I'm stopping—the evenings are really exhausting now. A sign. And it was good you were here.

Hugs,

Ingrid

---

3   In Germany, the State Security agencies consist of the Attorney General's Office, as the coordinating agency with the media, the intelligence agencies (BND, VS, and MAD) and the State Security departments of the BKA and LKA (for acronyms, see the Acronyms list at the end of the book). Some courts include State Security Chambers for political proceedings regarding "membership in a criminal organisation" (§129 of the Penal Code, later extended to §129a "membership in a terrorist organisation").

4   Philip Agee was a CIA secret operations officer from 1956 to 1969 and wrote a book about his experience: *Inside the Company: CIA Diary* (London: Penguin Books, 1975). Asked to appear in the Stammheim trial as a witness for the defence, he wasn't admitted by the court but, together with other former intelligence officers (Winslow Peck, Barton Osborn and Gary Thomas), he testified during a press conference. See footnote to Ingrid's letter of 16 December 1976, p. 149, footnote 33.

6 March 1974

Hello Sister. Mea culpa, mea culpa. Am okay really, but this damned writing job really is no fun. A necessity, obviously, an absolute must, part of the discipline. Oh well.

What you wanted to send me was a book about Africa by Basil Davidson. I came across the title of the book I wanted somewhere, but then forgot it again. Will be the right one, whatever you send, because the guy is good, well-informed. Second, during your visit we also discussed your ordering the *Economist*. The issue you sent was interesting—do you still have newsprint paper over there? Has become a dark country, this Angelland. Third, please ask the *New Left Review* for the September/October issue. It didn't arrive, although paid for? Or did the subscription start later? I did get the July/August and November/December ones. That's all for now.

Sending money would be a sheer waste and nonsense given the current exchange rates.[5] So leave it for now, we'll manage. Most likely the money's needed just as much where you are. Send something to the Price Sisters or the two blokes from the IRA.[6] An absurd proposal, do you think? Incidentally, do you know that quite a lot of these insane attacks are apparently carried out by members of the UVF (Paisley and the like),[7] and that it also tends to be a special tactic of the British intelligence services? The hint in the *Stern* article,[8] which I enclose, is not without basis—why should an imperialist country like the UK refrain from using such counter-insurgency methods? Especially as using the army against strikers isn't an isolated phenomenon but an imperialist strategy against class struggle. In West Germany, the border police

---

5   In 1974, the UK suffered a financial crisis because of extensive strikes, a three-day workweek, restricted use of electricity and major changes in national and local government.

6   Marian and Dolours Price, members of the Provisional IRA, were imprisoned in March 1973, with Gerry Kelly and Hugh Feeney, after a bombing campaign in London. On 14 November 1973, they began a hunger strike that lasted until June 1974 and included over five months of force feeding and the death of Michael Gaughan, who had joined the hunger strike. Their demand to be transferred to Northern Ireland was eventually granted a year later, as part of a ceasefire agreement.

7   The UVF (Ulster Volunteer Force) was a Protestant paramilitary organisation opposed to the IRA. Ian Paisley, the leader of the Free Presbyterian Church and the Democratic Unionist Party, opposed equal rights for the Catholic population in Northern Ireland.

8   *Stern* is one of Germany's weekly news magazines.

are trained accordingly, and special units (well known by now) are deployed against demonstrations and of course—primarily—against terrorists, using perfect ultra-modern equipment.

Don't talk to me about Amnesty.[9] They want to see corpses before agreeing that there's any torture in West Germany, even though it's almost at that point already. Kati is in Paris in a special clinic[10] where she was to be operated on, but it's too late now. She's been treated with morphine for months and is clearly in the final stages of her illness on account of the four-month delay here when NOTHING was done. The tumour was visible on an X-ray last August. I'll also send you an article, as I don't know how much you know about it.

The second example of torture is Astrid,[11] who has suddenly been released just like that in the middle of the night (despite being threatened with life imprisonment), simply totally broken by acoustic isolation and the combined collaboration of the judiciary with doctors and psychiatrists who tried to make the silent wing bearable for a longer period by using autogenic training. Like the doctors in Brazil and elsewhere who examine tortured prisoners to see how much more torture they might be able to stand, and who use "therapy" to get them back on their feet—only to torture them some more. Amnesty called 1973 "The Year of Torture"—but they won't accept it for West Germany, saying there isn't sufficient evidence to talk of torture.

Sure, attacking the shark's head does mean something. It means one step closer to realising the need for violence—and that question is gradually polarising Amnesty. And the fact that nobody was in that silent wing for a while was only the result of the protests by committees + lawyers + writers, etc. (Ulrike came out of it on the day lawyers lined up in their funny garb for a hunger strike in front of the Federal High Court.) Now they've got a new trick: loudly proclaiming some "relief" of prison conditions—with, in fact, now two in this unit instead of one,

---

9　As hinted in Ingrid's previous letter, the prisoners from the RAF were growing disillusioned with Oestreicher's closeness to the authorities.

10　Katharina Hammerschmidt, who was wanted on suspicion of supporting the RAF, surrendered to the authorities on 29 June 1972 and—contrary to her lawyer's expectations—was kept in custody. Three years later, she died of cancer that had been left untreated in prison. See the Endnote.

11　After her arrest on 6 May 1971, Astrid Proll was the first prisoner from the RAF to be held in Cologne Prison's "silent wing".

hence an intensification.[12] In Stuttgart, they are expanding a special isolation unit for the trial against the "core"—which will, incidentally, be the most expensive so far in the entire history of the justice system.[13] Not even Eichmann was treated with such hysteria.[14] Someone here said, "Aren't they ashamed to show their fear so openly?"

Moni's condition is so-so.[15] The Moabit Prison tower has hit her rather badly. Must be related to increased sensitivity—because the effects are less intense with us. Her blood pressure is off the charts sometimes.

Rather peculiar to learn that the situation of the two IRA Sisters would be "medically alright". Getting the tube pressed down your throat with utmost brutality every day (Dolours's description), with the cynical remark that it would be for their own good, what's alright about that? It should be the doctors' task to support their demands, instead of acting as henchmen of repression. The role of doctors in these things isn't at all well enough understood, just like their involvement in research, such as the torture research programme in Hamburg.[16] There is no neutral job. Everyone who insists that there is is an opportunist wanting to steer clear of something that can't be avoided: a human being is a social being.

Oh, yes, you were going to look for a new IRA book. If you find it, have them send it to me as well (everything direct from the bookshop or publisher).

And, no, the jumper for Susanna doesn't seem to get finished. Can hardly hold that stuff in my hands anymore, getting restless. But perhaps I'll manage by Easter.

---

12   Ulrike Meinhof was kept isolated in Cologne Prison's "silent wing" twice before she was transferred there again in early February 1974, this time with Gudrun Ensslin. The two women were both moved to Stammheim Prison three months later.

13   The trial against Andreas Baader, Gudrun Ensslin, Ulrike Meinhof, Jan Raspe and Holger Meins was to start in May 1975. It was considered to be the main trial against the RAF. It was conducted in a purpose-built bunker in the grounds of Stuttgart's Stammheim Prison; the prisoners were held on the top floor of the prison in a high-security unit specially constructed to hold them. See the Endnote.

14   Adolf Eichmann, one of the organisers of the Holocaust, sentenced to death and executed in 1962 after a widely publicised trial in Jerusalem.

15   Monika Berberich.

16   "Special Research Programme 115", based in the Department of Clinical Behaviour Studies at Hamburg University. It ran sensory deprivation experiments in a "camera silens", an acoustically isolated cell that was the model for Cologne Prison's "silent wing".

Well, the end again. And onwards with Labour into the next depression. The Reds under the beds—this kind of political irony and wit also manages to undermine political energy. A really strange affair.

Greetings and kisses to the whole troupe + let's hope for an early summer.

Ingrid

12 May 1974

Hello Sister, now it's happening. I'm pretty bad, but remember, everyone wants the same as you—a reply, and a prompt and extensive one at that—and that the mountain of paper grows above my head. You've no idea how much remains unattended to. Loads of books, Africa particularly neglected—everything's constantly put off again, the situation such that you can hardly concentrate for a minute from seven in the morning until midnight, because something's always going on that concerns you, directly or indirectly. And when there's some real peace you don't know what to do with it.

First, the books. Four have arrived—two on Ireland, one on Africa, one on sociology, though I only learnt this a few days ago, because they didn't tell me, so I've not started reading any of them. The *Economist* arrives regularly, but I don't understand a word of the specifically economic articles. The *New Left Review* too, really quite sophisticated and strictly traditional Marxist, so clever analyses of less important contradictions. The article about the Algerian women was quite scary, because nothing remains of the Algerian revolution and their strength. And because Boumedienne's official politics, the bourgeoisification, the sell-out to the capitalist centres, is a direct expression of this. His position can only be desperate—caught between solidarity with his neighbouring states and their increasing power and extortion by capitalism. You have to read Fanon over and over to understand what's happening.[17]

---

17   In *The Wretched of the Earth* (New York: Grove Press, 1963), 36–37, Frantz Fanon writes
     about the way colonialism perpetuates people's alienation and how "the 'thing' which
     has been colonized becomes [hu]man [being] during the same process by which it
     frees itself".

Yes, family visits are a bit too much lately, especially as I don't get anything in advance, but am simply confronted by *faits accomplis*. The parents next, but not before July, as far as I'm concerned, so best if you come in September. What kind of trip to the USA? With the kids? I get the impression you fear that soon you won't be able to get around to seeing the world any longer—not the way it's happening now, another continent every other month or so. Possibly one day, perhaps soon, *you* will find it impossible to travel the world as tourists, setting yourselves limits and asking, "What am I doing here?" when you stand in front of the Pentagon. The (bourgeois) "freedom" to travel criss-cross is really nothing but a lack of freedom in your own place. So you have to ask yourself what kind of need is that (no, you should *always* ask yourself this—to come to grips with this perverted complexity of needs within us, which is possible only *in the fight against*... because that's where the cause of the perversion lies).

How good old Marx dealt with that: he had the criterion of pangs of conscience. Old-fashioned but useful. Because these pangs of conscience came to him whenever he had understood an objective context, and when the understanding forced him to change this context, but his needs tried to convince him that it would be more opportune to make changes, to be able to express himself better. And what did Marx do in such a case? Did he listen to his needs? Yes! To come to grips with these pangs he tried to get a deeper understanding of the objective context, until the need for change removed the pangs and replaced the need to dodge the issue. This is how good old Marx's revolutionary need is supposed to have developed and grown. Not only his, because according to reliable sources it created a precedent, and that's why even today there still exists political cooperation. And that's why the struggle is daily, permanent. Just imagine all the baggage you're carrying around with you.

Heavens, already 4:00 p.m.—I started this letter at 8:00 a.m.! And outside a human mass is raging, a football game ten thousand strong. Hell. 6:00 p.m.—this terror finally ended. Some idiot once said that the football stadium is the place to win mass support. Crazy. Only fascism can win there.

Okay, this mangled writing is really bad. There's so much more to say and write, for information alone. But ask our mother for the address of Ulrike's sister. I don't have it. She's really good. So is Gudrun's sister.

At the press conference during the meeting of the relatives, they stated very clearly what was going on and didn't allow the media to drive them into a corner. Time and again, the media tried to get a statement about the RAF from them about whether the relatives approved of certain things, etc. With the relatives very clear each time that it was all about clarifying and denouncing the current methods and getting the two out of the "silent wing" in Cologne Prison.[18] They are both out now and were taken to Stuttgart, where this craziest trial ever will take place. The justice system's strategy for this trial was also sketched out by the relatives. I'll make sure you get the transcript of the press conference. And Wienke (Ulrike's sister) will surely have some things too. The fact that the two are out of the "silent wing" doesn't mean things are over or solved or whatever—it's only the beginning, because the system will now implement its programme, one that's very complicated and highly refined, in accordance with the sophistication/development of science in the capitalist centres.

I think it's excellent that our mother too "marched" to this meeting, and I'm sure it's the same for all the relatives, that there, within the solidarity of the group, they feel considerably "freer" than with me/us during visits and certainly spoke out about what they noticed and what disturbed them. Here she tends to represent the other side's position, defends it—always. And because with me she never experienced it like the relatives of prisoners in West Germany do, of course, it's more difficult to convey the nature of the dirty tricks. Although the two years in Moabit were also a fact. Probably, because at the time I hadn't really taken in what the "tower" meant for me, I couldn't convey that to others. You can only make sense of it afterwards, just like those in the "silent wing" understood the extent of the torture only after coming out of it.

There's lots of material around now about this type of torture, including from abroad, where people have a better understanding of what goes on. Oh, yes, try and find the March 1974 *Les Temps Modernes*, a French monthly.[19] Or, even better, I'm sending the title page and you can order it. It's quite a good journal, improves your French, provides material for your thoughts on social policies and their origins—because

---

18   See previous letter, p. 94, footnote 12.
19   The March 1974 issue of Jean-Paul Sartre's monthly journal *Les Temps Modernes* was dedicated to the prison conditions of the prisoners from the RAF and their resistance (https://socialhistoryportal.org/sites/default/files/raf/0319740300_0.pdf).

you simply can't investigate or analyse *anything* unless you consider it dialectically, using the Marxist method. Your pluralism ("not so one-sided", etc.) limits you at the same time, because you never reach a standpoint that can guide you to take action but, instead, stay trapped in non-committal "opinions". Promise me you'll get *Les Temps Modernes*.

About prison visits—if anyone came to look at my cell I'd throw them out regardless of their motives, no matter how pure, because these visits serve only to justify the prison system: how good it all is, the progress already made, etc. The real purpose is to convey make-believe to the world outside, irrelevant because most of the shit comes from the outside, that's where it starts and stops. It's sheerly impossible, a contradiction, to try and make prison "better". Prison can only be abolished—and that's only possible as part of the destruction of the whole. And after that (in the end, one distant day), there will only be political prisoners. There can't be one single change of *any use to the people* that comes from above. Useful change can only ever come from the people themselves. And for prisoners that means understanding their situation, as well as its causes, and knowing that only they themselves can bring about the changes they want to see. So when these "chosen ones" (on what criteria, really?) are so clearly peaceful, when their final assimilation to the demands of the bourgeois society has taken place, they have accommodated the fact that the "solution" for them always comes from the top: their final destruction is sealed, because they have abandoned their resistance.

The (so-called) reformed prison, the psychologising on every level (as happens outside, everywhere)—is *the* new weapon in the machinery of oppression. And because they can't use this weapon against political prisoners (i.e., everyone who, irrespective of their offence, understands the strategic purpose of the justice and prison system against the people and who fights it through politicisation and the organisation of resistance), because they don't join in the game, so they are being isolated. And because they can't be re-educated, so they are destroyed slowly by means of silent wings, years of solitary confinement, subtle psycho-terror that might be "normal" trivialities of life, but which gain huge significance for someone living in total isolation. This, in the context of *all* prisoners, shows the subtlety of the programme. And against this stands the solidarity, the unity of the political prisoners—whom they try to divide, of course, by differences in treatment and prison conditions: here a bit of relief, there an offer, somewhere else a little finger of advantage—all things that one must refuse, because they are being granted for this very purpose of division, not as a friendly gesture. *Every* means of State Security apparatus and intelligence agency trickery is applied to them: falsifications, alleged discovery of break-out plans, police informers, etc., etc. You see, *they* won't be deterred from anything—neither here nor globally. But here it's much more difficult to see through, because they can't work quite so openly.

Pure chance that I can write today; I'm banned from leisure time, and this is quite useful just now. Locked in because we didn't want to vegetate in front of the screen and instead sat outside the TV room and talked. This was re-interpreted as us "not following the instructions of the official on duty". A recent article (in the lying Springer press) gave a nice example of the total perversion, of how people are constantly being re-educated: in relation to Ulrike's punishment of having to take her daily walk on her own, it was said that—contrary to some "normal" prisoner X, who must share the courtyard with twenty other inmates— Ulrike has the entire courtyard to herself. This example is so extreme that everyone should be able to see what's going on—but normally the perversion comes through in more obscure forms.

(By the way, my strange way of splitting words here is lack of atten-tion when the machine gets to the end of the line. Our mother already assumes slow deterioration of my orthography. Anxious questions and the like.)

Let's end here. To Susanna, many thanks for the letter. Don't think an explanation by letter will be very fruitful. Will try it sometime.[20]

Don't you want to do something about your chronic sinusitis? Like at least getting a proper diagnosis.

Take care, hugs to all,

Ingrid

More in response to your last-but-one letter: "people" here means those who are aware and oppressed. They are both—and are being kept in ignorance forcibly—the function of the media! "Aware" because their

---

20 The children's questions about Ingrid linger on in the family, remaining difficult to answer.

entire *being*, their material situation as producers of surplus value, being exploited, gives them the "natural" awareness that also gives them power—and that's why they are oppressed by all means possible. And "people" means all those who politicise their own situation and use it to fight this terror, i.e., all those who identify with the people's need for the abolition of exploitation, who make it their own—and who in the process of revolutionising will *be* it, will become the revolutionary subject themselves. "People" is everyone, *provided* they develop class consciousness and resist exploitation. Whether consciously or unconsciously is the next question. So "people" is everyone who, from their conscious or unconscious situation/class situation, is being oppressed subjectively and objectively. Those who position themselves consciously on the side of the exploiters (through their job, actions or thoughts) and those who internalise the system's mechanisms and so become part of it (e.g., prison guards), they are *against* the people (even when perhaps a "proletarian" at birth). And they must be attacked for this—otherwise they won't become conscious of it.

Here's an excerpt from the latest RAF paper,[21] which I don't think you know:

> The exploitation of the masses in the capitalist centres cannot be covered alone by Marx's concept of the wage labourer from whom the surplus value is extracted in production. It is a fact that exploitation in the production sphere has reached an unprecedented form of physical strain, an unprecedented form of mental pressure, and a tremendous and increasing intensification with the further compartmentalisation of labour.
>
> It is also a fact that with the introduction of the 8-hour workday—the precondition for increasing the intensity of labour—the system has usurped people's entire leisure time. Adding to their physical exploitation in the enterprise is the exploitation of their feelings and thoughts, wishes, and utopian dreams; adding to capitalist despotism in the factory is capitalist despotism in all areas of life through mass consumption and the mass media.

---

21 The RAF's third paper, *The Black September Action in Munich: Regarding the Strategy for Anti-Imperialist Struggle*, published in November 1972. See Moncourt and Smith, 205–36 (see p. 57, footnote 5). The following quotes provided by Ingrid appear on pages 222–23.

With the introduction of the eight-hour workday, the system's twenty-four-hour-a-day domination of the worker began its triumphal march. With the creation of mass purchasing power and "peak income", the system has taken up its triumphal march over the people's plans, needs, alternatives, fantasies, and spontaneity. In short, over human beings as a whole!

The system in the capitalist centres has managed to drag the masses so far down into its own dirt that they seem to have largely lost their sense of the oppressive and exploitative nature of their situation as objects of the imperialist system. So for a car, some junk, life insurance, a mortgage, they will accept any crime on the part of the system and can hardly imagine or wish for anything beyond a car, a vacation, a tiled bathroom.

It follows, however, that the revolutionary subject is anyone who breaks free from these compulsions and refuses to take part in the system's crimes. Those who find their political identity in the liberation struggle of the people of the Third World, all those who refuse, all those who no longer participate: each one of these is a revolutionary subject—a comrade.

This means that we have to analyse the twenty-four-hour day of the imperialist system. That in all the living and working conditions of this society we must show how the sucking out of surplus value functions, how it relates to exploitation in the enterprise, what exactly is the point each time. With this axiom: the revolutionary subject of imperialism in the capitalist centres is the person whose day is the twenty-four-hour day under the diktat of the system's regimentation—we only outline the framework within which the class analysis has to be done. We are not claiming that the axiom would already be the analysis.

The fact is that neither Marx nor Lenin nor Rosa Luxemburg nor Mao had to deal with *Bild* readers, television viewers, car drivers, the psychological conditioning of young students, high school reforms, advertising, the radio, mail order sales, loan contracts, "quality of life," etc. The fact is that the system in the capitalist centres reproduces itself through an ongoing offensive against the people's psyche, not in an openly fascist way, but rather through the market.

Autumn 1974, to Her Niece Susanna

Written in English

Hello, Susanna!!!

You wouldn't imagine—I finished this jumper after half a year. At the end it really became a nightmare, because it was all finished and suddenly everybody told me that it's far too small for a girl of your age. Maybe it's now far too big, but that's better than the other way around. But I tell you: *never* again I'll do knitting but will write instead of that a letter or so to you, that's more reasonable. You must understand that—and I'm sure you do not like knitting either (if you've ever tried, which I doubt with good reason). But don't bother, it's ready now and I'm happy about it, hope you too.

How are you? Your knowledge of writing should be enough in the meantime for writing me a letter. I would be very glad about that. Try it together with Nicole, will you? I told Opa already that it would be a good thing to come here some time, when Mummy is with you in Germany, maybe in summer, though I do not know where you will have your summer holidays. I will write to Mummy about this idea—and you will speak with her about it, will you? There is no reason to be afraid of the place where I am, you know it's a prison, though it will be hard to understand the reasons why I am here and not outside. If you have questions about it, put them. Some day you and Marcus and Chris and all you children will understand it. As soon as you want to know it, I'll explain. But as we haven't seen for such a long time and you (especially you, the boys maybe do remember) cannot remember me, we have first to come together to talk for a little while, just to get to know each other. Is that right?

Now I will finish, because I am very tired, did a lot of sport today. What is it in English: you're playing with a little ball on a table, in German it is called *Tischtennis*?

With much hope for a good holiday with Omi and Opa in Koblenz and a nice party at Nicole's "communion", and many greetings to Marcus and Chris, Nicole, Oliver (if you'll meet him) and so on (gosh, what a lot of nieces and nephews). I kiss you.

Ingrid

8 September 1974

Dear Sister, your visit is in the can, but try not to come on 20 September, when I'm supposed to appear as a witness (though this may change).[22]

I wrote to our parents straight away.[23] But I *cannot* and will not write out of pity for them. There was a very concrete reason why I'd stopped writing, but for sure it was also wrong: after so many years and visits *in* prison, at some point it simply has to be clear that they shouldn't try and persuade me and that I can and must determine when visitors should come, which, considering the large number of family members, needs to be organised in a way that nobody feels upset if sometimes I have to say no.

And she was offended—for heaven's sake, the kind of stuff she comes out with, the family idyll at the Günther family—*the* example. Sickness, sure, shit—and what I appreciate and told her is that she doesn't give in but somehow fights on. But I don't relate to illness with pity; it's only one condition out of thousands. And the fact that she's got involved in the relatives' group is also very good—but the next step would have been to transfer the personal and *only* personal thing about me towards at least a basic political understanding of the whole issue, so as not to suffocate me. Sort of like this: now we've done something for you, and you're still not listening to me. I've let this go on far too long—family visits without obligations, and, don't forget, they had the closest contact with the pigs—and still this chatting with them every time they come. I simply cannot take that; there, I explode. And Pa says bluntly that they (in West Germany) had it coming to them, being treated like that, make sure you don't get treated that way.

And how often have they told me to talk, to unburden myself—to save me, save my skin. So sinister. Please understand. Ditto for saying that I should be nice and friendly. Once and for all, I do not want to hear that again. Plus, if you must arrange something with the authorities here, do it in writing beforehand or briefly when you're here, but no more chats from one class to the other. That's a decision you simply must take. At least that.

---

22   As a witness in the trial against Ulrike Meinhof and Horst Mahler regarding Andreas Baader's prison break. The trial lasted until 29 November 1974.

23   Ingrid had told her parents that she wanted fewer visits, which distressed them, and Gerti and Klaus intervened.

Four years here, twenty-four hours a day where the system's might and power are at their clearest, visible every minute. Doesn't leave a shred of collaboration with them. No room for blackmail, sweet talk, or any other diversion.

Something else: you needn't renew the *New Left Review* at the end of this term—really too sophisticated. Of little use. Am still not sure about the *Economist*; it's coming until the end of the year as far as I know.

Oh well, I start to spin when I see your postcards—can't relate to that, of course—because I see the other Amerikkka. See you then. Still lots to do today.

Hugs,

Ingrid

16 December 1974

Yes Sister, sure I can write. But there's so much going on in the mean-time that I can really only say: only our victory will convince anyone. So the question about how long things will go on is already answered—as long as it takes. Simple, right? It's hardly possible to convince someone who isn't part of *this* struggle that it's the right thing, because appar-ently everyone prefers to believe the media or government propaganda rather than the people themselves, those who know why and who certainly wouldn't make such a difficult trip if they didn't have every reason to do so. This too is simple. Everything becomes simple when you understand that and also why it's an either/or thing—then even dying becomes easy: you despise death like you despise disease or pain—because they stop you doing what you want to do.

"More liberal, more relaxed?" Or whatever you call it. Awkward concepts, the impressions people take from here: very subjective. What does feeling okay mean—after three months here and given what we want?[24] These can't be separated. The way you put it, it looks as if you'd be glad if I were fine at the expense of those who are dying. No, not that, never, out of the question to think "the main thing is that I'm fine".

---

24 In the trial against her, Ulrike Meinhof made a statement on 13 September 1974 in which she announced the start of the prisoners' third collective hunger strike, which lasted until 5 February 1975. During this strike, on 9 November 1974, Holger Meins died after being systematically force fed too few calories for two months.

In the enclosed article by Sigrist, and also in Seckendorff's speech,[25] this has been explained very clearly: the collective. This is exactly what the individual who lives isolated (in the family or otherwise) cannot understand, because they aren't doing that. And one isn't naturally part of a collective but must fight for it, and everyone who starts doing that knows how hard it is, the collective learning process. Here there's no "I"—only the group as a whole, all together in the struggle—the political dimension, the revolution, not ending up in "sects". The smallest indivisible unit, with responsibility for all, and which all have for each one of us.

That's nothing mysterious, just to say that. A political learning process that every group experiences in every country in the world where there's a guerrilla.

And that will then establish the unity, the identity with those in the Third World—on the basis of this dialectic. Absolutely lively, Sister— there is no other *life*. But enough. About coming here: only after this is over. It's too exhausting, and it's pretty shitty here anyway.

Well, and today the entire "secret" negotiations are already written up in *Der Spiegel*.[26] Naturally—they have close contacts with the State Security agencies and the Federal Prosecutors' Office. Let's see. Quite meaningless anyway, and most certainly their hopes for a peaceful Christmas party are a joke. I *had* to be so strict with Ma. Explained it to her again[27]—because it's simply impossible to hold one lawyer after another responsible for this action. Unbearable.

Well, am pretty tired again now, not much concentration left. Do you actually get the information from Hamburg or from the committees? There's a bunch of press conferences providing loads of information and insights. Let me know, so that it can be organised. In France/Holland/Germany an international defence committee is being

---

25 Christian Sigrist, sociology professor at the University of Münster, and from 1975 chair of the Amilcar Cabral Society, worked for many years as a researcher in Asia and Guinea-Bissau. The article mentioned by Ingrid was given as a presentation at a meeting of the Committee against Torture in Frankfurt on 11 May 1973 and published in the August 1973 edition of the periodical *Kursbuch*. The former prison doctor Ekkehard von Seckendorff gave his presentation at a similar meeting in 1974.

26 *Der Spiegel* reported in its issue of 15 December 1974 that "a British clergyman" would "conduct secret negotiations with the West German judiciary". See Ingrid's letter of 11 January 1974, pp 90–91.

27 See the next letter.

set up. We'll see what can be done in England.[28] Not much I guess, but with that guy Oestreicher something should be possible, in relation to the lawyers. He seems to have understood quite a bit.

In the meantime, did you get to read Kitson's *Low Intensity Operations*?[29] In Ireland, the "ongoing laboratory" for Europe, it's happening already: the computer that, unbeknown to the citizen, peeps into the living room, catching and scanning *everything*. And the counter-strategy in England itself, bombings that are targeted provocations and indeed fulfil their purpose. That's happening over here too.[30]

Until the next letter.

Ingrid

Your letter (card) took a week to arrive. Nothing Happy Christmas. But what bliss: at last, these terrible days without a full belly.

8 December 1974, to her mother

Written before Ingrid's letter to Gerti, above, to which a copy of this letter had been attached

Ma, extreme situations require extreme measures—and this was such a situation. I had to act that way to stop you storming headlong down the wrong turn that you had made. Certainly, very radical + shocking, for me too—and just as necessary, because in this situation *nothing* can be allowed that stabs us in the back unnecessarily. And from what I was told it seemed that you were close to doing something with the

---

28 The International Committee for the Defence of Political Prisoners in Western Europe (IVK), was established in Paris on 14 December 1974. It eventually had sections in West Germany, France, Holland, Italy, Belgium and England.

29 British Army General Frank Kitson is considered one of the most important counter-insurgency experts of the time. He gained his experience in Kenya, British Malaya, Oman, Cyprus and Northern Ireland. His book *Low Intensity Operations* (London: Faber & Faber, 1971) is one of the handbooks used by NATO special forces.

30 A reference to provocations imputed to the RAF, such as the threat of a rocket attack on the Hamburg football stadium on 29 May 1974 and the explosion of bombs in lockers at the Bremen and Hamburg central railway stations on 9 December 1974 and 23 September 1975. Each time, the prisoners published denials of the RAF's involvement. See Moncourt and Smith, 314–15, 376–80 (see p. 57, footnote 5).

press, or otherwise publicly with other relatives, against the lawyers "responsible", which would have damaged us terribly.

Never mind whether you really intended it, out of desperation, and how you understand the situation, which is very clear at every visit: it leads nowhere. And as soon as something like that lands in the wrong place, I must stop it.

I cannot explain to you here the whole concept of the hunger strike and its development (which will win—of that you can be sure, precisely because we are determined, and because they know this). But I must be able to expect from you that you don't try and get in the way, even if it doesn't seem like that to *you*. And be honest—haven't you been influenced by this whole press/TV propaganda (we too watched it all on TV), the full-page articles, the witch hunt? You cannot ignore it—because that is exactly how public opinion is formed, and that is also its purpose. Nothing to do with the fact that you consider the entire hunger strike a crazy undertaking. Well, okay, only victory can convince.

Gerti should now contact the guy she had been pushing so much. Maybe that's a help—for you. I didn't mean Kristine when referring to the phone calls—on the contrary, she defended you. But this is what's difficult: you act in good faith, and it is not good, because driven by panic—and that undermines our responsibility, which isn't right. Those are the contradictions in your life and mine that cannot be revoked, because I have different plans to those you've had all your life—and you cannot deny sixty years, those are your firm convictions in the meantime, and as long as you don't accept that, you will suffer—instead of accepting the struggle I'm engaged in.

Frau Mohnhaupt writes to say she can't come at Christmas, because she's still too weak.[31] And that she won't be allowed to carry more than one kilo from now on. And that you wanted to come together this time. So better later, at any rate not while all this is going on. And then it will be good to come together, good for both of you. For her it will be a great relief in her condition. Well, in yours too. Do contact her again—she somehow understands all this differently—as not in the sense of suffering and that the learning from each other *never* stops.

---

31 The mothers of Brigitte Mohnhaupt and Ingrid sometimes came to visits together when their daughters were in the same prison. Frau Mohnhaupt accepted Brigitte's decisions, whereas Frau Schubert believed almost to the end that she might be able to improve Ingrid's conditions by negotiating with the authorities.

No hurry with a Christmas parcel, but I enclose the permit anyway. Let's see. I told you, I think, about the five pounds of home-baked biscuits—and some new recipes as well! Don't forget strong tins to keep things fresh. Oh, yes, quite absurd to talk about this now—but also incorrectly rigid not to do so.

One day there will surely be much to talk about—as Gerti said.

Hugs for both of you,

Ingrid

Letters 1975

The hunger strike has ended. In the first letter of the year, Ingrid refers to a "debacle" between her brother and their mother. He and Gerti try to convey to their mother the strength of the prisoners' conviction that relatives should not interfere with what is happening to them in prison by trying to negotiate with the authorities. In April, the German Embassy in Stockholm is occupied by a commando demanding the release of twenty-six prisoners, including Ingrid. The occupation ends with the death of two members of the commando and the arrest of four others. All prisoners from the RAF are working this year to prepare for different aspects of the main trial against the RAF, to be held at Stammheim Prison. They also continue internal discussions about their collective struggle, as reflected in some of Ingrid's remarks and requests. It is her fifth year behind walls, and she is now back in Berlin's Lehrter Strasse Prison. Towards the end of the year, the judiciary orders her to be moved to a prison in Frankfurt.

11 February 1975

I'm writing now about fruit/vegetables to bring because I don't know when you will come. According to my calendar, it could well be as soon as the 20th or 21st. I'll try and get two hours at least once, as you're only here two days, but don't know if that will be possible.

I'll write another time about the debacle that occurred when Klaus and Ma came here—because it was important what happened, simply because I realised that I'd made a fundamental mistake, not only for the past five years in here but practically throughout my relationship with her: a negative one. And a damn mistake on my part to have hesitated that long with unclear and dishonest conduct, out of pity, etc. Shit. But no longer.

So buy here: 1 kg chicory
½ kg paprika
½ kg frozen raspberries, *without* sugar
parsley

In case you'll be rushing here straight from the airport, just buy it for the second visit, calmly.

Until soon, greetings,
Ingrid

Perhaps write soon about when you'll be coming.

June 1975

This visit on the 6th and 7th will be a job for early risers, because it's a weekend, and that means visiting time for everyone and not enough officers to listen in on the conversations. So you simply must get here as early as possible, to give us longer to talk. Around 10:00, you'll have to clear off, because then the other visits start. Best to come at 9:00, or even 8:30—then we'd have an hour and a half. Two hours hasn't been approved. If you arrive on the Friday, that will be easy. Shit, if Saturday morning. Well, we'll see.

Can you get that stuff? The address of the International Institute for Strategic Studies is 18 Adam Street, London WC2.

Until then. And my English will just about do. Greetings to everyone.
Ingrid

25 July 1975

No idea if you're in Koblenz or still in London—hence this letter with a carbon copy to both places. The preamble to these visits tends to assume the proportions of a State visit, but okay now, next weekend and three visits. They said something here about "sons" coming, then it was "son", but never mind. In any case, the young lot should be here. Don't know, but I really want to see them all and talk with them, which will of course be difficult at first and strange for them. You can tell Susanna she's called the little pancake here (based on her pictures), while I'm the big one. When will she come? And when Klaus + Pa come they should bring Oliver. But I'll write about that, as it would be good if they could combine their visit with Frau Mohnhaupt's—she's quite ill but doesn't want to miss coming. Let's see.

If you can come Monday too, the fruit-buying programme won't be a problem + we can decide it from here. Should I press Larry to drive you around? He recently gave some sign of life again from his tomb, and I rather gave him hell for saying the same old stuff for years (that he has no idea what else to do), and I don't know if he's offended. Can't imagine that you'll have fun with this resigned old fellow, but a car would be useful.

Was your hunt for books successful? The most important is Mao.

Does Michael know the Haldane Society?[1] They protested rather strongly against the wave of lawyer exclusions and arrests,[2] with signatures from a whole lot of defence lawyers. Michael isn't a lawyer, but he could still sign such a protest. I'll try to get more exact information.

Ah. Just got your letter, so it's London + hence a single letter. It's clear that this is going to be an expensive trip. (By the way, weekends

---

1   The Haldane Society of Socialist Lawyers is a movement of lawyers advocating for the rights of those caught up in the justice system for political reasons. The campaigns it supported or initiated include those against the fascist regimes in Spain and South Africa, the persecution of the Black Panthers in the USA, and the prison conditions of the prisoners from the RAF. Several of its members, including Pearce Gardner and Anthony Gifford, were also engaged in the International Committee for the Defence of Political Prisoners in Western Europe (IVK). See Ingrid's letter of 16 December 1974, p. 105, footnote 25.

2   During the first months of the trial in Stammheim, several defence lawyers were arrested and others excluded from defending the accused and other prisoners from the RAF. See Pieter Bakker Schut et al., *Fatal Shootings, Confinement in Isolation, Killings in Prisons, the Manipulation of the Right to Legal Defence, Criminalising of the Struggle against Confinement in Isolation: Documentation and Critical Comments About the Report Submitted by the Federal Republic of Germany to the United Nations Human Rights Committee in November 1977*. Copies in English and Spanish of the report, presented to the UN Human Rights Committee in New York in December 1977, are available at socialhistoryportal.org/raf/5979. (Subsequently, a German edition was published by Verlag Libertäre Assoziation, Hamburg 1985.)

here are regular visiting days, with the highest number of visitors—so quite normal and all possible anyway, as there won't be any officers present for you.)

I'll send Kristine the list about fruit, etc. Okay. Ha—no cherries, more exotic stuff instead. See when you're here.

Well, I'm very curious to see Marcus. I can imagine what he looks like now—after all, I did once have a teenage brother. But I think you're becoming an old hen already: 12:00 should be a good time for a guy like him now. I must say: very strange that you even notice. Beware of motherhood.

Until soon,
Ingrid

29 September 1975

Sister, I replied to your last letter immediately, then realised I had no address (for your old stone ruin in France) and in the meantime lost it again. But now I'll have to quickly send off the "sermon" to apply for the parcel—hope you'll have time.

Mother wrote that it would take fourteen days. Can't imagine that, could be sent as express parcel. But maybe there's another postal strike. Five kg isn't that much for so many people (packaging and glass jars can be deducted, 5 kg is the net weight—so you can calculate relatively generously). And because it's so little, and because every year we develop increasingly exotic desires (not surprising really), it should only be good stuff, fresh and from the best shop. Hmm.

- 1 kg bitter orange marmalade
- 1 kg bitter lemon (or ½ kg will do—probably a glass jar)
- at least ½ kg of butter toffee, flavoured with mocha, nuts, coffee, etc., anything *except peppermint*—those are horrible
- marshmallows (do you know them? but must be very good ones, otherwise they are tasteless)
- *English tea biscuits* (in my mind those very crumbly brown-white ones, am I right? If you can't get some of the other stuff, then more of those)
- and biscuits from several countries, just not so rich—Welsh or Scottish—isn't there some kind of rum cake—made with only

local ingredients? Or something like that with nuts. I remember seeing it in tins.

– and marzipan with Grand Marnier, or pistachios, or nougat. French nougat (the white sort, with hazelnuts)
– Turkish honey
– a small tin of chestnut *puree* (I had it once at your house)

That's about it, should be enough. The trick is this: nothing that we normally eat, and if possible varied ingredients, not ready-packed supermarket stuff with uniform taste and no imagination. The trick is to fit it into a parcel. I also remember small nutty round balls, nuts and all sorts of flavours. Can those be sent? And do you know those pistachio cakes? But not those pink and green things. Oh well, you'll manage. And take care you pack it properly, as most of your parcels arrive rather battered. Well, and only edible things, *nothing else* (like books). And most important, the orange and lemon marmalade—otherwise there'll be a rebellion here.

We're constantly annoyed here because mothers and others lug all sorts of stuff in here that *they* think is good—but stuff we don't like and didn't ask for. Should be logical that we think about and ask for exactly what we want, not just any old thing. (Like Ma with her thousand blouses that I never wear and no longer have.) If the glass jars (marmalade) are too dangerous to pack, use your famous Tupperware (I remember with horror those awkward Tupperware parties, but the stuff's useful all the same). Do you have such a thing as a bakery "By Royal Appointment" (like in Vienna)?

I'm sending you the declaration about the attack at the Hamburg railway station[3]—there are plenty of similar provocations in your country too. I could of course collect or send you more, but I don't know if you've got time. The office seems to keep you rather busy.

Dearest Sister, this is only a parcel letter, so you have it at last and in good time. (Ma made me quite nervous, saying you're so careless and would lose and forget everything and are oh so very busy.) My disinclination to write is starting to irritate me. It's not just you, the simplest letter is such an effort. Shit. Embraces to all.

Ingrid

---

3   See Ingrid's letter of 16 December 1974, p. 106, footnote 29.

7 October 1975

7 October (arrested five years ago tomorrow).

Well, Sister, put the brakes on. Why should I cram my brain with stuff that doesn't interest me in the slightest? And because it doesn't, it can't contribute anything to the rescue of my endangered brain. I respect your educational ambition for me—but I can do without it, because the better education comes from below, from being right *down* at the bottom, which we are in prison, both objectively and subjectively. Maybe this will stop one day: Ma wants to turn me into an idiot in the library here, and you want to get me into some psycho courses or whatever. Perhaps these helped you a lot and created opportunities for you to do what you're doing now—but my situation is different, and I truly can't complain about having too little to do here; my brain never had to work as hard as now. The mistake of my entire past was not starting to think early enough, and this still causes me difficulties. There's the danger of being isolated, of course; that's the intention, and I don't avoid that with these perverse thirty-minute visits. It's laughable really. I can only avoid that intention by fighting against it and, thus, preserving my identity. Difficult enough. And the intention can no longer be overlooked or explained away, look at Stammheim.[4] The prisoners alone are responsible for their annihilation.

Not much different from the prison police strategies used in England against the prisoners from the IRA. Still have to dig out the article on the Birmingham trial.[5] Even if one doesn't agree with what the IRA, RAF or ETA[6] are doing, is the alternative right, what the pigs do with them? No, certainly not, you say. Only, in this middle ground of "both sides are not quite right", it's a bit slippery, as always with

---

4   During the Stammheim trial, medical experts called by the court concluded that the prisoners' poor health was caused by the isolating prison conditions. This led the presiding judge, Theodor Prinzing, to issue an order on 30 September 1975 that the trial could continue in the absence of the accused, since they alone were responsible for their ill health.

5   In the trial against the "Birmingham Six" in August 1975, six men were each sentenced to twenty-one life sentences for the Provisional IRA's November 1974 bombing campaign. After three appeals and a sustained campaign, all six were released in 1991, based on new evidence of police fabrication of confessions and the suppression of evidence.

6   ETA (*Euskadi Ta Askatasuna*, Basque Homeland and Freedom), a Basque urban guerrilla group active in Spain, and to a lesser degree in France, between 1958 and 2011.

compromises. (Unless there are tactical reasons—but that's something else.)

Guardian Weekly hasn't arrived yet.

Well, and if the post is really that slow, better send the parcel now, even if it will arrive a bit early. Asking you to pack the parcel was probably not such a good idea, because you obviously have lots more important things to do. Well, we can only try; just say if it's too much work. Understandable, with the office so busy. (Hey, did my letter turn up in the end? Hope so, with the list and all that.) And please, *no* candied fruit. Horrid.

So this unpronounceable word "institutionalisation" does exist, but not in the sense you mean—I think. But never mind, it's not our problem—it's always a matter of tactics and strategy, especially in prison. Why do you think the State Security agencies are so interested in smashing our group, organisationally as well as mentally/physically?

What guy from Hesse?[7] Does that mean you're now the contact for the press? Don't know how that happened, which people and how they get to you. Try and find the address and names—you must be careful about the countless parasites and braggarts from the scene. Of those captured recently,[8] three are here, and the two guys are in Moabit—isolated again, of course, with all that that entails.

And a word about getting rusty: obviously, all this work collecting information makes sense only if it's concrete and has a *practical* purpose. Why else? Clearly not to accumulate knowledge for nothing. Understanding the theory about the practice and how to live it (the dialectic) is what it's about—our task and survival strategy.

A second question is how far everyone is able to do this—but it can be learnt, and it's a prerequisite for becoming, being and remaining able to act. Those who can do it are then authoritative on it—which is the opposite of a hierarchy. That only exists in the bourgeois world.

I'm off to watch TV now.

The absolutely important thing about the parcel is both marmalades (bitter lemon and orange), the toffees (maybe 1kg after all, if they're good ones) and the tea biscuits. And, as said earlier, the rest too if possible.

---

7   A journalist from the federal state of Hesse who tried to contact the prisoners from the RAF via their relatives.

8   A reference to the arrest on 9 September 1975 of five members of the 2nd of June Movement.

If you read *Der Spiegel*—recommended in any case (though always relative as far as factual truth and interpretation go)—you'll know about the reactions to Stammheim's "legal practice" and the recent arrests, etc. It was all in there.

Greetings to all.

Ingrid

The parcel needs to have a *duplicate* list of the contents. Prison bureaucracy.

October 1975

A few jobs for you—as soon as possible, please.

1)

"Sean McBride, former president of Amnesty International, demands UNO status for the Provisional IRA and, in this context, openly accuses the British of using torture in Northern Ireland". (from the West Germany/Ireland Solidarity Info)

As McBride is no longer with Amnesty, better to find a direct link to him with regards to UN recognition—that's important: international law (see the PLO now). But perhaps Amnesty too has something on that.[9]

2)

Mervyn Rees, minister for Northern Ireland, wants to rescind political status for prisoners from the IRA from 1 March 1976.[10]

Are there any statements, official bulletins, press statements? How long have they had this status? Since the ceasefire? What information material is there about it? Are there any statements by the IRA or Sinn Fein? Or other political groups? Is this Rees initiative understood in the international context (in line with the strategy of the Western European governments, particularly West Germany, to refuse political status—as part of their anti-terrorism programme)?

---

9   The information was wrong. Sean McBride, in the 1930s a prominent IRA member and in 1961 one of the founders of Amnesty International, wanted the European Court of Human Rights to deal with the treatment of prisoners from the IRA that had been publicly acknowledged as torture since 1971.

10   In an attempt to de-escalate the conflict in Northern Ireland, Special Category Status was phased out from 1 March 1976. As a countermeasure, internment was to cease and all existing sentences against Republican prisoners halved. See Ingrid's letters of 4 December 1973 and 29 March 1976.

(In Germany, the different ministries regularly publish government bulletins—this should exist on your side too. Or parliamentary records, like Hansard. Perhaps a journalist can help you further.) But best to go direct to the Rees ministry.

3)

The Institute for Strategic Studies[11]—whose job is *conflict* research. 1,500 employees from fifty countries (a super-apparatus, and the Pentagon relies greatly on much of their analysis, a lot of military and specialist personnel). They publish:

Military Balance—we don't need this right now

Strategic Survey

Adelphi Papers—we do need these, so try and get a list of their publications (ten or so per year), and then we can order what we need. These are analyses of particular fields of conflict, and they are the best, given their resources.

If you've got a relevant contact, try and find out about political analysis/material on the crisis in the UK during the winter of 1973/74: strikes, three-day workweek, crisis management, counterstrategy. (Kitson had a plan prepared for the military occupation of all industries—they clearly reckoned with the possibility of a revolt.) And enquire whether *Conflict Studies* is the same thing as *Adelphi Papers*, also published by them. We once had a few of these (*Conflict Studies*) but don't know where from.[12] The director of the Institute is a German, Christoph Bertram, a specialist on East Germany (we'll need something on that too: conferences of the European ministers of the interior, etc., but later, first do 1–3). If you can get a link to the Institute for Strategic Studies, you'll get more—it's a real think tank.

And something for our bodily well-being: could you send another small parcel—not more than 1 kg of the orange marmalade, two *light* bitter orange, one dark orange. (But *not* to be brought with you.)

Until soon,

Ingrid

---

11 The International Institute for Strategic Studies (IISS) is an international think tank based in London.

12 Until 1989, the series *Conflict Studies* was published by the Institute for the Study of Conflict (ISC), founded in 1970 by Brian Crozier as a propaganda organisation financed by the CIA. See Ingrid's letter of 15 March 1976.

October 1975

Gerti, briefly: *Guinea Pigs* has arrived,[13] Brigitte got it today,[14] and there's only one page on UN status for the IRA, the rest is descriptions of torture. The other things haven't come yet, but wait rather than send anything else. Better we ask the guy directly. Just send us his address and that of the Rees ministry.

The T-shirts are completely okay, especially the blue ones, very comfortable to wear.

The socks too. A pity everything's always so short.

The Strategic Institute stuff is still with the censors.

For this UN thing (McBride), please ask the Amnesty people; there should be more information than this one report for Strasbourg.

Well then, greetings to all (in case I had forgotten). Did you give Larry my special greetings? Do hope so. I'll let him visit after all.

Ingrid

Funny thing: the money you spent at the KaDeWe on Saturday was stolen today: two to three million was taken from one of the money transporters.[15]

5 November 1975

Sister—at last, the most ardently desired items have arrived. At the last minute, in three regards. First, because we'd already given up all hope; second, because we no longer had anything to chew on; and third, because we (Brigitte and myself) are "soon" to be transferred TO THE PRISON IN FRANKFURT.

Yes. Got the decision yesterday (we had smelt it coming for a while, based on our knowledge of the intention—destruction—and the

---

13   *The Guinea Pigs*: a book by John McGuffin about the use of sensory deprivation on fourteen prisoners from the IRA between August and October 1971 (London: Penguin Books, 1974). In 1976, McGuffin became a member of the International Commission of Investigation into the Death of Ulrike Meinhof. See Ingrid's letter of 10 November 1976.
14   Brigitte Mohnhaupt.
15   KaDeWe: Berlin's flagship department store. Throughout its existence, armoured cars collecting money at the store were repeatedly attacked and robbed.

situation here): "In agreement with Hesse's minister of justice they will soon be transferred to the prison in Frankfurt, etc., *close to their parents* for the subsequent duration of their sentence". Full stop.

The parents, of course, is a shit excuse—because they don't care a bit about our "resocialisation"—all they want is to close the last link in the chain: as we're the living proof refuting their propagandistic thesis that open prison conditions wouldn't be possible for us, etc., so they must remove that, bit by bit. The others will surely follow as soon as their sentences are confirmed (but in another prison—because isolation from each other is the purpose). Imagine, they confronted us with this scrap of paper yesterday—complete stress since then. The parcel just in time for the goodbye party. Shit.

Nothing can be done about it—some stupid complaint would be rebuffed in any event, because, of course, it's a centrally directed and ordered decision, for which fascist Buback has stuffed all authority under his hat,[16] to move closer to his final solution. But your parcel was great—everything right + everything unbroken + everything received (all your letters to the prison were also there, all okay). Though obviously, within the hour, it was all gone and distributed, and now this fat belly.

I'm not in the mood for writing to Susanna just now—perhaps if the transfer's delayed, but we reckon no more than a few days, because on their side there's no reason to wait. I'll also have to sort out and pack a few things. Or you sit there for weeks without any stuff, as we well know. An obscure clink there, with buckets and no basin and nothing that we achieved during our five years here, just silly psycho-groups from outside that everyone goes to, because there's nothing else, and because they've no idea about wanting something for themselves and doing something about it.

Oh well, let's stop for today. The next one from the Hesse dungeon perhaps.[17] Maybe by then I'll write in the Hessian dialect.

Greetings to all, and thanks again for the parcel.

Ingrid

---

16 Attorney General Siegfried Buback would later be killed (7 April 1977) by the RAF's Ulrike Meinhof Commando.

17 Hesse: one of Germany's federal states. Ingrid's transfer there with Brigitte Mohnhaupt (to Preungesheim Prison in Frankfurt) was delayed until April 1976. See Ingrid's letter of 5 May 1976.

13 November 1975

Well, yes, a real hoot when those flowers appeared. Saturday afternoon, we were crammed in one of these tiny holes, music on full volume. The door opened, the roses standing there, and nobody knew what it meant. Naturally nobody thought of turning the music down. A long dialogue ensued between the deaf and the dumb—who were they for, and where did they come from, and finally the female guard shouted in my ear: THE ENGLISH!! So then it became clear. And the flowers even found a space in our hole.[18]

Very touching how everyone's trying to find something positive, no matter how small, about this push to Frankfurt—I know it myself, but anyway. Just so no misunderstanding: I really do not love this shithole so much that I'd want to stay because of that. Well, let's try, see what's possible.

Sunday again. Pretty hectic again for the moment, and because everything happens so fast, one constantly runs back and forth and never catches up. Reading is out of the question, and newspapers have been piling up for two weeks. No idea when I'll read them. Perhaps when I need to find something. Don't think my lecture to Marcus was particularly clever, me as teacher-like as his teacher-like sentence on aggression. He should simply say if he finds it stupid. Don't understand that reverence. I prefer something cheeky, because livelier.[19]

What on earth would Oestreicher know about this plan to transfer us? You are strange—I mean rather naive. And more importantly, what could he do, especially as he doesn't care. Doesn't even care about the facts in Stuttgart—which would have made *sense*. Understand me, one can only understand this transfer (transferring us after five years, and only three of them not in isolation) when one grasps the underlying intention in the coordinated decisions about our prison conditions. And we had attacked those with our hunger strike. And he didn't want to acknowledge them, otherwise he couldn't have talked about "alleviations" in Stammheim that would have made the hunger strike superfluous + made us out to be ill-advised fanatics, etc. But, in the

---

18 Ingrid was thirty-one on 7 November 1975.
19 Marcus, fifteen, had come to Berlin for his first prison visit. He and Ingrid talked about violence, but there wasn't enough time to reach any common ground or real understanding.

meantime, things seem to be grasped better abroad: what the trial shows is fascism's new quality in Germany, in the form that is necessary in order to stay in power: under the mask of social democracy, and only in that form do they have a chance of retaining their dominant position (as in Portugal, for instance), without being attacked by the countries of the Third World and those they want to co-opt.

My head is spinning, full of music and chatter. We mostly listen to records at weekends. I'm just following the traces of our dear brother's somewhat obscure endeavours. Don't know if you're aware of this uranium story between Germany and South Africa + the Nuclear Research Centre being fully involved in it + STEAG,[20] where he once thought of applying for a job. He always wanted to convince me that all that was for purely peaceful purposes, but I could tell him even then which dangerous fantasies he was chasing, such as "neutral sciences" and "value-free" and what not—things that simply don't exist. Just couldn't back it up with facts for him.

Is Susanna's birthday the end of October or November?

Well, that's it, am dead tired. Greetings to all + Susanna and Chris, of course.

Again, a thousand thanks for the drawing (didn't know Susanna could draw my face so accurately!). Will reply when I feel up to it.

Ingrid

---

20 Electricity provider STEAG (Coal & Electricity Company) owns several large power plants in Germany and has been involved in the construction and operation of power plants in South Africa, Turkey and the Philippines.

Petition by Prisoners in Lehrter Strasse Prison against the Transfer of Ingrid Schubert and Brigitte Mohnhaupt

We, the undersigned prisoners at Lehrter Strasse, demand that Ingrid Schubert and Brigitte Mohnhaupt not be transferred to Frankfurt but remain here.

Berlin, 11 December 1975
(forty-seven signatures)

Statement by the West Berlin Senator of Justice on 29 January 1976 Regarding the Transfer of Ingrid Schubert and Brigitte Mohnhaupt
Extracts

Of the sixteen women currently connected to anarchist circles, at least eight will be transferred to West German prisons in addition to the two applicants.[21] Most of these are still on remand and need to be available for their trials. Some of these transfers have already been prepared. For other women there are agreements for their transfer with several German federal states. Short-term transfers cannot be considered because of cost. Transfers can only be done with charter flights, because persons resisting travel are not allowed on regular flights.

Due to the obvious physical structure of the prison for women and the long-standing and extremely overcrowded situation here, conditions have arisen where young, adolescent and adult remand prisoners and convicts, drug addicts, prisoners in preventive detention, women kept on substitute or civil confinement or detained awaiting deportation cannot be kept sufficiently separated from each other, not even on different floors. Each prisoner can communicate by calling out to other prisoners at any time. Also, communication by swinging objects from window to window can hardly be contained. This group is united, knows how to persist and is intellectually largely superior to the other prisoners, whom they succeed in coercing to do what they want, thus undermining the running of this institution considerably.

---

21 A reference to the application by Ingrid and Brigitte to be transferred to Stammheim Prison.

The collection of signatures is an outstanding example of the effect of the solidarity emanating from such a strong anarchist group. It may be assumed that some of these signatures were given only because the persons in question were unable to resist the pressure of the dominant group. The aim of changing social conditions through agitation is also being pursued within the prison.

The guards are the declared enemy, rudely and hatefully deni-grated. Brigitte Mohnhaupt was formally sentenced to three months' imprisonment for causing bodily harm and resisting a prison guard. Ingrid Schubert was charged with instigating a mutiny amongst the prisoners. This charge was later withdrawn in accordance with §154 of the Penal Code.

Loud noises during the night have repeatedly led to in-house penalties and complaints by other prisoners. Resistance by prisoners had to be quelled on several occasions with the assistance of male staff from the remand prison.

The special security measures necessarily entail more rigorous restriction of movement for other inmates than would normally be required—joint events, leisure time, courtyard walks, visits—and lead to greater physical and mental stress for our female officers. During the last two months, Inge Viett made two escape attempts, Juliane Plambeck one. The tools used got into the building despite the stringent controls. Events such as the week-long hunger strike could be repeated at any time. Moreover, there are indications of a planned attempt from outside to free prisoners.

In the meantime, the pressure to take in more people has escalated. With a capacity of 126 prisoners, there are now 147 in this prison for women. Admissions have had to be limited, using alternative penalties and not accepting those with sentences of less than a year. The transfer of every single prisoner from the anarchist group improves the running of this penal institution.

Letters 1976

Ulrike Meinhof dies in Stammheim Prison. Her friends and relatives do not believe the official version of suicide, and there are widespread demonstrations. An International Commission of Investigation is constituted and concludes that she was most probably dead before she was hanged. Ingrid and Brigitte Mohnhaupt are transferred from Berlin, and then Frankfurt, to the high-security unit in Stuttgart's Stammheim Prison, where Gudrun Ensslin, Andreas Baader and Jan Raspe are also held. Weeks later, a plane is hijacked to force the release of fifty-three political prisoners—including Ingrid—from Israel, Germany and other countries. The operation ends with the death of the hijackers at Entebbe airport. Throughout the year the prisoners continue to work on various subjects regarding their struggle and the Stammheim trial.

2 February 1976

It's okay with me for the 26th—could also be a week earlier. Or whenever the special fares are being offered. Ma and Frau Mohnhaupt are coming on the 6th and 7th, which is fine, because I've still got visits in my quota. Please state the exact dates you'll be coming—I'll then apply for a permit. No need for you to write to the administration here.

Heaven knows when the transfer will actually take place. Certainly not depending on the snow. But I really don't care when—we no longer wait for it, otherwise the whole madness of prison becomes even madder. Waiting for something is wrong anyway—be it here or outside—because the fixation on it robs you of the ability to think or act, and in here that's even stronger, of course, because there's that door with the lock. That definitely forces you to deal with the conditions as they *are*, to work and not let it get on your nerves: that's how it is, so do something with it. It takes ages until you can do that + often enough it doesn't work. For instance, when you know precisely that you've just got to wait because some idiot is too lazy to pick up the phone, time and again, honestly every time—so you already know it—like when we have sport and they don't collect us + every time act as if it's something completely new to have sport on a Monday. Sure, we've only had it for three years at the same time every week. Like that, but with a thousand variations a hundred times a day. You can't get used to that—unless you give up and conform to their objective of "adaptation" (= dying miserably).

Well, such poor creatures exist in droves here. Clearly five years is too long. And the "crises" or whatever you want to call them happen umpteen times a day or three times a year, it's all the same: it's a condition, and you either freak out and almost certainly destroy yourself, go crazy from this shit—or you do something about it, asking what's the core of the crisis, what's the reason, what's the real problem, and each time you conclude that only you can change it. And if you don't, you're a pig that doesn't feel responsible towards the others. Because they don't need people who are destroyed but people who have thoughts on all the problems and questions, and you use that to work on yourself, by having to take decisions, evaluate something or some situation or person, and, thus, constantly control what's happening to you. If you don't have thoughts about things, you aren't interested—don't feel responsible for clarifying and developing things that you are part of. In other words, collective thinking and acting. That's something one simply couldn't do because of not knowing it. Instead, you do the opposite, based on how things are organised in this society. Well—difficult, but there's nothing better.

As for Larry (every now and then a letter arrives, and each time I think this guy must have some crazy streak, given the way he writes: no normal sentences, everything jumbled and mystified and psycho, unbearable), that's someone already waiting to get old (says he). I can only say this: take the rope now, what are you waiting for + anyway, why wait at all? I simply don't get it, how someone can be so resigned and only focused on one's own psyche. I mean I do understand where that comes from, but I cannot (ever) forgive someone who is intelligent enough to understand. You see, when someone just sits there waiting for the others to jump into the fire, so that at some point he gets the better life he dreams of, ridiculous.

In the end he's leaving this up to his children. I mean someone in *his* (or a similar) situation, who has or had every opportunity. For you, the situation is quite different—when you're confronted with powerlessness in your work—and that's normal, because you can't break through the boundary, can't jump across the dividing line—that's an experience that perhaps would make you think: okay, that doesn't change things either; it's limited, but I can't do more without changing my situation completely, so I'll do what I can.

Well, and you're no way near the end of your possibilities yet, as far as a clear stand is concerned. Social engagement is also something that drives you either to resignation, because you struggle to death—or to radicalisation, where you discover the system, and the fronts that put you on one side. Which is a very practical matter: you attack where you can. You take action, solving problems, such as people clinging to you, because they're not capable of acting themselves (how could they be?). Because you can't tell millions of people that they should act independently; that's no use to them, because what they should be acting against doesn't change. So you must do something to make it change. (For instance, I can't tell the poor creatures here to stop grovelling, I can only do something myself. It wouldn't be of any direct benefit to them, as they don't grasp it; it wouldn't help them, because their only example is this rotten system. If I did this, it would be like preaching or welfare, and I would be deceiving them.)

The problem is not philosophical consideration of the differences between one's own life and that of others, but which side you're on—that's what changes one's life. In the way that perhaps one day you will simply feel like puking when you hear the usual social chatter of arrogant middle-class circles who allow themselves to make judgements about the *struggles* taking place on umpteen fronts or the revolutionary perspectives here, while not taking part in these but, instead, going after their fat job from their big house. Well, you too sit in a big house, and there you are in the contradiction that's bothering you, and that's good in a way, because you don't like it.

"Guilt" is something you have when you do nothing to remove the "discrepancies", and that doesn't work without a struggle. How else could your situation change? What you are now trying for is a kind of compensation, to reduce the "pile of guilt". To provide yourselves with a clear conscience. But you understand: slipping into routine + activity + tilting at windmills, because in reality this can't change anything about the causes. So the next step to consider must be this: *Where* are the pigs' attacks the most severe + how can I intervene at the most important points? Which of course means exposing yourself to being attacked.

That's only possible if one's current life has lost its importance, with all that that implies—property, society, a certain standard of living. It loses its importance or becomes repulsive to the extent that one discovers what's really important. When I hear what's important to the women in here, I feel repulsed, remembering this from earlier times—I no longer want it, either subjectively or objectively. I don't want it because I cannot accept it. In other words, it's causal or dialectical. The idea of enjoying the earth's happiness on a quiet piece of land—no thanks. (Even though I understand only too well those who sit in their little garden in the countryside cultivating their own carrots, especially when one tastes so-called progress in the form of ever-growing plaaastic [with a very long "aaa"] mountains of food. Unavoidable in here as well: everything machine made and tastes so too. What's good about that?)

This has become a long epistle today. Probably because of the porridge I just made. I'm terribly hungry for something, because for weeks there's been nothing but horrible grub in here.

Let me know when you'll come so I can start the application, or call Ma and tell her, in case the letter gets to her in time. She flies on Friday.

So "pardon" doesn't exist for us. You really don't have to look into that. The only path to pardon is via the pigs: when you repent and preferably divulge some information that they like. Apart from that, nothing else will do the trick. So the next eight years are certain for me. Just take a look at reality.

And something else: please stop those unnecessary deliberations (Ma + you too) about how you might *occupy* me. You can't do that anyway, because you constantly suggest something different from what I want, and what Ma imagines always results in what the pigs want too: diversion, followed by accommodation, followed by dumbing down. And what should I do with ART?

Where does this butterfly suddenly come from? And what does
one do with it? Perhaps put it in my hair. I'll certainly look pretty.
Greetings to all,
Ingrid

2.2.

von mir aus ist das gebont mit 26. - kann auch ein woche
früher sein.oder wann gehen diese spezialfahrten ab.am 6./7.
kommt zwar ma mit fr.mohnhaupt,aber das macht nichts,da es
bis dahin wieder 14 tage sind und ich noch besuche offen hab.
schreib genau an welchem tagen ihr dann da seid - den besuchs-
antrag stell ich,dann brauchst du nicht extra schreiben an
den knast.
wann die verlegung nun läuft weiß der himmel.am schnee liegts
sicher nicht.ist mir jetzt auch scheißegal wann - warte da nicht
drauf,sonst wird man bei dem ganzen irrsinn,der knast ist, noch
irrer.auf was warten ist sowieso falsch - xob nun draußen oder
drin - weil man durch die fixierung dadrauf wirklich denk-und
handlungsunfähig wird,und hier potenziert sich das natürlich noch,
weil da die tür ist mitm schloß.das zwingt dich unheimlich,mit
den bdingungen,wie sie d a sind,zu arbeiten,also nicht dran auszu-
ratten,sondern:es ist so,also mach was mit.dauert wahnsinnig
lange bis man das kann+ oft genug gehts nat.nicht.zb wenn du
genau weißt,daß du nur warten mußt,weil irgendwo ein idiot hier
wieder zu faul ist das telefon zu bedienen,und das jedesmal,aber
wirklich jedesmal - so daß mans schon weiß - zb wenn wir sport
haben.und die uns nicht holen + jedesmal so tun als wärs was
ganz neues daß wir montags sport haben. wir hams ja auch erst 3 jahre
jede woche zur gleichen zeit. und sowas in tausend variationen
1oomal am tag. da gewöhnste dich auch nicht dran - oder nur wenn
du eben resignierst und ihr erstrebtes ziel xxx 'anpassung' (=ver-
recken) vollziehst.naja,die armen kreaturen gibts hier nat.zuhauf.
- klar ,5 jahre sind zu lang,und die 'krisen oder wie man das
nennen mag,hast du zigmal am tag oder 3mal im jahr ,und damit ists
genauso.: es ist eine bedingung, und entweder flippst du drauf
ein und gehst kaputt zwangsläufig,wirst an der ganzen scheiße
verrückt - oder fängts was mit an,also was ist der kern der krise,
woran hängts,was ist das problem,und du kommst immer auf den
punkt,daß es an dir liegt es ändern zu können.und wenn du es nicht
tust bist du ein schwein,daß sich den anderen nicht verantwortlich
fühlt.weil dienat.nicht n kaputten typen brauchen,sondern einen
der sich was überlegt zu allen problemen und fragen + damit
sich selbst be-arbeitet,indem du entscheidungen treffen mußt,
etwas beurteilen,eine situation oder n typen,und so ständig
kontrollierst,was mit dir selber los ist. wenn du dir nichts über-
legst,interessiert dich es nicht - fühlst dich also nichtx verantwortlich,daß klarheit entsteht,entwicklung läuft,von der du
ein teil bist. also kollektiv denken und handeln. - das ist etwas
was man einfach nicht kennt,weil mans nicht kannt,sondern immer
nur das gegenteil,aus dem heraus wie der ganze laden eben läuft.
naja - schwer auf jeden fall,aber es gibt nichts besseres.
la! (ab und zu mal n schrieb von ihm,bei dem ich jedesmal denke,der
junge muß ne starke macke haben nach dem was er schreibt:kein
normaler satz,alles verschlungen und mytifiziert und ein psycho,hälste
nicht aus) , das ist einer der wartet schon aufs alt werden (sagt
er) . kann ich nur sagen:nimm dir besser gleich den strick,worauf
denn da noch warten + wieso überhaupt warten.versteh ich einfach
nicht,wie man derart resigniert sich nur noch um sich selber und
seine psyche drehen kann.d.h.wie das kommt ist mit schon klar,aber
ich verzeih (sowieso nie)das niemandem,der einigermaßen durchblickt.
verstehste,wenn da einer hockt und drauf wartet,daß die anderen für
ihn ins feuer springen um ihm mal irgendwann das erträumte bessere
leben zu bringen,na warte.nicht zuletzt überläßt ders ja auch seinen
kindern.ich mein jemand in s e i n e r (oder ähnlicher) lage,der
alle möglichkeiten hatte. für euch ist das eine ganz andere situation

15 March 1976

Hello, I got all the stuff on the giant list. Brigitte says it's quite good as far as the wealth of information is concerned.

Now, I'm sending you a few titles of the texts we want, not that many, but the prices are horrendous, shit. Some are still only available as photocopies, hence the price.

From the Institute for Strategic Studies: *Strategic Survey 1975* (to be published in April) (nothing else from them).

From the Institute for the Study of Conflict, ISC:

I. *Conflict Studies*:

No. 15—*The Coming Confrontation in Southern Africa* (Gutterich)

No. 53—*Oman: Insurgency and Development* (Price)

No. 63—*Guerrilla Politics in Argentina* (Johnson)

II. ISC Special Reports:

Sources of Conflict in British Industry (February 1974)

Revolutionary Challenges in Spain (June 1974)

The Changing Scene in Spain (sections 1 + 2) (recent and £3 more expensive)

That should be enough for now. Anyway, I don't know when all this work is to be done but am feeling good at the moment + have also started working on South Africa again, am back at it and now have a better understanding of what's what and how it all hangs together. The joint ZANU + SWAPO attack and all that can only be victorious in the end (of course with setbacks).[1]

Did you send the marmalade? Would love to eat it again on a slice of bread.

Big kisses for the three kids and Michael. And you.

Ingrid

19 March 1976

Hello, I've already done some of what you asked—I wrote to To + also to Ma.[2] (Copies enclosed so you know. No idea if she'll understand,

---

1   National liberation movements in Zimbabwe and Namibia.
2   To: Larry's wife at the time.

but I tried not to be too harsh, because, in fact, there's nothing to be understood, except to act, and she cannot do that.)

I find it really good how you two go about things, given your situation (integrated middle-class position, glued to this whole material stuff of house, property, family, etc.). How you develop and do projects *together* through an engagement with something that can only teach and enrich you more, even if it becomes increasingly difficult then—when the *limit* of what can be done comes ever closer. The narrow path between resignation and a complete change. It's real, though. (Larry: *nothing*, only crazy fantasies about symbiotic life and ideals, unbearable. He really drones on, just like he writes. I never thought he'd do that.)

I too would walk past a burning house or drive away and, as you said, what's a burning house when every day the apocalypse fills the TV screens? I never understood Berlin as a frontier town with its corresponding absurdities—but today I'd flee its narrowness as quickly as possible.

I still read books on and off, and why not, it's as much part of our life here as rock, beat or eating poppy cake, and just as relatively unimportant. Everything seems to get so important inside (seen from the outside), because it's connected to so much hot air and the eternal tug of war. Today, Larry spouted again about the parcel (I've now ordered it, should he/she do it): how you need to free yourself from such low cravings that were in complete contradiction to our otherwise "highfalutin" stuff, etc. (whatever that means—he couldn't explain it concretely). But about ordering it through him—a simple mistake. Obvious now. Dear me.

So back to more orders (it's quite a lot again—Brigitte is working very hard indeed; me too, though not as fast; I seem to be a bit thicker and slower). White Papers are constantly being published by every ministry or the government or someone else (currently over anger with the Budget). Can you or even better the guy over there get the following two:

White Paper on Defence, published 12 February 1973 by the British government, and

White Paper on the Future of Northern Ireland, published 20 March 1973.

And let me know what weeklies there are and their likely political angle. Brigitte would perhaps like to order one more, but a daily newspaper is too much. Apart from the *Economist*, not needed. *Guardian Weekly*—is that only about the unions? Publisher?

And dailies or Sunday papers—different perspectives. For instance, is the *Guardian* worth it, or what's with the *Herald Tribune*? One should have some sort of overview.

And could you cut out more of those articles from the *Times*, not everything on Ireland, just things like internment, UN status + if there are military reports on British army activities. Again, I'll ask Brigitte what she wants exactly, as we wouldn't need the whole paper. She still needs to think about it, so wait a bit longer.

That's all. Hugs,
Ingrid

29 March 1976

Oh God, I think the marmalade was sent long ago, curse the postal service. So you: only the marmalade, 3 x 300g is fine—so it will go as a small parcel (1 kg) and won't need three weeks to arrive. Or send it express, if that will be quicker. The rest will be brought in fresh from here from the illustrious couple. To is coming to visit on Friday + she'll bring it then.

How did Ma react? If she wants to put these parcels together and send them, selflessly and quietly, that would be good. But I believe she will do it in a suffering-in-silence way, instead of really understanding what it all means. That would also require a bit of self-analysis and criticism. Oh well.

Can you get all the stuff I wrote down for you? But the requests continue:

1) The address of the Anti-Apartheid Movement in London.

2) The *Cunningham Report*, about the Northern Irish prisons being too insecure. We don't know who published it + when. Sounds like a government report.[3]

3) Can you look in the *Times* for articles about the internationalisation of anti-terrorism policies, what the UK says and does about it. It's been a while that the European ministers of the interior have

---

3   The *Cunningham Report* was the annual report of the Northern Ireland Prison Service.

been conferring about it + Germany's policy seems to win through. Jenkins and Maihofer have just met.[4] And we want to know in particular whether the cancellation of the political status for the prisoners from the IRA has been the result of this alignment,[5] i.e., this pretence of all criminals and no political prisoners. (Thieu insisted on this until the day before Saigon's final fall: there are only criminals in his prisons, all revolutionaries are criminals.)[6]

Well, that's a pretty full list. I hope you will stick to a certain degree of order as, given your sloppiness, things aren't all that easy. I can see this in my own "archives", it's devilishly difficult. Have no real over-sight, *like* I used to, chaos and useless collecting, because I had no clear contexts, or only vague ones, which stopped me organising different subjects correctly. Found it tedious too—now, I slowly manage. Learning, learning.

Bye + finally, send the marmalade (only light orange, bitter).

Spring is coming...

Ingrid

Klaus just sent an express letter: I should immediately write an express letter to Koblenz + confirm that, of course, I want to maintain the connection + from now on state my opinion clearly. As if it were that easy—the result might be much worse than now. It's shit, really. It really bothers me, this insoluble knot.

---

4 Roy Jenkins was UK home secretary from 1974 to 1976, and Werner Maihofer was his German counterpart from 1974 to 1978.

5 The political status was cancelled in March 1976, one of various measures intended to de-escalate the conflict in Northern Ireland (see Ingrid's letters of 4 December 1973 and October 1975). As a result, on 14 September 1976, the political prisoners started their Blanket Protest, refusing to wear prison clothes. This culminated in one of the longest IRA hunger strikes, lasting from 1 March to 3 October 1981, during which ten prisoners died: Bobby Sands, Francis Hughes, Patsy O'Hara, Raymond McCreesh, Joe McDonnell, Martin Hurson, Kevin Lynch, Kieran Doherty, Thomas McElwee and Mickey Devine. See: Bobby Sands, *But an Unfinished Song* (New York: Nation Books, 2006).

6 Nguyen Van Thieu was president of South Vietnam from 1965 to 1975. He had come to power via a military coup supported by the CIA and the assassination of the then president Ngo Dinh Diem.

12 April 1976

Hello, I wasn't affronted at all. On the contrary, I took it as intended: seriously. And learnt a lot about myself, nothing edifying. It's like with every mistake: it bites back and how.[7] You learn from it, but it doesn't justify the (probably irreparable) damage inflicted. Shit. It's this pointless boastfulness, nothing new. The kind of criticism once described here as "steamrolling". And I could have known, and I should have. What you said is right overall: the use of a world revolution "to cut the umbilical cord" (ridiculous really) and "imaginary shackles", etc. I'll have to think about this much more before doing anything. Anyway, it's given me lots to think about. Wait.

Your marmalade parcel probably won't arrive in time if it takes another three weeks. Next week is probably my departure time. Brigitte was taken to Frankfurt last Wednesday + writes from there that our suspicion of why all this happened was correct (because logically there's no other reason): self-isolation because of our refusal to integrate into the prison community. It's a perverse concept, which in reality means a psychologically supervised process of integration until they have you at the point where you're fulfilling your role as a woman/prisoner. Of course, they know in advance that this doesn't work with us + so they cleverly engineered the whole thing: a scheme whereby non-integration means no exercise time, no shopping (because no work) + the hole is shut and the hatch is sealed. Over there, almost everything is possible that you can hardly imagine possible here anymore, because we managed to deconstruct this whole nonsense (that's why they have to dismantle things here). Brigitte was sent earlier, because for me a decision is expected on Wednesday about our trial appeal + so my transfer was postponed. I was to be transferred too, but we complained + I got a period of grace. The appeal will be refused, of course, but this way it looks legally more correct.

Oh—the marmalade has just arrived, that was quick.

The new address will be Homburger Landstrasse 112, 6 Frankfurt am Main 50.

---

7   A reference to Gerti questioning the tone of some of Ingrid's recent letters to her parents.

Sister, I'm somewhat pressed, because there's still so much to do here—it's an incredible rift. When you know you're bound to end up in a situation that's shitty from start to end + with the purpose as obvious as here (i.e., conditions will now be brought into line with those for all the others + at the same time with the propaganda confirming that integration doesn't work with us, because we aren't able to conform, etc.)—then there's a lot to think about, about what can be done against it. It can't be stopped, that's clear. We can only constantly denounce it.

Have fun on your holiday. The next letter will be from Frankfurt. Greetings to all.

Ingrid

I see you've gone already.

Early May 1976

I'd have to write a whole novel to describe how it is + you still wouldn't be able to picture it—because nobody can imagine what prison is + especially not this one, where someone who looks at it from the outside must think, "Oh, but something is being done there".[8]

In the attempt here to create an artificial unity between prisoners and guards—who are dependent on each other and, therefore, need to work with each other—the entire project shows its limitation, the fact that some people are prisoners and some are guards and there's nothing in between. It *is* the front, and that's what they try to obscure in every way possible + they succeed in so far as the prisoners don't see through it. That makes sense. The result is totally broken people who comply to the utmost degree.

The system is this: on arrival, you are put into the so-called admission station or "intensive care unit". There you get intensive training on how to behave in order to receive the least possible bullshit, or the most essential items like tobacco and coffee. It's called learning "group behaviour", social thinking, etc. Social in one direction only: in line

---

8   Ingrid is now in Preungesheim Prison in Frankfurt. Its section for women had a reputation for being progressive in its approach, with its unit for mothers and pre-school
children, a policy of open doors within units, and a complete battery of psycho-social
reintegration programmes.

with the house rules. Here people work half days and get forty pennies a shift—a way of making them want to work full-time, which they can do after two months. Those who don't want to do this idiotic work are locked in and not allowed to buy anything, meaning they have *nothing* (the system won't let you have your own money, as that would undermine the entire system). That works, but not with us.

So they got this idea that we should do a correspondence course, which they would count as "work"—to keep up appearances + leave the system intact. We had told them: only on condition that we stay in the same section—because they wanted to separate us after two months. Well, it's all useless now anyway, because it will be either Stammheim or here—but certainly without this dirty charade that they want to sustain. No way. The first thing they told us, and repeated every minute, was about getting "equal treatment". But the reality is different + we aren't the idiots they hoped we were. (That idiotic course had Ma's enthusiastic approval again, of course: "It seemed to make sense".)

For the past week the men's prison here has been incredibly lively, a rumpus *raging* every evening—it's an iron/concrete machine, with concrete shades in front of the windows, so with human destruction already programmed into the architecture. We hear it over here + until a while ago, there was a never-ending demonstration, scores of vehicles circulating around both prisons and honking away on their horns—and just now the sound of people being beaten up—the pigs have arrived. A solidarity hunger strike is going on here too, but we're not taking part, as it was organised and arranged *jointly* with the prison administration. Well, thanks.

Finishing now. Will be a while to the next letter. The articles arrived and the flowers (which one of you sorts that?). What am I supposed to do with all that Solzhenitsyn stuff? That guy means absolutely nothing to me; he only functions as a slanderer and an instrument of anti-communism. Some articles in the first lot of material were very good. Who are Chris and her friend?[9] I didn't get anything from them—those lazy fools at the Lehrter sent everything back to sender. So for weeks I didn't get any newspapers, plus there's the printers' strike (or was).

---

9   Chris and Milo were Irish friends of the Wilfords. Chris worked in Michael's office while she was studying.

And, yes, about all your questions at the beginning. The hatch isn't sealed, because their plans didn't work: the others threatened to shout and rebel if they locked us up + did the opposite of what the guards tried to persuade them to do: hate us because we don't work ("isolate themselves" was how they put it). On the contrary, they find it completely right + good, of course; nobody wants to do this idiotic work, but they aren't strong enough to resist the pressure. Many here are like the girl you write about in your work. Almost all of them are like that + they carry the total experience of the world on their backs.

I don't need anything right now + we aren't getting anything in here anyway.

In the plane here, I thought, "Ah, finally, away!" Here the doors are open all day long + there's no loo in this hole. It's terrible; every morning it's congestion over there.

The latest thing with dear Mama will dampen your sense of relief again, because she can't resist it. And I can no longer grin and bear it.

Greetings to all. Visits here are ten times more difficult. Frau Mohnhaupt came today + was totally exhausted with anger. No pigs present—but after such a struggle.

16 May 1976

Hi Sister, so much has happened in the last three weeks, and there's so much to think about and reflect on that writing is the last thing on my mind. It's damn difficult to concentrate, by which I mean that I need to make sense of things so I can deal with them.

The anger first: I heard on the radio that Oestreicher made more comments about Ulrike.[10] What he said was so sinister that it's crystal clear to me what a cleric is, him especially, and I would advise him to keep his mouth shut if he doesn't want to denounce us. Saying that Ulrike had "lost her will to live" as long as two years ago is a dirty

---

10   Ulrike Meinhof had been found dead in her cell the previous week, on the morning of 9 May.

denunciation of her and all of us. He doesn't have the *slightest* idea about her or of what it means to fight + she did fight. And the fact that she didn't manage it conveys an idea (but truly only an idea) of what isolation really is, known *only* by someone who has actually lived through it, and so would know how terrible the pressure is and how unbearable for anyone. His drivel is as bad as the shit about "tensions within the group", insinuating that we had driven her to suicide—or what? He'd better stop spouting any opinions about us—because he knows *nothing* + his "insider" fabrications fit the function of psychological warfare exactly.

No wonder our dear Mother managed to do another one of her things, and all I could really say was that I'd had enough. She phoned the prison psychologist here, asking how I'd "coped" with the news of Ulrike's death + then saying how good it would still be for me if I did the Spanish language course. Out of "concern" for me, of course. Nice concern, that strangles me over time, with not a bit of sensitivity for my situation—only wants to satisfy her own concern, regardless of where and with whom, even if it means siding with the pigs. If I don't write to her about what we feel and think, it's precisely so that nobody finds out about it + especially not this way. It would also be useless, because she has no idea what it means for us, given that she considers us to be misguided, seduced and obsessed people, with no idea of what goes on in the world. While she, of course, seems to know it all. Oh boy, I'm so sick of always considering her self-centered concern, because it's increasingly clear that nothing changes + these things are the absolute limit.

The cops now want to take me to Stammheim Prison as a replacement for the corpse there. You need to know the background in order to understand the dirty scheming of this. In Berlin, we both applied to be transferred to Stammheim instead of Frankfurt, because that's what we want and need: group association, *against* their destructive isolation strategy (and *that* it destroys should be clear to anyone by now). This was refused. Now that they have killed her, *one* of us must go there to make up the number + thus, enable the smooth continuation of their destruction. I refused, and we demanded that we both go. It's not been decided yet—probably the ruling will be made some time this week, so we will either both be there soon or neither of us for the moment, i.e., we'll keep trying. Let's see. I hope you understand.

Well, and here—a totally different prison + other people. Am damn glad I'm away from that island,[11] and it's only after leaving that you realise how broken it all is. The guards here are ten times livelier and more natural in their thinking and reactions. More direct—honest. While the prison here + its system is a well-oiled blackmail apparatus on the psycho-level: "our house community" (which didn't work in Berlin, because we resisted the methods they used on us).

Don't send me any visitors please! By the way, I've got no pictures on the wall—and the entire "household" consists of three boxes with books, one with files, one with clothes. I don't need more property.

Dear Gerti, another brief addition—just got your letter + I do think you understand why I am or was so angry about Oestreicher. Although he's relatively unimportant, within this whole propaganda he fulfils a function *for* the pigs. Just like they tried to medicalise Ulrike posthumously after not managing it while she was alive,[12] *because* she fought *from* within the context of the entire group. Only in this way can the relationships between us be understood, and they have nothing to do with all the bourgeois rubbish about suffering and grief. (That's why such phone calls are so unbearable. If only Ma could understand that, or at least *refrain* from doing such things.)

The *Strategic Survey 1975* has been published. Could you please get it and post it to me? It will get through okay—everything does here. You can also send the rest of the articles, no problems there either. But no rubbish, thanks. And no French either—I'd need years to understand that properly. (By the way, the same report on Cambodia appeared in *Stern*.)

Nothing new on Stammheim.

A kiss and big firm hug back to you.

Ingrid

A funny thing here—all my home-town representatives are here, from everywhere: Bamberg, Saarbrücken, Sendorf. This is the only big prison for Central Germany, and everything is concentrated here. I had totally forgotten the different dialects + it's quite funny how Berlin has affected such small details. Really glad to be finally away from there.

---

11   West Berlin.
12   In the year before her death, the Federal High Court had decreed that Ulrike's brain should be examined against her will; the order was abandoned only after a wave of public protests.

27 May 1976

Dear Gerti,

I hope you received the last two letters—this isn't always entirely clear here, some disappear. As to our transfer, nothing has been decided yet, i.e., the decision seems to be to maintain a completely unclear situation + to undermine our application by asking others for information. It will still be a long, drawn-out struggle. And when you can imagine that a suicide seems increasingly impossible, you know what kind of struggle it will take to counter the violence they've already inflicted. (Considering *all* that we know, and what we know about Ulrike herself, she was assassinated.) Our demand is group association and not the transfer of one of us as a replacement—and the fact that we demand this is the result of our five-year experience, which objectively and subjectively makes it necessary: for each of us, as well as out of political necessity.

The few weeks back here again have made this clear in the shortest time: you either get smashed up in this mill by adapting and participating fully—or you must stay away from it, isolate yourself + that's impossible. The only logical conclusion is to come together + do what's important.

Please send the interview with Rory O'Brady in the *Sunday Times* of 23 May,[13] where he declares "no unification". It must be that date, because it was mentioned this week in a German newspaper.

When will you come next—holidays will soon be here. I only want to know in order to plan somewhat in advance, which is necessary here with these stupid timeframes of three weeks + one-hour visit. And perhaps I can try to get a bit more time, etc.

This is it for today. Loving greetings to you all + send me a letter with the article.

Ingrid

---

13   Rory O'Brady (Ruairí Ó Brádaigh) was president of Sinn Fein from 1975 to 1976. In the *Sunday Times* interview, he proposed an independent Republic of Northern Ireland.

1 June 1976

Hello, another sign of life. I do appreciate that it's pretty bad not to write—and I think this will improve sometime soon. Perhaps it's partly because communication is somewhat "saturated" + the rest of the time is crammed with x journals, books, etc. You know—what can be said here is damn little and also so frustrating.

So, simply: come whenever you want and whenever you can. All the same to me and no matter anyway if another visit gets cancelled as a result (talking to you is a bit different from talking to Ma).

And, meanwhile, you can also see me again at full "strength"— which I regret (and despite my best daily resolve).

So, until soon, Sister. And firm hugs for all the people.

The Mao hasn't been published yet, has it? But damn, I haven't even finished all the other books you sent. I thought Craig would be something quite different.

People's News arrives every few weeks or months—well, not very interesting, full of local colour. Such stuff exists here too.

Greetings,

Eva

14 June 1976

Hey, you're rather on the wrong track with your anxieties about this place, well, not just rather, but completely. I can't blame you for that— because it could only have been me who gave you that impression. "Theorising", etc. What concerns you can only be resolved by under- standing the things that are conveyed over time.

As far as that guy's concerned—don't take it any further, no way, it's suspicious, and only creates a legitimate entry for him (through the back door—family, because anyone working in this field knows where to get the information they need) to concoct a book whose impact can only turn people against us, because he can't really know anything about the reality of prisoners and policy. If he really wants to do some- thing *for* us, then it would be in a political context that's useful for us. On the contrary, selling Ulrike is sheer infamy. And glorifying her as well.

We're boiling here—the cells like ovens, a concrete block that acts like a stove.[14] Brigitte and I together in one hole. On arrival (in a police helicopter from Frankfurt—quite something) we were pushed like cattle, and, without being asked, into what was Ulrike's cell. At the time, we didn't know it was hers, completely repainted, even the tiniest scratch, and the window sealed hermetically. Then things went very fast. Gudrun came, and we went into her cell next door and simply stayed there—she'd been transferred into the high-security unit with Andreas and Jan the day before. We can all have *Umschluss* for a few hours during the day,[15] and we have asked to be moved into their unit too—because this situation is so impossible. The section that includes our cell is precisely the one where murder was possible. And we know that's what it was. (Had it been suicide, we wouldn't have a problem with saying so. To conceal it or turn it into a "signal"—that's what people do who prefer not to see reality, so they don't have to confront their own reality as passive spectators.)

What's happening *is* counterinsurgency at a level that conveys the scope of the confrontation—the State reactions reveal the explosive nature of the policy: guerrilla. And not, as you might assume, because the Germans are being particularly thorough and hysterical once again, but *because that's how it is.*

I'll see that you get a few of the last texts that Ulrike wrote—some booklets have been published already.[16] You'll understand, because they are an expression of maturity: the false tones of the past gone, now

---

14 At Stammheim Prison, the prisoners from the RAF were kept in a separate unit on the seventh floor. Directly above this floor was a flat roof with an enclosed structure that was their exercise yard. In summer, the cells on the top floor were unbearably hot and the air stagnant, because the very small windows were covered with fine-mesh screens.

15 *Umschluss* is a term used by the prison administration to signify a situation in which two or three prisoners are allowed to be together for a few hours in one of their cells. At one point, the prisoners from the RAF in Stammheim could spend several hours a day together in the corridor of the high-security unit where they were held, a change introduced following court evidence by medical experts about the prisoners' need for social interaction. They were not, however, allowed to enter the cell of a prisoner of a different gender. See sketches of the unit, p. 225.

16 Some of Ulrike's texts were published in a booklet (socialhistoryportal.org/raf/5535) and have been translated into English with other writings by her in: Ulrike Meinhof, *Our Gun, Our Consciousness, and the Collective* (Montreal/Oakland: Kersplebedeb/PM Press, 2025).

clear—simple—witty, sharp. It's the result of the process here and of the group + then you will *know* that she did not commit suicide.

Well, our mother remains a problem, because she is part of the problem. I don't feel like getting upset about this right now, but I really see no prospect of contact working in the current circumstances here. Let's see. Visits need to wait a bit; I'm not so keen on them right now. Helke, well, that's another problem. Visits here are only every four weeks anyway (apparently, fewer visits the further south we come).

You could send another parcel with marmalade, four of the bitter orange like the last ones, they were very good. Please send it soon. And, please, not next year, hey.

And the stuff you wanted to send ages ago, articles, *Strategic Survey*, etc., this year too, if possible.

Greetings to all of you.

Ingrid

15 July 1976

Hi, I wrote to you during the action,[17] but then didn't send it because it seemed no longer relevant. Well. What can be learnt is that there's nothing they wouldn't be prepared to do, whatever the material cost, including human lives. Their reaction gives you an idea of the current state of war that exists + the role we play in that. We were totally isolated in here for five days, no radio, no newspaper, no lawyer, no *Umschluss* + then, suddenly, Sunday morning *Umschluss* again, when it became clear what had happened. You'll have heard about the offer of collaboration while the negotiations were going on.

I wrote to Ma (a bit cool or distant or whatever you want to call it) saying there's no basis right now for a visit, given the situation. I really don't know what we'd talk about. Writing briefly like this isn't a problem anyway, so that's okay.

The marmalade—you dummy, two jars were broken to pieces, two okay. And I had said different kinds and didn't mean different kinds of

---

17   On 27 June 1976, a joint RZ (Revolutionary Cells)–PFLP-EO (Popular Front for the Liberation of Palestine–External Operations) commando hijacked an Air France plane and rerouted it to Entebbe, Uganda, demanding the release of fifty-three prisoners, including Ingrid.

orange, but jelly jam made from blackberries or bitter lemon or whatever. Never mind. Until the birthday parcel.

Good that you got the material. Just think (particularly from
Ulrike's texts) that someone writes like this after four years of destructive detention as a result of a collective learning process + that tells you
something about the "miracle" of them not having achieved their aim
of moral and political annihilation. Hence the physical destruction.
And at a point when it was necessary for them.

The whole thing continues right now in this civil war bunker with
the crown witness who made it a condition of his appearance that
Ulrike would not be present in court,[18] using false statements to kick
out her lawyers. Buback called this "sealing the cells".

Five people in isolation—doesn't seem to you like isolation. Well,
even Amnesty International calls it small-group isolation, with the
same impact as single isolation. And you, like everyone, are a victim
of the psychological warfare—all invented, etc. It's hardly possible to
break through the artificiality of this vacuum here—except by more.
It's this reference to the old fascism with its horror and tanks and
torture—but in the meantime Kissinger and Brandt and Schmidt,[19] as
protagonists of this system, have long understood that *they* no longer
need these to survive. They are determined to replace the ugly and
open fascism with the new fascism, by force, if necessary, in countries
that don't want it, i.e., with economic pressure etc., like for instance
in Chile, Spain, South Africa. The new clean reform fascism—SPD[20]—
social democracy. That's the method: Vorster suddenly showers down
presents for the Blacks:[21] electricity, permission to speak their own
language—after Kissinger's plea. They are biding their time. They know
that open fascism creates immediate resistance, Vietnam, their fear,
which they would openly have to oppose militarily throughout the
world. Which would deprive them of their last base. Hence, the covert
way, covert warfare.

---

18 Crown witness Gerhard Müller had been arrested in July 1972 with Ulrike Meinhof.
19 Henry Kissinger was President Nixon's national security adviser (1969–1975) and US
    secretary of state (1973–1977). Willy Brandt and Helmut Schmidt were SPD politicians
    and German chancellors (1969–1974 and 1974–1982 respectively).
20 SPD: Germany's social democratic party.
21 John Vorster, prime minister and president of South Africa (1966–1979), was an advo-
    cate of the country's apartheid regime.

I'd like to know if you've got Ulrike's last texts. There's a lot in there about the role of the SPD. And that's our understanding of the situation, which continues to develop, of course. Not doctrine—but a process. Put simply, we're not making things up.

In one of those early talk shows (Sunday at midday—six journalists from different countries and the personification of fascism, Höfer, in the middle), a long-faced woman from the *Guardian* said she had discussed things with colleagues and they all thought that the secret service should take over! Drive down there and somehow kill all these people! She meant us, of course. She just verbalised it. Quite a woman.

Yeah, Berlin, quite a thing.[22] Here, of course, a lot of nonsense, new locks, etc., though nobody can get in. But they know that too, of course.

Oestreicher—you know, that guy will never set foot in here again, such a slime ball. I'd like to know what kind of stories he still spreads about us. My request was to get Amnesty International to support our demand to be together in a group; he had no permission for anything else.

I've not yet read your article about your line of work, as we've only just returned from our *Umschluss* (taking place where Andreas, Gudrun and Jan are, in a separate part of this section, with a gated door in front, where three or four guards sit permanently, with *nothing* to do but observe us).

The dissemination of the texts in England has started already, as far as I know.[23] But you can ask Wienke. She's quite a good source for this kind of work—and through Ulrike she understood *how* things are done *here*. Hidden + with each acting according to their possibilities. And by acting one understands what's to be done next; you understand quite simply how the machine functions. Just as it's the reactions that tell us what's important. We recognise ourselves in those.

Well, finished. Oh, visit. As I wrote before, only every four weeks here, and I want to have some other visits. Let's see, maybe you can get a special visit on the grounds that you're coming from England just for this. You might try that.

---

22 Four political prisoners had escaped from Lehrter Strasse Prison. See Timeline 7 July 1976.

23 Only a few texts were published in English at that time. See Ingrid's letter of 16 December 1976, p. 148, footnote 32.

Do you make marmalade too?
Greetings,
Ingrid

18 July—Forgot to send it off. We moved yesterday: *into* the unit, which means we're in single holes again. Total silence. Like under a bell.

28 July 1976

Hey you, very briefly. About this profane matter of money (which is only there to be spent). We need quite a lot here—for technical stuff, such as radios, a recorder, microphones, tapes, and for warm blankets, thermos flasks, etc., etc.—which all must be bought by the institution and can't be brought in by visitors (amounts to the same, of course). Not ideal to always ask the parents. The problem with you is the rather weak pound + the miserable exchange rate. Are there other ways of providing us with some? (No upper limit, hey!)

When are you coming to Germany? Try and come with one or two of the kids.

And a kiss,
Ingrid

Tomorrow I'll say something down there (in court—we'll all say something there now).[24]

14 August 1976

Hello. Greece doesn't really seem to be a dream destination—as a tourist you can easily get busted.[25]

So your visit—here, half an hour. I don't know what it's like for someone coming from abroad, should be easy + in any case, because of

---

24 In July and August, fourteen prisoners from the RAF testified in court about the structure of the RAF, mainly to counter the testimony of Gerhard Müller, the prisoner who had turned crown witness for the prosecution. Ingrid testified on 3 August.
25 A reference to Rolf Pohle, a former West German guerrilla, arrested in Greece the previous month.

some misunderstandings no visits have taken place here so far. Klaus should call Schreitmüller, who calls himself the prison director + say when. They will then book the LKA officer,[26] and that's it. He can then also arrange for how long and whether twice would be possible; I don't know about that. If the kids don't want to come—I'd completely understand, even though I'd certainly be more curious than they seem to be.

Bring three pounds of fruit, plums, peaches or whatever. And try marmalade. Nothing else. Money—by postal cheque to Croissant's office, Langestrasse 3, 7 Stuttgart 1,[27] indicating that it's for me/us here.

This "telegram" will have to do. The papers + letter have arrived. I know nothing about a cheque for a radio. Father paid for that. It doesn't matter what date you come—only Monday to Friday is possible. I've no calendar. I've written to Klaus.

Ingrid

19 September 1976

Hey you, what I wanted to say at the visit was that you've never looked so overwrought and shocked about I don't know what—fear or what, but of whom? Fear I understand—it's always the reality that elicits this reaction, exerts pressure. Well, your situation seems pretty clear to me—perhaps more to me than to you, as I view it from the other side, the other side of the river, and the look that you tend to put on here doesn't really affect me, but somehow also grows tedious over time.

It's a bit different with you—but you're in a kind of vicious circle that doesn't allow such a thing as an understanding of resistance—because then you'd have reached the limit that would make it subjectively impossible to continue in the old way. I don't know if you're familiar with the feeling that at some point you can no longer do certain things, i.e., don't want to—and then why not have confidence in yourself, believe in yourself.

---

26 An officer from the Regional Criminal Investigation Bureau (LKA) in charge of surveillance during prison visits.
27 Klaus Croissant: one of the lawyers defending the prisoners in Stammheim and elsewhere.

I do understand (i.e., your limits + sure I don't like it) why suddenly such sentences appear as "not with that label", etc.[28]—because in the meantime we have a situation where everyone understands what it means for them to do something for us, where it's always a decision that no longer leaves you as an outsider but now defines you, irrespective of how clear that might be to you.

The stuff from the Conflict Institute is needed really urgently (even if you can't imagine that we work with such things—it is after all something we can do here). And, then again, and also soon, a parcel with cake or if possible plum pudding in a tin like the other parcel, only twice the size. And jelly, but packed better: blackberry and whatever else is available.

Ma's marmalade, well, I don't have particularly clear memories of that. And, hey, as I've said before, such requests are always thoroughly thought through.

The line to Koblenz is more than arduous. But, okay, they will be coming for my birthday. It's one of these things that objectively no longer work + then only through pity + that's a really bad foundation for communication. For sure, no basis to build on. But please understand that I no longer say that the way I used to, as personal antipathy—but they are as far away as anyone else.

Something else, the money—even though it's shitty to spend more words on it; I suppose you were disappointed that I didn't rejoice over the amount—much as it's a lot, it's also nothing + just money. Only to be despised, much as one is forced to need it. So am relating coldly to it.

Well, will this make any sense to you? Greetings.

10 November 1976

Hi, the journal arrived today, the socks (really good this time—congratulations!) a few days ago (enough for now). Only the cake is missing. I don't understand—but the problem with the postal service isn't new. Ma said that all of it can be got here too. These visits are cruel—for her

---

28 Gerti was aware of a growing distance and possible misunderstandings between herself and Ingrid, which may have been due to the hardening situation and the fact that Ingrid's priorities were now discussions within the group of prisoners in Stammheim.

as much as for me. But that's contradictory. I really think in the mean-time that some sort of delusion has developed there—the example of that journey is already at a limit that nobody understands. Greetings and fitness—the social democratic programme, no?

Did Wienke inform you about the IUK?[29]

Have you seen the film *Traces of the Past*, by Marcel Ophüls (son of the old Ophüls). I read that it was shown on your TV (on 8 November). Even in its cut version, it's still a document that affirms us: aggression infringing on people's rights—a principle developed at the Nuremberg World War II Trials—*always* legitimises the right to resistance.

Do you know whether Ophüls lives in England?

Greetings.

The whole thing is so crooked because of the way I'm lying.[30]

16 December 1976

Oh no, how could I find it bad that they're now sitting on a steamboat travelling around the world. I found it terrible that she didn't want to go, with that pitying look.

I might have known that you'd be taken in by those peace women.[31] Here are a few articles for your information, commentaries by the legal Left, whereas I'm still thinking a bit differently. You seem to be in danger of sinking into a bog of ideology or unreality—whereas we act on facts + it's rather irrelevant whether one considers war stupid or not. It's the reality: war against the war. I do wish you'd read a thing or two.

The texts are now published as a book in several countries—for England it's still not certain.[32] Agee is going to be expelled—do you

---

29 The IUK was the International Commission of Investigation into the Death of Ulrike Meinhof. Its final report was presented in January 1979 at a press conference in Paris and published in French and German. See the Endnote.

30 Refers to Ingrid's handwriting in this letter.

31 In Northern Ireland, Women for Peace was an organisation financed by the Institute for the Study of Conflict (see Ingrid's first undated letter of October 1975).

32 At the time, the book with texts by the RAF and the prisoners was published in German and Swedish only, and in a different format in French. In English, some of the texts were published much later in Moncourt and Smith (see p. 57, footnote 5).

know his statements and those of the other former CIA agents for the trial here?[33] If not, I'll send them to you.

The relatives are now meeting more regularly again. There are some things to be done. Looking at what the Irish relatives are doing + those over here + in Spain, for instance, one sees that they all want the same things. Let's see.

Do you still get information from Wienke?

Fried[34] also knows about the latest developments of the IUK; the next session is in Brussels. Its membership speaks for itself. The thing has power.

Well, here again it's the encirclement policy at work: following a raid + the arrest of Haag, they want to prevent lawyers coming unless they or we agree to a search down to their underpants. Well, that's how it is.[35]

The cake has arrived. Thanks. A sadistic time, Christmas.

---

33 Former CIA agent Philip Agee and others had been called by the defence in the Stammheim trial but were not admitted by the court. They reported on CIA activities in Germany at a press conference in June 1976. See Ingrid's letter of 11 January 1974.

34 Erich Fried, a writer and poet who fled Austria under the Nazis and settled in England. He supported the demands of the prisoners to have their isolation lifted.

35 Following the arrest on 30 November 1976 of lawyer Siegfried Haag, who had gone underground, the prisoners' cells were searched again by officers of the Federal Criminal Investigation Bureau (BKA), and lawyers visiting the prisoners had to submit to being searched down to their underpants.

Letters and Reports 1977

In late March, the prisoners from the RAF call their fourth hunger strike, this time demanding to be brought together in groups large enough to enable social interaction. They end the hunger strike after a month, following assurances that, as an initial step, the group in Stammheim Prison will be enlarged to up to eight prisoners. In the meantime, the RAF's Ulrike Meinhof Commando kills Attorney General Siegfried Buback, whom they hold responsible for the death of three prisoners from the RAF.

The year continues as a period of escalating confrontation. Ingrid describes the mounting tension in the prison and a brutal attack on the prisoners by a group of prison guards that results, amongst other things, in another hunger strike and Ingrid's transfer to Stadelheim Prison in Munich. A contact ban of more than six weeks is imposed on all the political prisoners following the abduction of the president of the Confederation of German Employers' Associations by the RAF and the hijacking of a plane in support of the RAF's demand for the release of eleven prisoners, including Ingrid. Ingrid writes about her experience of the contact ban.

She is moved to Stadelheim Prison and applies for a transfer to Frankfurt, to be nearer to her family. Her last letters describe her plans for the future. She writes to her sister Gerti about the imminent visit they have arranged. Before the date of the visit, Ingrid is found dead in the isolated cell she had been moved to a few hours earlier.

Early 1977

Hey you. Your letter arrived + the socks (? that bad—what I need exactly are *ski* socks, really warm ones) + jumper. Well, let's leave it. But thank you.

Another study by the Conflict Institute: *Terrorism versus Liberal Democracy—The Problems of Response* by Paul Wilkinson. Must be quite new. It's extremely urgent. Really.

In great haste, greetings,
Ingrid

4 May 1977

It's clear that writing's a problem and almost impossible, because what needs to be said can't be said + "discussion" in this no man's land turns out to be flat, stale. I'm okay—yes, that's what you can always assume. And don't presume alienation when you hear nothing for months, because all this writing is much more alienating if I don't feel like it, and then it's just chat about any old stuff.

You see, what strikes you with panic is to me the opposite. What more is there still to explain. And particularly because from your situation it's clear that there's a limit to "understanding"—whereas there's nothing to be justified. So to Ma's anxious question, that I surely would never have wanted "this": I have.[1] So that's how it's developing, and it's only the beginning. Wow—such shallow words.

I'd rather see you, and you're always welcome. Okay?

It's a bit barren here, but do understand.

The books arrived some time ago, thanks.

---

[1] "This" refers to the killing of Attorney General Siegfried Buback by the RAF's Ulrike Meinhof Commando on 7 April 1977.

Report of the Attack in Stammheim Prison, Stuttgart, on 8 August 1977

The prisoners in Stammheim Prison's high-security unit are provoked and attacked by prison guards. At this time, the prisoners from the RAF who are held there are Ingrid, Gudrun Ensslin, Irmgard Möller, Jan Raspe, Andreas Baader, Wolfgang Beer, Helmut Pohl and Werner Hoppe. The following report by Ingrid about this attack analyses the facts and circumstances. Ingrid's report was drawn on subsequently by several lawyers, quoting sections of her account in their submissions on behalf of other prisoners. Extracts of the report were later translated and submitted to the Human Rights Commission in New York.

The overt brutality of the attack this morning is the signal that the State Security, the Baden-Württemberg Ministry of Justice and Bender are preparing for the final solution in Stammheim within the next few days.[2] The direct physical assault is certainly not the end of the offensive that was fuelled systematically in Stammheim last week, in parallel with escalation at all levels—the campaign against the lawyers' office here in Stuttgart, the false allegations, the attempts to connect Croissant to Ponto's death,[3] the fascist image of us as enemies or "terror furies"—all of that is intended not just to stoke up the manhunt outside but also to prepare public opinion for the targeted liquidation of the prisoners. It is a pattern of psychological warfare, using military, ideological, psychological and economic means to liquidate an opposition movement.

The background that makes the issue so urgent is the high probability that the follow-up conference of the CSCE in Belgrade[4] and—following the rejection of the appeal—the European Court of Human Rights in Strasbourg, as well as the UN, will be concerned

---

2   Traugott Bender, minister of justice (1972–1977) of Germany's federal state of Baden-Württemberg, where Stuttgart is the capital city.

3   Klaus Croissant (one of the prisoners' defence lawyers) was arrested in July 1977 after announcing the establishment of an International Commission of Investigation into the Death of Ulrike Meinhof. Jürgen Ponto, chair of the Board of Directors of the Dresdner Bank, was killed by the Red Army Faction on 30 July 1977. For days afterwards, all political prisoners were denied access to radio, newspapers and all external contacts, just as happened after the killing of Attorney General Siegfried Buback.

4   The Conference on Security and Co-operation in Europe (CSCE or Helsinki Accords).

with the direction of the dramatic show trial for which Rebmann, still Germany's top prosecutor, is responsible,[5] not to mention his shared responsibility (as permanent secretary in the Ministry of Justice of Baden-Württemberg) for the wiretaps in the cells during lawyer visits and for the deaths of Ulrike and Siegfried in Stammheim.

It is clear that this Swabian—who in the most literal sense has furthered his career by walking over corpses, those of the prisoners and his predecessor—wants to use a combination of smear campaigns and murder to rid himself of the trouble looming ahead. What was already clear after Buback's death—that we are hostages of the Federal Prosecutors' Office—is now made crystal clear in a new way with the death of Ponto.

The Individual Phases of the Escalation

After the "binding promise" from Rebmann,[6] at that time still the person responsible at the Ministry of Justice, we suspend the hunger strike. For seven weeks nothing happens. They are taken up with constructing the perfect machine that will control and register our every movement, an architecture that is a cross between a bulletproof bank counter, behind which they lurk and observe us every minute, and a wild animal's cage, where we sit composing our twelve thousandth secret message and—judges and politicians never lie—brooding over new sensational crimes.

Crammed with electronic surveillance and alarm systems, they don't understand it at all, pressing the wrong buttons and setting off the alarm. At night, two video cameras equipped with the latest electronics observe every movement and react to every fly or fluttering bit of paper, triggering the alarm.

Construction work drags on for seven weeks, then three of us are moved, and we are now eight instead of six. Verena isn't brought into this high-security unit, despite her six weeks on hunger strike and Nusser's firm promise. Günter is moved from Stammheim into the total isolation of the Weissenau madhouse and from there to the infamous

---

5   After his death in April 1977, Germany's Attorney General Siegfried Buback was succeeded by Kurt Rebmann.
6   The promise to bring political prisoners together in a larger group in Stammheim Prison.

psychiatric prison unit at Hohenasperg.[7] Nusser and Schreitmüller make it clear that the Ministry of Justice is pursuing delaying tactics in conjunction with the Federal Prosecutors' Office.[8] The federal states suddenly no longer know anything about agreements and refuse other transfers; it becomes clear that their promises are not being kept.

The Federal Prosecutors' Office formulates the absurd charge of attempted murder against Newerla and Müller, because they cannot dissuade Verena and Sabine from the hunger strike.[9] The Office wants to eliminate the last two lawyers from visiting prisoners here, and, thus, shut out any oversight.

At the same time, the ideological *Volkssturm* is mobilised.[10] The child stars of the Student Movement, grown fat and false, and the old hands of the Ban the Bomb movement—all come together in the anti-terror front of the SPD. Here, they suddenly have at their disposal against the prisoners something that never occurred to them to use against the State: militancy. Cohn-Bendit spreads blatantly false news about Klein in *Der Spiegel* and, in parallel, Gollwitzer uses the main leftist disseminators—*ID*, *ED*, *Links*—to neutralise the Left's reflexes, where they still exist, against more killings of prisoners, following the model of State Security journalists. And Albertz appears on TV with the same kind of humanity that made him resign in 1967.[11]

---

7   Verena Becker, a prisoner from the RAF held in another section of Stammheim Prison, and Günter Sonnenberg, who had been arrested with her in May 1977 after being shot in the head. It was a long struggle before he regained his cognitive faculties.

8   Hans Nusser was the prison director, Ulrich Schreitmüller his deputy.

9   Armin Newerla and Arndt Müller worked at the same office as Klaus Croissant and were persecuted after defending prisoners from the RAF. They were arrested in August and September 1977 respectively and spent several years in prison. Sabine Schmitz, accused of supporting the RAF, was arrested in December 1976 and imprisoned for three years.

10 *Volkssturm* (People's Militia): a reference to the Nazi Party's last desperate attempt to win the war, when they mobilised men who were not already serving in a military unit and conscripted women and youths as auxiliaries.

11 Daniel Cohn-Bendit was a student movement militant in the 1960s in France and Germany. Eventually, he became co-president of the European Greens in the European Parliament. Hans-Joachim Klein was a member of the Revolutionary Cells (RZ) who ended up providing information to the media and police. Helmut Gollwitzer was a well-known pastor in the Ban the Bomb and student movements of the 1950s and 1960s. Heinrich Albertz, a pastor and SPD politician, had to resign as mayor of West Berlin following the killing of student Benno Ohnesorg during a demonstration against the Shah of Persia in June 1967. *ID*, *ED* and *Link* were leftist periodicals.

Rebmann, barely on Buback's throne, begins a propaganda offensive against the prisoners and their lawyers, especially the Stuttgart office. In late July, a State Security article against the lawyers is published in *Der Spiegel*, which from start to finish is a fabrication by the police and the intelligence agencies, stripped of all trace of journalism and, thus, setting a new bar for State Security journalism. It includes pretty much every State Security lie against the lawyers from the past nine months. By the end of July—two days before the Dresdner Bank loses its collaborator who had made it into the most aggressive monopoly bank in Western Europe—Rebmann bluntly states that, as attorney general, he will not keep the promise he had made as permanent secretary in the Baden-Württemberg Ministry of Justice, and that the group of prisoners will not now be increased.

One hour after the fatality, the most massive smear campaign to date goes into effect, concentrating more and more on Gudrun and Andreas and escalating throughout the week.

On Sunday, it's the turn of the Stuttgart office. Zeis, armed to the teeth and posing as the Skorzeny of the Federal Prosecutors' Office,[12] organises a raid on the lawyers' office and subsequently launches the wicked fake news that a draft version of the Ulrike Meinhof Commando's statement has been found there, and that Gudrun has been identified as the author. In the list of searched documents, there is only a reference to "one envelope".

As usual, things come to a head in Stammheim. As always, when they are preparing something, the prison staff is changed. Grossmann, the guy who had opened Ulrike's cell that morning, is back again, despite being on leave. The guards become provocatively aggressive, an atmosphere that indicates on every level that we must reckon with some kind of attack.

Friday evening, while Gudrun is still with her lawyer and the evening meal is brought in, Andreas goes into her cell to get something, as usually happens several times a day. All the guards must have seen that. Shortly afterwards, Gudrun appears and goes into her cell, and a little later Irmgard appears from the cell where the fruit is,

---

12   Peter Zeis was one of the federal prosecutors in the Stammheim trial. Otto Skorzeny had been a high-ranking officer (lieutenant colonel) in the SS, the Nazis' paramilitary organisation. After the war, he advised the police in Franco's Spain and in Egypt, Argentina and Israel.

and the unthinkable must be thought—Andreas is in the cell with two "ice-cold, calculating and highly-trained female murderers" (article by Zehm in *Die Welt* newspaper[13]). The guards who saw this suddenly bolt the door, in front of my eyes, which we found rather strange, because, normally, as soon as two of us aren't visible, they get annoyed. I stood right in front of the door, and it was completely obvious that they knew where Andreas was. I noted that all of them were nervous, whispering to each other in front of the glass cage. The three in the cell must have been surprised too, because the alarm lights lit up at once and the door was opened again. Irmgard comes out, goes to her cell to fetch something. Münzing, the senior unit manager, who was posted here only a week ago, goes past me into the cell, walks across to the windows, knocks at the bars of both windows then turns around and walks out again past Andreas, who had clearly been searching through the folders near the bookshelf while eating an apple and watching him, not hiding at all.

I briefly discuss with Irmgard that I will go to Verena for the night. Verena is isolated from us in another section of the upper floor, but we can see her at lunch and at night. Then I go out to the table in the middle of the corridor, and Münzing, without saying a word, immediately closes the door behind me. As this "comedy of manners" unfolds, at least five guards are standing about in the corridor.

We established later that, at this point, none of us knew what the whole thing meant. I'm not in the mood to explain why, after six years of isolation, we wish to be together—even in a violent situation that sets out to make every feeling, every thought and every movement unreal or turned into the extreme torment that we call torture, because it is planned consciously, deliberately, scientifically.

We were amazed but also found it quite funny, because it's not our business to support the dirty spying that follows and registers every movement we make.

In fact, during the year and a half we've been together in here, the system is such that a guard—one of them must watch us continuously until relieved after twenty minutes, and previously three of them sat on three stools in a row staring at us—makes a noise as soon as two of us not of the same gender can't be seen for a moment, while

---

13   Günter Zehm was deputy chief editor of the Springer newspaper *Die Welt*.

simultaneously sending in three other guards who are on standby behind a curtain, ready to intervene immediately. In addition, when one of us can't be seen, they note down which of the two open cells we might be in. It's a wicked and perfect system of total control, from which no sign of life within the high-security unit can escape.

The others found out what it all meant an hour later, when Andreas came out of the cell, and then the next morning, Saturday. The provocations and aggression they are exhibiting since Ponto's death are now accompanied by fat smirks, and they exacerbate things by announcing that on Monday "the rest will follow". The two doors that had been open so far remain closed, the guards stay in the unit until the door is closed, and so throughout the weekend, throughout the whole time we are together having *Umschluss*, at least three and sometimes four guards are standing around in the corridor in a threatening manner, in addition to the one sitting in the bulletproof cockpit. Asked why they seem keen on trouble and why they started this thing on Friday, they react aggressively, threatening "you'll see" and "things are going to change here".

It becomes clear that they believe they can ride the popular wave of psychological warfare, getting on our nerves with their piggish projections, slipperiness, jabbering insinuations. In a direct way, they demonstrate to the prisoners that they are convinced they are in the right not only as pigs but also as men. Even though it should be clear, including to the densest guard, after eighteen months of watching us incessantly, that the intimacy within the group, and certainly in prison, happens at another level, where sexuality—different from sensitivity—has practically no role. The three of us in that cell on Friday evening certainly had other problems and at neither 4:00 nor 5:00, when they fetched Andreas, had anything like that in mind.

From that moment the guards—when they talk at all—talk of fucking. Grossmann literally "I didn't think that of you, that you'd do that, fuck". In such a way that Andreas's blood boiled and he said to him "If that doesn't stop, I'll shut you up". That was the only threat uttered. And it's clear from the jargon that the wording in Grossman's testimony is pure invention.

On Monday morning, everything is ready for total confrontation: from 9:30 onwards, the guards are standing in the unit watching our every movement. During the half-hour conversation—during which we requested that they leave—Nusser, Schreitmüller, Haug, Bubeck, etc. stood behind the curtain listening, and amongst them was the little one with the pock-marked face and weasel features, who often boasted openly in the canteen that he'd go up and shoot Andreas dead in his cell.

Around 10:00, in storms the riot squad. I reckon there were forty to fifty in all, at the head the trumpeting Nusser, and just behind him Schreitmüller, fat and grinning, and, of course, Haug, as broad as he is tall—the most hated guard in the whole prison. This army general staff alone tips the scales at six hundred pounds. Most of them we've never seen before. The guards who normally work here, like Misterfeld, for example, aren't there, as is usually the case when they are planning something. The entire bunch moves up to us and the open doors, and Nusser, without even an attempt at listening, orders, "Shut the doors. No discussion!" Andreas tells him calmly that they seem to be expecting an escalation.

We position ourselves in the doorway of Andreas's cell, whereupon Haug immediately assaults Wolfgang. Jan shouts at Haug to let go of Wolfgang and to begin by explaining what they want. A fat guard stinking of beer, standing behind Nusser, starts to punch Helmut. Andreas, who until then had stood there with a cup of coffee in his hand, throws it against the bars of the corridor. Schreitmüller later turns this into "aimed at the head". The cup had hit the floor some meter and a half from the guard, while Andreas was standing only two meters from him. Schreitmüller, a State attorney himself before worming his way into the State Security detention system, was the guard in charge when Ulrike and Siegfried died here. He simply lies and can do so knowing that his contribution to the country's security—setting fifty brutalised pigs loose on the prisoners—will certainly win approval and understanding from all branches of the judiciary.

Then it started: six guards grabbed Werner, who had only shouted that they should let go of Wolfgang, and hit him. At the same time, six guards jumped on Andreas, and both were thrown into random cells. Then they jumped on Helmut and Wolfgang, knocking their heads and backs into tables and shelves. In front of Andreas's cell, they start to beat Jan. I shout at them. Haug pushes me away. Next to me by the radiator, I see Gudrun lying on the floor—and it seems to me that the bestiality of it all is culminating with her. One of the pigs has her whole face in his hand, pressing her down, two are pulling her legs apart, a fourth is twisting her arms and trying to knock his knee into her side. The whole thing looks like murder. I'm trying to get to her, and at that moment I'm grabbed by six guards—can just see Gabi who has also been thrown onto the floor—and am being thrown back and forth, and then to the floor, banging my head.

As I tried to defend myself from kicks to my sides and kidneys, Haug knelt down on my head with all his weight, pressing it hard into the floor, then lifted my head and banged it on the floor five or six times, over a good five minutes, until they dragged me the thirty metres to the other end of the unit and, holding all four limbs, threw me into Helmut's cell such that I fell on my head and back. All I can remember is waking up lying on the floor. I don't know if I was out for seconds or minutes. Then vomiting and completely wrung out.

At 2:00 p.m., the second wave. They take us out of the cells they had kicked us into and put us into other cells one by one. Ten guards, led by Haug, Grossmann and the drunkard, fail to get Andreas out of his cell. They don't touch him. Instead, they fetch Wolfgang from my cell and push him—I hear the blows—into an empty hole. Passing my cell, Haug threatens me with "your turn soon, bitch".

When they open the door and come in, I immediately go out into the corridor, ask for Jan and Andreas, and haven't even tried to approach his cell when the drunkard grabs me from behind by my hair, twisting my scalp and tearing out my hair in tufts. Now the other guards grab me too and hit me with sadistic precision in the neck, back and sides saying things like "here's what you deserve, dirty bitch" and "we'll show you". They drag me to my cell, and there Haug, roaring "disappear, you bitch", gives me such a violent kick in the small of my back that I end up at the other end of the cell.

Apart from bruises over my whole body, kidney pain and pulled tendons, I have a painful swelling on the right side of my head behind my ear and a swollen ear. About two hours later severe headaches, pressure on my eyes, shivering, nausea, faintness. The whole thing was forty-eight hours ago, and I still have severe headaches despite the strongest painkillers they have here.

Since the beating we are completely isolated, we cannot see or speak to one another, the walk in the yard has been cancelled, every step in the corridor takes place in the presence of five guards.

We have communicated by shouting through the door slits. We have started a hunger strike and have explained that we will start a thirst strike unless the old situation is reinstated within a few hours and without a single restriction.

I am certain that the brutalities and humiliations of the type of detention practised here, and for which Stammheim has by now become internationally renowned, will stop—if not, they will carry us out of here dead, one after the other.

Ulrike said, "We can only be repressed if we stop thinking and stop fighting. People who refuse to stop fighting cannot be repressed—they either win or they die, rather than losing and dying".[14]

Ingrid Schubert

9 August 1977

---

14   This is a quote from the statement announcing the beginning of the third collective hunger strike in September 1974, paraphrasing George Jackson (George Jackson, *Blood in my Eye*, Black Classic Press, Baltimore 1990, 86–87); see Moncourt and Smith, 285 (see p. 57, footnote 5).

Report on the Contact Ban in Stadelheim Prison, Munich, in October 1977

After the abduction of Hanns Martin Schleyer, president of the Confederation of German Employers' Associations, by the Red Army Faction on 5 September 1977, all prisoners from the RAF are isolated, searched and denied any contact, under a contact ban order that will be subsequently enshrined in law. The ban lasts for more than six weeks, until 20 October. In an undated handwritten note, Ingrid describes her time in Stadelheim Prison during this period.

Schmidt's assertion that "nothing illegal" is happening is true in so far as they now have every law legalising the prisoners' hostage status and every kind of torture, or can produce one in no time.[15] The law on the contact ban is the codification of the hostage status—the execution of total power over defenceless prisoners—hostages of the State. The basis of every kind of stress manipulation (according to Amnesty's definition, torture).

We have described in all its forms and effects what isolation is and means subjectively—there is a limit, where someone who experiences it doesn't understand what's happening. The contact ban is ten times that: an absolute vacuum of utmost permanent stress—during an action in which your life is at stake. A hundred revs a minute—for six weeks. The absolute vacuum creates absolute irritation—every stimulus is multiplied, uncontrollable, irrational. Every telephone ring, every step, every helicopter triggers a hyper-reaction. Hallucinations: hearing large numbers of police cars, doors banging, weapons rattling, etc. Start packing, am sure things will move. Etc. Receptive to the smallest stimulus.

Examples of stress manipulation in this situation:

1) During the whole time, the guards utter not one word to me or in front of my door or even nearby. It is as if the action is not happening. Sunday night, five days after the abduction, when all calculations were telling me that I *had* to expect a decision, two guards stage the following drama outside my door: the first calls out loudly and deliberately to the second, "Hey, Schleyer is free, thank God". The second calls back, "When was that broadcast, that Schleyer is free?" No further

---

15   Helmut Schmidt, West Germany's chancellor 1974–1982.

reply, some whispering, silence. "Schleyer free"—had to suggest this: the commando encircled, dead or whatever, in any case, that the action had failed big time.

2) The same guards—night duty—turn up the radio every evening, leaving their door open. When it's time for the news, guards from different sections come and gather, the door is closed deliberately—I can hear that the news is on but can't understand anything, of course. Babble of voices. After the news—door opens again, one says, "Silence now, not a word"—they all return to their sections. This happens every night.

3) Steierer, the prison director, speaks openly of our hostage status. Not one conversation with him that doesn't begin with "Murder gang..." and "Mr Schleyer hasn't..." or "Who knows under what circumstances Mr Schleyer..." or "You lack absolutely nothing... legally you are not at all entitled...", etc. After the end of the abduction, and with an attitude of revenge, he moves me without any (security or other) reason into a freezing tiled cell with opaque windows, in a silent wing, where I am alone. When I fall ill, he has to put me back—which proves that it was sheer vindictiveness.

4) Tuesday—one week after the abduction—an officer of the BKA-SG comes with the questionnaire.[16] His precise words are that Mr Schleyer "shall and *will* be exchanged". So a definite statement corresponding to his general behaviour. He conveys the impression that the exchange will happen—when the decision not to exchange had already been taken, two days after the abduction. I leave him, assuming that things may take only a few days more. But for five more weeks: nothing, absolutely nothing.

5) Until, on 15 October at 8:00 in the evening, the same security guard is back, tells me about the plane hijack + asks a question about Somalia. So a decisive phase—the tension becomes unbearable, stretched to breaking point + no information.

6) Tuesday morning, I am suddenly called into the medical room. There, an assembly of doctors, nurses and the prison's deputy director.

---

16   The BKA-SG, the federal police's security group in Bonn, was responsible for the security of politicians and State visitors. Initially co-ordinating everything to do with the RAF, this function was later integrated into the BKA-TE (Terrorism) Department. All prisoners to be exchanged for Hanns Martin Schleyer were given a questionnaire asking them whether they wanted to be released and which countries they would suggest being flown to.

I am to be submitted to a body search, and my cell is to be searched too—they are not able to give me a reason.

I refuse the body search when I realise that it is to be a gynaecological search. I am then assaulted by four male nurses, three female doctors, two female guards who forcibly undress me, two male nurses who force my legs apart. I shout and defend myself as best I can (for which I am punished later with a ban on buying things). Back in the cell: everything had been removed—mattress, blankets, every scrap down to the dish-cloth and handkerchiefs. A little later, a prisoner whispers through the door: Andreas, Gudrun, Jan and Gabi have hanged themselves.

I am in something like shock: the brutal, degrading and humiliating assault suddenly explains itself + at the same time, it is clear that everything is over. I do not know how or what. Have a crying fit for hours, see and hear nothing, totally crushed. Indescribable. Slightly clearer in the afternoon.

7) At 5:00 p.m. they call on me again: two officers from the Federal Criminal Investigation Bureau. Had I heard about the events of the last few days? I say no, they should tell me. One tells me about Mogadishu—then that Baader, Ensslin and Raspe had committed suicide this morning and that Möller had attempted suicide. Both observe me closely—obviously expecting some shock effect or collapse. I don't react but demand to be moved back to Stammheim immediately, to Verena Becker, and that the permanent surveillance be stopped. Hausmann: "Oh, yes, you are just making demands here. What do you think is going on? The three who committed suicide this morning surely thought something was. Think about it. The clock is ticking. Be clear about that". So first they try to shock and intimidate, then paternalistically: "Think what awaits you now. Don't you want to make it easier on yourself? When you make demands, you also have to show that you're willing to make concessions. Mr Schleyer is still missing... So if you know something...".

I get up and want to leave, when the other one starts again. Maurer: Stammheim would have been a real base and "that's how it was. Let's talk sensibly. We are on the other side...", whether I knew and could I explain how Baader and Raspe had weapons in their cell... finally, I leave.

So an interrogation attempt in a shocking situation, i.e., with the intention of provoking a shock and using it to get information.

8) Next day, in one swoop: moved back into the slaughter bunker, shopping ban, announcement that the total isolation is to continue.

24 October 1977, to her parents

Dear Parents,

I have told Bendler that you can visit me,[17] but I am not sure what it will be like. I will not talk about what you want to say—and I can hardly be silent about that. But let's see.

Since I don't know whether I will ever get the stuff left in Stammheim, I need some trousers. Cord jeans, Boston, waist 31, inside leg 32, light brown or light grey or black. Also, my watch is broken. There are cheap *quartz* watches with a date window. (Quartz lasts longer and doesn't need to be adjusted or wound up, etc.)

Please bring the birthday parcel. I have nothing here anymore, with a monthly shopping limit of 26 DM. Urgently:

- 200g Nescafé (repacked)
- 6 packets of black tobacco, Samson or Schwarzer Krauser
- 1 packet of cigarette papers, in 20s
- 1 simple gas lighter, 2 refills
- 2 Roger & Gallet soaps (Carnation)

Plus: home-baked stuff, you will know what, and fresh cheese: Brie, French Camembert, Gouda, Gorgonzola.

No more than 3 kg in total.

When are you coming? Let me know the date a bit in advance, please.

See you soon,

Ingrid

26 October 1977, to her father

Pa, I only received your letter on Wednesday; didn't know you wanted to come on Monday. In case you haven't left before the letter arrives, I would be very happy if you could bring the parcel or that, at least, it may be sent by express mail. Trousers and watch are not so urgent and shouldn't be in the parcel anyway. The batteries are important, because I've been told I'm now barred from shopping.

---

17   Wolfgang Bendler: Ingrid's chosen lawyer in Munich.

Why isn't Ma coming with you? I think I know why, and perhaps it's better for the time being, until we can talk more calmly. I know you both suffer a lot—I cannot change that without denying myself completely.

I need nothing else—meaning, I get *nothing*.

What happened to the subscription to the *Süddeutsche*? It hasn't arrived but did in September. Perhaps you only ordered it for September. Please renew the subscription. Also for *Der Spiegel* and *Stern*.[18] As I shall remain in isolation for the time being, I have to get everything myself.

Greetings,

Ingrid

I'm no longer in the hospital wing but in a unit with nobody else present and blinds in front of the window.

ANOTHER THING: there is only one condition from my side: that you do not engage in any of your beloved talks with people from the prison administration here.

30 October 1977, to her parents

Dear parents, another brief note about the parcel: as things stand, you can pack 300g of Nescafé, eight packs of tobacco—the exact black brand, "Samson" or "Schwarzer Krauser". Don't forget the twenty x cigarette papers. And six x batteries. Two x soaps enough (small ones). And a packet of marjoram. And add in a few (genuine) "Mozart" chocolates. Cheese: only French camembert and brie. That stuff is so heavy—I prefer more of your cookies, okay. Felt tips are no longer necessary, as I now have biros. Don't forget the lighter refills. The *Süddeutsche Zeitung* must be ordered and paid for directly through the prison administration here. I've done this now for November. Please order it for December from outside; it must be done by you. I no longer have any books to read, as I've read everything of the slightest interest in the library. So I'm sitting here and am freezing to death. The temperature

---

18   *Süddeutsche Zeitung* is a German daily newspaper, *Der Spiegel* and *Stern* are weekly news magazines.

is always too low because of the tiled floor and walls in here, a real slaughter bunker.

Have you been to Stuttgart, and did you hear anything? The decision must come soon.[19] Aichach Prison is out of the question. You might be able to intervene on that one, as the journey is too arduous for you in your old age, as well as being too expensive. That dump is even further away and very difficult to reach. Apart from that, there's nothing for me in Bavaria. One possibility besides Frankfurt is Bühl. That's near Karlsruhe.

The parcel permit must be stuck on the outside. (If there's none in the letter it means it doesn't work here—so send it by express mail.)

Warm greetings,

Ingrid

3 November 1977, to her parents

Dear parents, how could one guess that? If I'd known Nescafé wasn't allowed anyway, I wouldn't have made it so urgent—what an absurdity, as it can be bought here. The parcel clearly only needed one day to arrive. Everything was very good, and I'm already feeling sick with overeating, but in future I'll have to plan the contents of what's to go in these parcels differently. I'm no longer so keen on sweet things. The watch is also fine (though I'm really against such small lady watches).

The window blinds have been taken down, and maybe I'll be moved back to the old warmer cell; depends on the doctor, as I am now ill. The rest remains darkness, total isolation. And if one reads what the plans are, apparently for the final solution. If you do anything: the "official legal rule" (that's the wording) is that convicted prisoners are not allowed to be kept in solitary confinement for more than six months— I've now been isolated for three months—and that's after seven years in prison with every form of isolation. I've already indicated that I have some plans—but don't want to broadcast them here—and it's too

---

19   The decision about where Ingrid would be transferred to from Stadelheim Prison in Munich. Munich and Aichach are both in Germany's federal state of Bavaria.

complicated and multi-layered and subject to constant change for me to want to feed it into their computer. This is just a hint.

Warm greetings,

Ingrid

Still waiting for the subscription to the *Süddeutsche Zeitung*, I'll continue to do it from here, as long as I'm here.

4 November 1977, to librarian Max Witzel

Dear Witzel,

Obviously, some brains were racked over your letter—it only arrived today. Good that you wrote. I had no idea where to get your address, as it appears to be a final decision that I will not get back to Stammheim and, thus, not get hold of our (irreplaceable) material, which will disappear into the Federal Police storage room. I'm not too keen on writing by hand, but it seems that a typewriter, as well as books and simple scissors, etc., belong with immediate effect to the things endangering the security of the Federal Republic.

Your voice is one of the familiar ones, and so for the first time I was something like happy again. But while trying to answer, I realise the horrible fact that I cannot speak anymore, after three months of silence and all that happened. In this schizophrenia between "enough" and "let's see", a lot is happening, but it happens only with oneself—no possibility of seeing yourself in relation to anyone else. No dialogue through which you feel alive. And one cannot describe it.

There's nothing I'm so hungry for as the people I love. And books, which I need but don't get, at least not here and, considering what they are planning—metal cages and permanent surveillance (already happening here day and night)—not for a long time. But I'd appreciate it if you could let me have the list of the books you sent to Stammheim, for the possible time ahead. I didn't have time to read them there, and I can possibly get them back—or Gabi or Werner,[20] who are in the same

---

20 Werner Hoppe and Irmgard Möller. Irmgard was transferred to Stammheim Prison in late December 1976. Werner, together with Wolfgang Beer and Helmut Pohl, was in Stammheim Prison from July to August 1977, until the group of prisoners was broken up after the attack on them.

situation (i.e., all prisoners have been totally isolated, as you know—and, on top of that, we have been atomised).

Müller is a (smart) diplomat.[21] "Difficult" is not something I've applied to myself so far, but it's right. Those who I love most are dead—they had a tough time with me and I'm tough with myself. Let's see, maybe I can write about that once I'm able to speak again. For the moment, everything just comes out shit, poor stammering. A report such as the one you've read was only possible from this intensity of relationships, from the power of the collective[22]—which is actual counter-power. And, yes, I am very different from Gudrun. You'll hardly find her in me, but we wanted the same thing—at least that's what I think. Although that's a very differentiated thing.

And write to Gabi—please do that. She's in that madhouse at Hohenasperg—and that means total incapacitation.[23] Could be that I'll suddenly write to you from time to time, because I can imagine something about you and your life. The picture of the "terrorist" and the postage stamps were taken out of your letter.[24]

I greet you,
Nina

Letter from Gerti to Ingrid, 4 November 1977

Part of a letter from Gerti to Ingrid, found with Ingrid's papers after her death

Dearest Sister,

Time flies. We haven't forgotten your birthday, just that it's next Monday.[25] I wrote to you a few days ago, but then decided not to send the letter.

So first of all "many, many returns of the day", as they say here in England, while the "happy" will return, definitely, and soon we hope. All

---

21 Defence lawyer Arndt Müller.
22 Ingrid's report about the attack on 8 August 1977. See pp. 152–60.
23 See Irmgard's testimony in the *Remembering Ingrid* section of this book, pp. 200–2. Hohenasperg is a prison hospital some twenty kilometres from Stuttgart.
24 A photo of Witzel's two-year-old daughter.
25 Ingrid was to turn thirty-three on 7 November.

our best wishes and thoughts are with you; in fact, they are with you all the time, because we can imagine how damn difficult it must be for you now. I can come at the end of the month and have written to the prison administration about whether we could have two visits, one on Friday and one on Saturday morning.

Please let me know if you would like that or if you'd rather see someone else. And if you want books, let me know—the thought that you might read the *Sunday Times* is exciting. I try to imagine what might be of special interest to you, and regularly come to the conclusion that there's lamentably little of interest in there. How about the *New Statesman*, a politically Left weekly, a respectable journal, or the *New Scientist*?

Mother told me that you felt cold. Can I send you one of those thick jumpers, or more of those thick Shetland socks? Let me know soon. Right now, I've no idea what I can tell you that's relevant, or what I'm allowed to write—the whole story has raised a lot of interest here, and thoughtful comments.

The rest of the letter is missing.

10 November 1977, Ingrid to Max Witzel

Dear Witzel,

I'm now allowed to study philosophy (and will probably get a typewriter someday for this purpose), and since I've been curious about Sartre, Benjamin and Lukács and wanted to get to know them better, this is to ask you to please send me their most important works.

I don't have the titles of Benjamin's main works, or even the interesting smaller things he wrote—so I am trusting you completely. By Lukács, definitely *History and Class Consciousness*—otherwise, as with Benjamin, just put something together.

Sartre: *The Words, Critique of Dialectical Reason, The Imaginary, The Transcendence of the Ego, Colonialism and Neocolonialism*, and maybe something from his novels (I know none of them, no idea if they're worth it).

Camus: *The Rebel*. Bataille: again, I have no titles, but his philosophical writings.

And whatever else you can think of. Include catalogues + the list I already mentioned. As someone poverty stricken, as far as external stimuli are concerned, I'm already licking my fingers, all ten of them, in anticipation of your parcel. From what I've been told, the books must be in their original packaging.

In haste.

Greetings,

Nina

12 November 1977, Ingrid's last letter to her sister

Dear Gerti—your visit application arrived today and has been approved for 26.11, that's in 14 days. Without coffee or ice cream. A few of the external conditions have changed in such a way that I can breathe again without asking myself why.

mir aus ist das gebont mit 26. - kann auch ein woche
er sein.oder wann gehen diese spezialfahrten ab.am 6./7.
t zwar ma mit fr.mohnhaupt,aber das macht nichts,da es
dahin wieder 14 tage sind und ivh noch besuche offeh hab.
eib genau an welchem tagen ihr dann da seid - den besuchs-
ag stellk ich,dann brauchst du nicht extra schreiben an
knast.
die verlegung nun läuft weiß der himmel.am schnee liegts
er nicht.ist mir jetzt auch scheißegal wann - warte da nich
f,sonst wird man bei dem ganzen irrsinn,der knast ist,noch
r.auf was warten ist sowieso falsch - xob nun draußen oder
- weil man durch die fixierung dadrauf wirklich denk-und
lungsunfähig wird,und hier potenziert sich das natürlich no

Photographs

da die   as zwingt dich unheimlich,mit
bdingungen,wie sie d a sind,zu arbeiten,also nicht dran aus
en,sondern:es ist so,also mach was mit.dauert wahnsinnig
e bis man das kann+ oft genug gehts nat.nicht.zb wenn du
u weißt,daß du nur warten mußt,weil irgendwo ein idiot hier
er zu faul ist das telefon zu bedienen,und das jedesmal,abe
lich jedesmal - so daß mans schon weiß - zb wenn wir sport
n und die uns nicht holen + jedesmal so tun als wärs was
neues daß wir montags sport haben. wir hams ja auch erst 3
woche zur gleichen zeit. und sowas in tausend variationen
al am tag. da gewöhnste dich auch nicht dran - oder nur wen
ben resignierst und ihr erstrebtes ziel xxx 'anpassang' (=v
en) vollziehst.naja,die armen kreaturen gibts hier nat.zuha
ar ,5 jahre sind zu lang und die 'kriæn' oder wie man das
en mag,hast du zigmal am tag oder 3mal im jahr ,und damit i
uso. : es ist eine bedingung, und entweder flippst du drauf
und gehst kaputt zwangsläufig,wirst an der ganzen scheiße
ückt - oder fängts was mit an,also was ist der kern der kri
n hängts,was ist das problem,und du kommst immer auf den
t,daß es an dir liegt es ändern zu können.und wenn du es ni
bist du ein schwein,daß sich den anderen nicht verantwortl
t.weil die nat.nicht n kaputten typen brauchen,sondern einen
sich was überlegt zu allen problemen und fragen + damit
selbst be-arbeitet,indem du entscheidungen treffen mußt,
s beurteilen,eine situation oder n typen,und so ständig
rollierst,was mit dir selber losk ist. wenn du dir nichts ü
t,interessiert dich es nicht - fühlst dich also nichtx vera
lich,daß klarheit entsteht,entwicklung läuft,von der du
teil bist. also kollektiv denken und handeln. - das ist e
man einfach nicht kann,weil mans nicht kann,sondern immer
das gegenteil,aus dem heraus wie der ganze laden eben läuft
- schwer auf jeden fall,aber es gibt nichts besseres.
(ab und zu mal n schrieb von ihm,bei dem ich jedesmal denke
e muß ne starke macke haben nach dem was er schreibt:kein
aler satz,alles verschlungen und mytifiziert und ein psycho,
t aus) , das ist einer der wartet schon aufs alt werden (sa
. kann ich nur sagen:nimm dir besser gleich den strick,wora
da noch warten + wieso überhaupt warten.versteh ich einfac
t,wie man derart resigniert sich nur noch um sich selber un
e psyche drehen kann.d.h.wie das kommt ist mit schon klar,a
verzeih (sowieso nie)das niemandem,der einigermaßen durchbl
tehste,wenn da einer hockt und drau wartet,daß die anderen
ins feuer springen um ihm mal irgendwann das erträumte bess
n zu bringen,na warte.nicht zuletzt überläßt ders ja auch

Ingrid age 3

Visiting the grandparents in St. Ingbert
1948: Hedwig Schubert with (clockwise)
her children Gerti, Ingrid, Klaus and Helke

First day
of school,
September 1949

First year at elementary school in Maroldsweisach 1949/50 (Ingrid second row, third from the left; Klaus back row, second from the right)

Birthday of grandpa (Opa Best), circa 1950: mother, Ingrid, grandpa, father, grandma (Omi Best)

Typical Schubert family evening in Koblenz, c. 1953: Helke, Gerti, mother, Klaus, Ingrid

In grandma's clothes on the roof of the Rei factory in Koblenz, c. 1954

Koblenz, summer 1955

Holiday in the Allgäu, 1957

At Schwaltenweiher, 1958

In the Allgäu, 1957, with Helke (left) and Gerti (right)

Ingrid on the family car, with her friend Sabine, 1958

Ingrid, c. 1958

With parents and sister Helke after Gerti's wedding, 1959

Summer party, c. 1960

School trip to Kolmar, 1961

Holiday in the Allgäu, 1961: Michael Wilford, Ingrid's friend Bärbel, Ingrid

Waiting for the ferry to England, Calais, 1961

Klaus, Larry and Ingrid at Helke
and Manfred Stiebel's engagement
party, Koblenz, 1963

Ingrid, taken
at Manfred
Stiebel's photo
studio, c. 1964

Ingrid with niece Nicole
and nephew Marcus at
their grandparents' home,
Koblenz, 1968

Studio picture by Manfred Stiebel, 1968

At the shared apartment Bregenzer
Strasse, Berlin, 1968

Bozener Strasse, Berlin, 1969

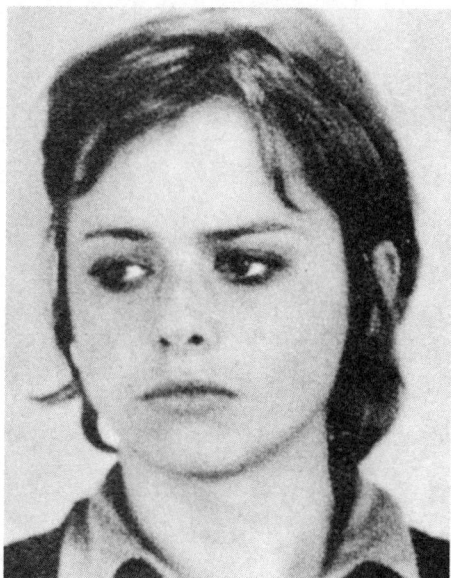

ID picture, c. 1970

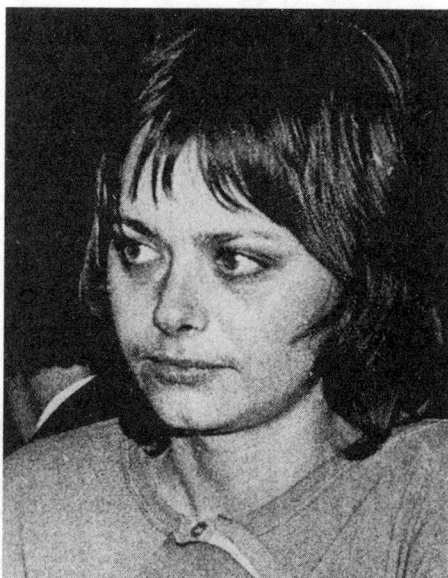

At the first trial, Berlin, 1971

At the first trial, 1971

Ingrid and Irene Goergens at the first trial, spring 1971

mir aus ist das gebont mit 26. - kann auch ein woche
r sein.oder wann gehen diese spezialfahrten ab.am 6./7.
t zwar ma mit fr.mohnhaupt,aber das macht nichts,da es
dahin wieder 14 tage sind und ich noch besuche offen hab.
ib genau an welchen tagen ihr dann da seid - den besuchs-
ag stell ich,dann brauchst du nicht extra schreiben an
knast.
die verlegung nun läuft weiß der himmel.am schnee liegts
r nicht.ist mir jetzt auch scheißegal wann - warte da nicht
r,sonst wird man bei dem ganzen irrsinn,der knast ist,noch
r.auf was warten ist sowieso falsch - xob nun draußen oder

Remembering Ingrid

weil man durch die fixierung dadrauf wirklich denk-und
lungsunfähig wird und hier potenziert sich das natürlich noc
da di   unheimlich,mit
dingungen,wie sie d a sind,zu arbeiten,also nicht dran aus
en,sondern:es ist so,also mach was mit.dauert wahnsinnig
e bis man das kann+ oft genug gehts nat.nicht.zb wenn   du
u weißt,daß du nur warten mußt,weil irgendwo ein idiot hier
r zu faul ist das telefon zu bedienen,und das jedesmal,abe
lich jedesmal - so daß mans schon weiß - zb wenn wir sport
n und die uns nicht holen + jedesmal so tun als wärs was
neues daß wir montags sport haben. wir hams ja auch erst 3
woche zur gleichen zeit. und sowas in tausend variationen
al am tag. da gewöhnste dich auch nicht dran - oder nur wenn
ben resignierst und ihr erstrebtes ziel xxx 'anpassung' (=v
en) vollziehst.naja,die armen kreaturen gibts hier nat.zuhau
r ,5 jahre sind zu lang und die 'krisen oder wie man das
en mag,hast du zigmal am tag oder 3mal im jahr ,und damit i
uso. : es ist eine bedgingung, und entweder flippst du drauf
und gehst kaputt zwengsläufig,wirst an der ganzen scheiße
ückt - oder fängts was mit an,also was ist der kern der kri
n hängts,was ist das problem,und du kommst immer auf den
t,daß es an dir liegt es ändern zu können.und wenn du es ni
bist du ein schwein,daß sich den anderen nicht verantwortli
t.weil die nat.nicht n kaputten typen brauchen,sondern einen
sich was überlegt zu allen problemen und fragen + damit
selbst be-arbeitet,indem du entscheidungen treffen mußt,
beurteilen,eine situation oder n typen,und so ständig
rollierst,was mit dir selber los ist. wenn du dir nichts ü
t,interessiert dich es nicht - fühlst dich also nicht verab
lich,daß klarheit entsteht,entwicklung läuft,von der du
teil bist. also kollektiv denken und handeln. - das ist e
man einfach nicht kann,weil mans nicht kann,sondern immer
das gegenteil,aus dem heraus wie der ganze laden eben läuft
- schwer auf jeden fall,aber es gibt nichts besseres.
(ab und zu mal n schrieb von ihm,bei dem ich jedesmal denke
e muß ne starke macke haben nach dem was er schreibt:kein
aler satz,alles verschlungen und mystifiziert und ein psycho,
t aus) , das ist einer der wartet sxhon aufs alt werden (sa
kann ich nur sagen:nimm dir besser gleich den strick,wora
da noch warten + wieso überhaupt warten.versteh ich einfach
t,wie man derart resigniert sich nur noch um sich selber un
e psyche drehen kann.d.h.wie das kommt ist mit schon klar,a
verzeih (sowieso nie)das niemandem,der einigermaßen durchbl
tehste,wenn da einer hockt und draf wartet,daß die anderen
ins feuer springen um ihm mal irgendwann das erträumte bess
n zu bringen,na warte,nicht zuletzt überläßt ders ja auch

Irene Goergens, June 2015 —in conversation

Irene was in prison from October 1970 to May 1977.

After the Arrest
At some point during the night I was brought to the Gothaer.

The Gothaer was the police headquarters?
Yes, in the Grunewaldstrasse in Schöneberg. In the morning I heard a voice asking, "Hey, is there no toothbrush here?" And I think, "You know this voice, it's Moni" and call out, "Is that you, Moni?" and she answers, still sleepy, "Yes, yes", and I go, "Wow, who else is here?"—I didn't know who had been caught. Well, it became clear pretty soon: Eve, Brigitte, Moni,[1] and me. That was important, because that day more of us had intended to come to the apartment for a planned meeting....Then they tried to interrogate each of us separately, and the next day we were brought to Lehrter Strasse Prison.

All four of you?
All four, though we didn't see each other there either. Lehrter Strasse is built in a U-shape, with short sides and a long bit in the middle, and, of course, they separated us. But I was on the side of the yard where we each had our walking time, and that's where I saw Eve again for the first time and was really happy. During the first one or two weeks, we were interrogated almost daily, brought before the Political Police. Several times they also put my grandmother in the hallway and told

---

1   Eve, Brigitte, Moni: Ingrid Schubert, Brigitte Asdonk, Monika Berberich.

her that if I talked she could take me home with her. And she believed it. They wanted her to sit there when I was led past, using her to exert pressure on me. Meanwhile, Eve and I were put into the same section at Lehrter Strasse.

Were there other women there too?
Yes, about twenty-five or twenty-eight prisoners who had already been convicted, who didn't want to have much to do with us, because the guards told them there would be no TV anymore because of us and this and that, and that we were nasty murderers.

And in the yard you could walk together?
No, no, we were never in the yard together, we only had cells next to each other. And I was only there with Eve for a short time. Moni and Brigitte were transferred relatively quickly to West Germany, sometime between October and December, and I was transferred in December. The first trial was due to start, and I was transferred to Kantstrasse Prison, because I was a minor.[2]

In the Tower at Moabit Prison
One evening, as so often in the evening, we contacted the guys around us.

How far away from the tower were they?
Hard to say, but about the width of two houses… from the right side of the tower, where there were two cells—to the left, there were two cells on the side where the street is—we had a view onto another prison block, where Shorty was as well,[3] and where Eve may have seen Mahler in the yard once. I never saw that, because my cell was further to the left.

Shorty was tall enough to get to the window without any help, whereas we always had to climb on a chair standing on the bed to reach the hatch. It was so far away that we couldn't communicate, even if we shouted, but we could make signs and simply be aware of each other. And one of those times we could see how Shorty was hauled away

---

2   Kantstrasse Prison was used for female minors and those on remand.
3   Shorty was the nickname given to Alfred Mährländer, because he was rather tall. He was arrested in June 1971.

from the window, and not long after they came to us and transferred us down into the hole.[4]

For us in the Moabit block it meant that the pigs dragged us down six flights of stairs, hitting and kicking us—and six flights can be a very long way. In addition, as we had to wear the clothes of convicted prisoners, that meant skirts for us. So it was not only unpleasant because of the beating but also because both the pigs and the male prisoners who stood at the bottom were looking up our skirts. When they came into our cell, they immediately forced my arms up behind my back and dragged me backwards to the stairs. I heard Eve's screams and the noise of hitting, they hit her more than me. The hole in Moabit was at the end of the basement, and there was hardly anything there. It really was one of the most horrible holes: first the six staircases, where you were punched in the kidneys and in the chest or whatever, over and over again. Eve came downstairs shortly after me, and I asked her what had happened to her, and she said, "Boy, my face hurts so much".

You could speak to each other?
Yes, but only from the outside, through the window, and it was very hard to make out. I told her to ask for a doctor at once, which she tried to do. But it didn't happen then, in the night. She must have bled a lot, as she told me later. A doctor came the next morning. She had a broken nose that was really bad. Then it was quiet for a while, but there was always the threat of the goon squad when they pulled us away from the windows.

How long were you in the hole?
I don't remember. Generally we were taken back upstairs after three or four days, once the signs of the mistreatment weren't so visible anymore. It wasn't a one-off thing there, but that was certainly the heaviest time.

In Lehrter Strasse
Okay, now comes a nice thing.

At some point we were convicted, and in Lehrter Strasse that meant we had to wear prison clothes. A dark blue dress, a white apron as long

---

4   The "hole" consisted of empty cells in the basement used for punishment, with no bed at all or just a plank bed.

as the dress and for winter a blue coat that looked ridiculous. And a white collar for the blue dress, which we had to sew on ourselves. So the blue dress, which was a normal cotton frock, white apron, white socks. Shoes too, dark ones, can't remember the exact colour. Then, at some point, we both had to go to the storeroom where they gave out the clothes, and there were these unbelievably terrific underpants, with long legs, and suspenders too, but we never used those. We were given a whole pack and had to go to different cells to put them on. We did, as we had to wear something.

Earlier, we had thought that we wouldn't hand over our personal clothes, not voluntarily, but some had already been taken from us, and it would have been impossible to tuck our trousers under this dress every day. So we went with it, and then we met in the corridor, completely dressed up, and Eve and I roared with laughter, because it was such a sight for each of us, we couldn't stop laughing and crying at the same time. We both looked so peculiar and strange. Not that Eve didn't like wearing skirts or dresses once in a while, though for me that was quite unusual—it was such an unbelievable sight with us in those white aprons. We altered things, of course, and Eve always had better ideas about that than me. Naturally, I refused to wear that white collar, and the apron too. Eve shortened the dresses, so they constantly brought us new dresses, and then reduced our spending money, claiming we had damaged their clothes by shortening them. But that encounter, when we met in the corridor and practically collapsed in laughter, will always stick in my memory.

And the walks we had in the yard together. (In my mind it feels like I walked alone for almost five years, but that cannot be true. In Lehrter Strasse, we often had to exercise at the back of the coal yard when something special was going on. I remember, because Moni would then hide a piece of margarine[5] for us in the rain gutter, and we would pick it up when we walked by later, not letting the guard see us taking it up to our cells.) Anyway, at some point, we were in the larger exercise yard in Lehrter Strasse, with other prisoners, not just Eve and me. Eve and I always ran a lot, and this had already got us into trouble, because we were supposed to walk only—no running allowed, maybe because they thought we were training to jump over the wall, no idea. So we would

---

5   Margarine was made into candles because the cell lights were switched off so early.

run, and if they told us off, we did one round of walking, and then ran again. But then we discovered what would be even more fun, because in that yard there was a grassy patch in the middle. Where we ran it was only concrete.

We must have told the other prisoners what we planned to do, otherwise they wouldn't have reacted so quickly. Eve shouted: "Okay, now!!!" and five women lay down on the grass one next to the other just like for leapfrog. Then Eve did a forward dive over them all, then did the same again, and then we ran around again very fast, and the guards couldn't see what was going on. We did this two or three times, then the free hour was cancelled, and we were punished. It wasn't allowed, but it was such fun, and energising. Otherwise, we could only do something in the cell, like sit-ups using the frame of the bed and press-ups. So running around the yard and jumping was something really special, a lot of fun for us and for Eve too, who was laughing the whole time.

I want to say one more thing. I really liked Eve a lot, and the time we spent together outside and inside prison was a very important period for me, because I think that, although we were very different, something totally clicked between us. In many ways, we complemented each other. I simply really liked her a lot. I want to say that again here. To everyone, but especially those inside, she was very important. I know it so very clearly for those inside, and I also know that when she really liked someone, she simply gave everything. Yes, that's it for now.

Brigitte Asdonk,
June 2015

Brigitte was in prison from October 1970 to May 1982.

When US President Nixon announced the extension of the Vietnam War on 30 April 1970 by invading Cambodia, hundreds of thousands demonstrated across the world. Mutinies occurred in all parts of the US army. The State of Ohio declared a state of emergency. At Kent and Jackson universities, six students were shot dead and twenty-one were injured, some severely. Following these massacres, four million went on strike in 450 universities and high schools.

In West Berlin, 1,500 people marched through Kreuzberg and Schöneberg to the *Amerikahaus* on 9 May.[1] Police cordons along the route kept up their attacks, trying to break the unity of the demonstration. In front of the *Amerikahaus*, barbed-wire fencing was intended to funnel the demonstrators through a small tunnel to disperse them. Mounted police threatened them. In so-called "self-defence", police officers fired into the demonstration. At the Technical University, the entire dining hall, where many had taken refuge, was flooded with tear gas.

This is where I met Eve. She radiated a great calm, despite the dire situation. We predicted that a domestic fascist process would be re-enacted. She spoke with great conviction about the urgent need to build clandestine groups for armed resistance. We sensed the historic time in which we found ourselves.

---

1 *Amerikahaus* (America House) was the US Information Agency's propaganda institute in West Berlin and West Germany.

In February 1968, at the International Vietnam Congress in West Berlin, Rudi Dutschke had spoken to us all:

> We don't have much time anymore. We too are defeated on a daily basis in Vietnam.... Historically, our options are open. How this bit of history will end depends primarily on our determination. If the Viet-Cong are not joined by American, European and Asian Cong, the Vietnamese revolution will be defeated like others before it.[2]

With these words, Dutschke expressed what hundreds of thousands of mostly young people were feeling at that time. Shortly after, a young right-wing guy, incited by the Springer press, made an attempt on Dutschke's life.[3]

A strong inner assurance is what characterised Eve (as we used to call her in Berlin), as well as a deep connection with those with whom she wanted to undertake this journey.

After our arrest in October 1970, Eve and I were together for a short time in Lehrter Strasse, in cells on the same corridor. We lay on our stomachs near the cell doors and played chess. I still have that chess set today.

---

2   SDS West Berlin, *Internationaler Vietnam-Kongress Februar 1968 Westberlin* [International Vietnam Congress 1968 in West Berlin] (West Berlin: INFI, 1968), 123.

3   Rudi Dutschke was one of the main voices of the student movement of the 1960s. He was shot by an unemployed, unskilled worker incited by the media's smear campaign against Dutschke. Dutschke survived but died twelve years later of the long-term consequences of injuries suffered during the attack.

Anne Reiche,
October 2010

Anne was in prison from November 1973 to January 1982, following two previous periods of imprisonment in 1970 and 1973 (each lasting 10 months).

Ingrid, Eva, Nina. I knew her mainly as Eva and a little as Nina.

The first time I saw her was at one of the shared apartments in Berlin. I entered as she was leaving. Laughing, with a fluttering coat. I knew immediately who she was. Georg had told me about her. He really liked her. But she didn't know me.

Then I met her again in Lehrter Strasse Prison. I had been transferred there six weeks before my trial, because it was closer to the court than where I was being held, in the Kantstrasse Prison for females on remand. Eva and Irene were in the Lehrter Strasse, normally used for convicted women. They had their exercise time together in the yard, and I had mine alone. During that time, we mostly stood chatting under each other's cell doors.

Eva was a bundle of joy, very calm and composed. Mostly in a good mood. Her face was always laughing, even when she did not laugh. I think it was her eyes, green with amber dots that always sparkled with mirth. Her eyes lit up her face. She conveyed such a warmth and a joy that came from deep inside. She was also pretty open and forthright, like overflowing sparkling water. It is said of some people that they have charisma. Nina not only radiated, she sparkled, with sparks that jumped across from her with the energy of life.

When I was released (July 1971), we remained in contact through winding prison pathways. We wanted to get Eva and Irene out. One night, at the agreed hour of 3:00, we stood with our tools at the back of the prison wall and sent our light signals. They signalled back: it won't work. I was seized with fright. We hadn't reckoned with that possibility at all. More signals; I wasn't mistaken. But we hadn't agreed on so many signals. We were dumbstruck.

As we didn't know what had happened, probably something had been discovered inside the prison, we wanted to disappear from the scene as fast and unobtrusively as possible. Everything was very quiet. We left the long extendable ladder behind.[1]

It turned out that nothing had happened; they just couldn't saw through the bars, because at night time it made too much noise. Had we reacted with greater cool and taken the ladder with us, nobody would have been any the wiser, and we could have tried again another time. The pigs only noticed the attempt when they discovered the ladder the next day. Eva and Irene were transferred at once to the tower at Moabit Prison.

---

1   The attempt to free the two prisoners took place during the night of 14 October 1971. See Ingrid's letter of 28 October 1971.

Brigitte Mohnhaupt, September 2015

Brigitte was in prison for almost 30 years: from June 1972 to February 1977 and from November 1982 to March 2007.

We saw each other for the first time in December 1972, in Lehrter Strasse Prison. Only from a distance—I was down in the yard and Eva and Irene were at their cell windows on the third floor. As my cell was on the other side of the prison, the half hour in the large yard was our only opportunity to acknowledge each other and call out a few sentences.

Of course, we all hoped that they would both remain in Lehrter Strasse, but as early as January they were transferred back to the tower in Moabit Prison. Eva shouted this bit of news to us in the evening, when it was less noisy—I think she was the only one who could do it so well: shouting at full volume and yet very clearly, so those of us on the other side of the building could hear, and, most of all, understand her. At the time, I admired that enormously; my voice was still completely untrained.

As the prison in the Kantstrasse had been closed that summer, Lehrter Strasse was full; along with the minors and remand prisoners, there were now more women who didn't accept the prison regime and who, most importantly, stuck together. Signatures were collected on a petition opposing the transfer of Eva and Irene, and, in mid-January, when we started our first collective hunger strike against isolation, some of the women joined us in solidarity for a while (as in all subsequent hunger strikes).

In autumn 1973, both finally returned from the tower. At that time, the prison authorities wanted to attach mesh screens to all the windows that overlooked the yard. A week of protests, raids, bunkers and bans from exercise time in the yard ensued. In the end, the windows remained as they were.

Katja fell ill,[1] and for a long time it was unclear how bad it was. She had been moved from her cell overlooking the yard to a corner at the back of the prison, where she couldn't talk to anyone. On one occasion Eva was able to reach her cell door—she had come back from a visit and noticed that the grill in front of the remand section had been left open, so she ran through it. Kat came to the spyhole, barely able to speak. When she was finally released in late November, an inoperable cancer was diagnosed.

It was during this period and the following year (when we had the confrontation with Mahler, the split with him and our long and intensive discussion about the timing of the next hunger strike)[2] that I got to know Eva better—still from a distance, a few sentences in the yard or on scraps of paper—and I was extremely glad that she was there, with her calmness, her thoughts about everything, her considerations that were thorough and always geared towards our aims. I asked Irene, because I wasn't sure anymore, but she also remembers that we actually met there briefly one time. Irene and Eva had come down the stairs to the yard as I was being taken up to my lawyer on the first floor. A mistake, but not forgotten.

It wasn't until the summer or autumn of 1975, when my verdict had been confirmed, that I was held in the same section as Eva and Irene and we could walk together in the yard. One afternoon in the yard, Irene mentioned that Eva could do a somersault. Of course, we all wanted to see that and teased Eva until she finally got up, concentrated briefly, took two or three steps, then, whoops, and she was upright again. Very cool, as if in passing.

We spent about nine months in that section. Our cells were round the corner from each other, so we could talk relatively normally from our windows, without shouting. In Lehrter Strasse the windows were high up, but you could get to them by climbing up from the bed, and, because the walls were so thick, you could sit on the window ledge in relative comfort, with the horse-hair blanket as a seat and our small

---

1   Katja, Kat: Katharina Hammerschmidt. See the Endnote.
2   Horst Mahler was expelled from the group in September 1974. See the Endnote.

medium-wave radios, tobacco, lighter. Later on, Anne joined us in the cell next to me, with Moni below, on the corridor of the remand section. We often sat there, sometimes for hours, even when not talking much, until one of us said, "I'm off". That's one of the most intense images I retain of the time in Lehrter Strasse, and even now, once in a while, a bit of the feeling of that atmosphere comes back to me.

Eva did a somersault another time, when we were in Stammheim. This time I had told the others about it. We were on the roof, concrete everywhere, no grass like we had in Berlin.[3] We moved as far as possible away from the guards, and behind a steel girder she did it again, exactly as before, completely casual, as if in passing.

---

3   In Stammheim Prison, the political prisoners had their open-air exercise time in a
    large cage-like structure on the roof.

Irmgard Möller,
June 2015

Irmgard was in prison from July 1972 to December 1994, including eight months with Ingrid in Stammheim.

At the end of 1976, during one of our hunger strikes at Lübeck Prison,[1] I was flown to Stammheim, because a new trial was to begin there against me (and Bernhard Braun), based on Gerhard Müller's crown witness testimony against us regarding the attack on the US Headquarters in Heidelberg in May 1972. Otherwise, I would have been released around that time, after serving my first sentence of four and a half years. I had to continue my hunger strike there in Stammheim in order to get the same conditions as the others on the seventh floor, and when I was taken upstairs I had a bowl of porridge in my hand. Andreas, Jan, Brigitte and Nina were there. I had never met Nina before, but I knew her from the *info*.

A few weeks later, Brigitte was moved to Bühl Prison and then released. On the days when the other three were in court at Stammheim, Nina and I spent many hours together in the high-security unit. We could move around relatively freely, though when Jan or Andreas were present we had to keep part of our body outside their cells. Nina introduced me to a lot of things—music, books, etc.

In 1977, several books were published about stereotaxis, i.e., changes in behaviour through interventions in the brain. This was widely celebrated news as a possibility for finally coping with rebellious prisoners

---

1   In December 1976, the women in the high-security unit in Lübeck Prison were on hunger strike to protest against the lack of fresh air and daylight in their cells.

or for "healing sick people". The apologists were not only from Germany but also from the USA. Nina read and analysed it all—I don't remember the titles just now. When we were extremely alarmed by Federal Attorney Zeis's attempt to have forensic surgeon Witter from Bad Homburg operate on Ulrike's brain, Nina was able to read and interpret the specialist literature for us.

A few weeks after Günter was shot in the head while being arrested in May 1977, he was brought to the hospital section of Stammheim Prison for a while. They tried to interrogate him while prodding him in the chest like a baby: "You Buback"—to which he didn't reply. We heard this from the prison doctor and from Weidenhammer, Günter's lawyer. Günter couldn't speak, he had to learn how to use words again. Nina put a lot into his case and prepared herself to work with him, either inside or outside prison, to help him regain his lost faculties.[2]

After the big hunger strike in March/April 1977, when Rebmann promised us that we would be held together in larger groups,[3] the authorities, particularly the Federal Criminal Investigation Bureau, wanted to disband these groups as soon as possible. The pretext for that was soon created: the brawl on the seventh floor in August 1977. The most detailed report about that was Nina's.[4]

We had no other means of defending ourselves than by repeatedly going on hunger and thirst strikes. The three prisoners who had arrived from Hamburg early in July were transferred back to Hamburg on 12 August. The heat of August during the thirst strike caused frequent fainting—and the authorities used this as an excuse to transfer Nina to Stadelheim, claiming that the medical facilities available in Stammheim were insufficient to keep all five of us alive. It was easier for them to transfer Nina, because she was the only one of us who had already been convicted. This meant that they didn't have to ask the Stuttgart court, or in my case the Heidelberg court, for a transfer permit.

Before Nina was taken to Stadelheim, she asked for the hatch in Gudrun's cell door to be opened (the doors were closed throughout August) and said goodbye. I was sitting on the floor with Gudrun, and

---

2   Recovery of his cognitive faculties was long and slow, before and after his release from prison in May 1992.
3   Kurt Rebmann was then secretary of the Baden-Württemberg Ministry of Justice, later becoming West Germany's attorney general.
4   See Ingrid's report of the attack of 8 August 1977, pp. 152–60.

it was the last time I saw Nina; she was completely confident of being back with us soon. That was the firm commitment we had been given. She had a fresh face and large sparkling eyes. She called out to us, "Find me a lawyer in Munich!"

We ended the hunger and thirst strike on 2 September; it was a Friday. We were looking forward to Nina's imminent return. On Monday 5 September, Schleyer was abducted, and all promises ceased to be relevant.

Later on, in her letters to Witzel, I read that Nina thought I'd been moved to the Hohenasperg psychiatric section after 18 October. In fact, after an initial period in the intensive care unit in Tübingen, I was at Hohenasperg for four weeks, but in a unit next to the psychiatric section. I wasn't placed in the surgical unit, because Günter was already there. In my room, I was constantly guarded by one or two guards from Stammheim. I had no radio, etc.

In the corridor, someone turned up the radio, and I heard the news that Nina was dead.

Ron Augustin, April 2015

Ron was in prison from July 1973 to March 1980.

The prisoners called her Nina in the *info*. That's how I got to know her—in our struggle against the prison conditions. Until then, I had only known her from hearsay, because my first contact with the group underground took place in October 1970, only days after the arrests in the Knesebeckstrasse. After that, I saw her briefly once at the window of her cell during a demonstration in front of the prison. Apart from that, there were the pictures and comments in the press, reducing everything to sex and crime, which had already found their way into the counter-culture scene as well. Particularly when talking about women.

Initially, I didn't know anything of an attempt to free Nina and Peggy (Irene Goergens) from Lehrter Strasse. However, the folding ladder used for it was kept in a safe house disguised as a graphic design workshop used by me and others. When I arrived there one evening, I surprised Georg and another guy assembling the ladder. They showed me the ID papers for the two women, with only the pictures still to be inserted. At a meeting a week later, Gudrun drew me a picture of some of the prisoners. I remember that she described Nina as a particularly fearless and lively girl with a strong will and a keen sense of humour.

The picture I got of her during our time in prison was that of a strong and sensitive personality, who threw herself heart and soul into her struggle for political consciousness. And so full of joy. Naturally eager to learn, self-critical and demanding, she exacted the utmost of herself in every situation. In the discussions and hunger strikes she didn't accept any half-truths, neither from others nor from herself. In every situation she was there *fully*, open minded, quick witted, consistent, persistent.

Like most of us, Nina read a lot, and in her letters we saw the speed with which her thoughts and insights developed. In the daily confrontations and decision-making moments we had to deal with, I learned a lot from her way of handling things. I could recognise myself in much of it: the collective interaction that I miss so much today.

When I look at her picture, I not only see her fair face with the thoughtful look but am carried back to the sharp observations, advice and suggestions she was always eager to share with us all.

Ten years after her death, our daughter was born—we called her Nina.

Susanna Wilford, October 2021

Susanna, Ingrid's niece and Gerti and Michael's daughter, is the child Susanna in the prison letters.

It is somewhat ironic that I sit here in Aotearoa (New Zealand) in 2021 in lockdown, effectively imprisoned from the rest of the world due to this government's "elimination plan". It is the government's response to the Covid pandemic, and we are currently in the Delta variant phase and their plan is to limit entry to the country to a select few. It's an intractable position for all concerned. The talk of increasing isolation in this current era through lockdowns and the consequent shrinking of human connections is acutely affecting as I re-read Ingrid's letters about isolation and its impact.

My earliest memory of Ingrid is through her letter writing. My relationship to these letters started as a child—I was five in 1970. I distinctly remember the daily splat of letters dropping through the letterbox. Some more welcome than others. Today, it's a sound on the device or a red dot pulsating on a screen that announces the arrival of a missive. A particular time I remember is of Sunday evening, when the family regrouped at the end of the weekend for tea and toast, as a time when we drew pictures and wrote letters and poems to Ingrid. It probably only happened a few times, but the potency of the image transports me to favourite spaces and times: together with family, and a sense of safety and calm.

Another vivid memory is when, with one of my brothers and our German cousins, I met Ingrid in Stammheim Prison in the summer school holidays of 1976. I remember going through the locked gates and corridors. The image I have of her is wearing an army green combat jacket and jeans; perhaps as an eleven-year-old I was expecting black and white stripes of prison gear, as in the movies, yet the identity she presented to me was not so much of a prisoner, only the context informed me of that. Her attire was starkly different to that of the other adults in my life at that time, and perhaps that's why it sticks out in my mind.

We children (aged thirteen, eleven, six and one) sat with my mother and uncle in a grey room with no natural light, under the eyes of the prison guards. We sat in a line on one side of the grey table, with Ingrid opposite. My memory of that visit is that nobody except Ingrid said very much. Any questions we children had rehearsed were snatched away by the culture shock of the experience. Ingrid was the liveliest and most relaxed. One thing I remember she said to me, "Promise you'll never cut your hair". Her hair was short, and I thought it was a curious thing to say. Perhaps there were some regrets.

It was the evening that Gerti got the call from her father letting her know of Ingrid's death that stands out for me as the next potent memory of Ingrid in our lives. I was in my bedroom. My mother was downstairs, by the phone. I heard her wail: the sound of the pain at the loss to a sudden, unexpected death of someone close. Ingrid was very much part of family conversations at home and continued to be so while Gerti remained involved with the political prisoners' rights in Germany. These experiences, I think, contributed to the direction that I chose to work in, areas striving for social justice.

In autumn 2012, in the same house that we lived in during those years while Ingrid and Gerti corresponded, I encountered the letters again. It was a turning point in reviewing the narrative I had held about Ingrid. Living in Aotearoa (New Zealand) had helped me acknowledge the inter-connectedness and inter-relationship of all living and non-living things. Scanning the lightweight onionskin writing paper, with the indented words of typewriter keys or biro ink, had a visceral effect on me. Holding in my hand the very same pages that Ingrid had scribed, as I delicately fed them through the scanner, brought me into contact with Ingrid after many years of imagining her.

As children, we didn't particularly come across these letters. They were for my mother, and she would relay to us news about Ingrid. Reading the letters gave me a different perspective. I distinctly remember as a child the drawing she sent to us of her cell, yet it was only as an adult that I noticed the clenched fist running along the edge of the page, often a symbol of political solidarity, and also used as a salute to express unity, strength or resistance. She wrote to us then that we would one day understand why she was in this situation, and I hope this is what this book is trying to achieve. I wonder if the publication of her letters will mean that the years of isolation and writing were not for nothing.

Those few weeks of scanning, transcribing and mulling over the words stand out for me, and they also secured a different kind of connection with my mother: we were collaborators in taking up a relationship with Ingrid again. I was moved by the love she voiced for us, the children. I had many questions, and as I read the letters I was introduced to stories about Ingrid that I hadn't encountered before. The demands she made upon my mother for the home comforts, despite rejecting the context they came from: the cakes, cookies, clothes, books, news, money. And the condemnation by Ingrid of the efforts of Gerti and their mother to help in other ways. As a parent now, I think what it must have been like for my mother and her parents to be called to action in that way.

Gerti shares with us Ingrid's voice, for us to take from it what we need. She spoke to me along the way about how this process brought forth buried emotions and thoughts. I'm moved to wondering how she did this, what steps she took to not avoid those expressions of pain or sorrow but somehow galvanise them to shine a light on a story that for me and perhaps for others too resonates more with the intentions than with the actions taken. What these letters also confirm for me is the notion that people's lives are made up of multiple storylines, and that following different strands reveal different expressions of their life. These letters offer us some insight into some of the more marginal storylines of Ingrid's life. They are ones that I think deserve to sit alongside the dominant narratives that are in public circulation.

mir aus ist das geboht mit 26. - kann auch ein woche
er sein.oder wann gehen diese spezialfahrten ab.am 6./7.
t zwar ma mit fr.mohnhaupt,aberx das macht nichts,da es
dahin wieder 14 tage sind und ich noch besuche offen hab.
eiß genau an welchem tagen ihr dann da seid - den besuchs-
ag stell ich,denn brauchst du nicht extra schreiben an
knast.
 die verlegung nun läuft weiß der himmel.am schnee liegts
er nicht.ist mir jetzt auch scheißegal wann - warte da nich
f,sonst wird man bei dem ganzen irrsinn,der knast ist,noch
r.auf was warten ist sowieso falsch - xob nun draußen oder
 - weil man durch die fixierung dadrauf wirklich denk-und
lungsunfähig wird und hier potenziert sich das natürlich no

Appendices

 da die ...... das zwingt dich unheimlich,mit
tdingungen,wie sie d s sind,zu arbeiten,also nicht dran aus
en,sondern:es ist so,also mach was mit.dauert wahnsinnig ,
e bis man das kann+ oft genug gehts nat.nicht.zb wenn du
u weißt,daß du nur warten mußt,weil irgendeo ein idiot hier
er zu faul ist das telefon zu bedienen,und das jedesmal,abe
lich jedesmal - so daß mans schon weiß - zb wenn wir sport
n und die uns nicht holen + jedesmal so tun als wärs was
 neues daß wir montags sport haben. wir hams ja auch erst 3
 woche zur gleichen zeit. und sowas in tausend variationen
al am tag. da gewöhnste dich auch nicht dran - oder nur wen
ben resignierst und ihr erstrebtes ziel xxx 'anpassung' (=v
en) vollziehst.naja,die armen kreaturen gibts hier nat.zuha
ar ,5 jahre sind zu lang und die 'krisen' oder wie man das
en mag,hast du zigmal am tag oder 3mal im jahr ,und damit i
uso. : es ist eine bedingung, und entweder flippst du drauf
und gehst kaputt zwangsläufig,wirst an der ganzen scheiße
ückt - oder fängts was mit an,also was ist der kern der kri
n hängts,was ist das problem,und du kommst immer auf den
t,daß es an dir liegt es ändern zu können.und wenn du es ni
 bist du ein schwein,daß sich den anderen nicht verantwortl
t.weil die nat.nicht n kaputten typen brauchen,sondern einen
 sich was überlegt zu allen problemen und fragen + damit
 selbst be-arbeitet,indem du entscheidungen treffen mußt,
s beurteilen,eine situation oder n typen,und so ständig
rollierst,was mit dir selber los ist. wenn du dir nichts ü
t,interessiert dich es nicht - fühlst dich also nichtx vers
lich,daß klarheit entsteht,entwicklung läuft,von der du
teil bist. also kollektiv denken und handeln. - das ist e
man einfach nicht kann,weil mans nicht kennt,sondern immer
 das gegenteil,aus dem heraus wie der ganze laden eben läuft
 - schwer auf jeden fall,aber es gibt nichts besseres.
(ab und zu mal n schrieb von ihm,bei dem ich jedesmal denke
e muß ne starke macke haben nach dem was er schreibt:kein
aler satz,alles verschlungen und mystifiziert und ein psycho,
t aus) , das ist einer der wartet schon aufs alt werden (sa
. kann ich nur sagen:nimm dir besser gleich den strick,wora
 da noch warten + wieso überhaupt warten.versteh ich einfac
t,wie man derart resigniert sich nur noch um sich selber un
e psyche drehen kann.d.h.wie das kommt ist mit schon klar,s
verzeih (sowieso nie)das niemandem,der einigermaßen durchbl
stehste,wenn da einer hockt und drauf wartet,daß die anderen
ins feuer springen um ihm mal irgendwann das erträumte bess
n zu bringen,na warte.nicht zuletzt überläßt ders ja auch

Endnote by the Publishers of the German Edition

Compiling this collection of letters has taken a while. As Gerti explains in the introduction, her sister's letters were published in a small print run some years ago, at the time only for family and a small circle of friends and close acquaintances. Gerti was particularly concerned that the younger generation in her large family, who had not known Ingrid directly, should get to know her through the letters and form their own view of her. Following this first publication, encouragement from many quarters to make the letters available to a wider audience has resulted in this new edition.

It is "family correspondence," a limited and controlled communication, but it is genuine and direct, an intense, open exchange. Even though only Ingrid's part of the correspondence still exists, one can sense from her letters the extent of the closeness between the sisters and their absolute determination to understand each other.

In 1968, Ingrid moved into a shared apartment in West Berlin, after commuting between West Germany and West Berlin for more than a year. It was the time of the International Vietnam Congress, the large Vietnam demonstration in West Berlin and the Vietnamese National Liberation Front's Tet Offensive. A time when all the mendacity of the post-war period and the trash of consumer society were being radically called into question by a large youth movement.

By the middle of the 1960s, the growing protest movement had turned more militant, compared to the pacifism of previous years. It derived its strength from an awareness of being part of a world-wide upheaval. Everywhere things were moving, with mobilisations and struggles for fundamental change. Demonstrations took place almost everywhere, and institutions were attacked, occupied and used for day-long and night-long discussions. Almost everything was being challenged politically. A "New Left" emerged, primarily informed by the Black liberation struggle in the US, the revolutions in Cuba and Algeria and the anti-colonial liberation movements in the Third World. In Germany, confronted with the alienating and authoritarian social structures and the still massive presence of Nazis in the institutions, it considered itself "anti-authoritarian". In December 1966, it constituted an extra-parliamentary opposition (APO), which mainly made its presence felt in the universities and on the streets.

From the start, this New Left was confronted with police violence and media hate campaigns. After a phase of demonstrations and provocative happenings, people were looking for ways to more effectively stand up to the existing power relations—power relations that, following their dealings with the Vietnam War and their own experiences of repression and consumer culture, they began to perceive as being part of a single system.

They tried to break through the amnesia in the capitalist centres with popular actions. In fact, there were moments where they succeeded in reaching a broader section of the population, for instance during the anti-Springer demonstrations after the attempted assassination of Rudi Dutschke and in the mobilisations against the German Emergency Acts.[1]

The fundamental issue was emancipation—the emancipation of women, but also more generally: in universities, schools, apprenticeships, youth centres, neighbourhoods, prisons...

But the manifold forms of protest and attempts at organisation were increasingly confronted with the problem of being absorbed by

---

1   West Germany's federal parliament passed the Emergency Acts (*Notstandsgesetze*) on 30 May 1968, adding emergency clauses to the country's constitution to ensure the federal government's ability to take action in crises such as uprisings, war or natural disasters. Preparation for these laws had started as early as the 1950s, as the Western occupying powers' main precondition for lifting West Germany's occupation and reinstating its sovereignty. In addition to its internationalist perspective, Germany's extra-parliamentary opposition of the 1960s organised broad campaigns against the press of media mogul Axel Springer, the judiciary and the emergency laws. The Springer press in particular was held responsible for the aggressive atmosphere that led to the death of a student, Benno Ohnesorg, during a demonstration against the Shah of Iran's regime in June 1967 and to the attempted assassination of Rudi Dutschke in April 1968. The latter attack triggered riots (the "Easter riots") in several cities against Springer establishments. A month later, large-scale mobilisations took place against the emergency laws, which were nevertheless adopted against the backdrop of a worldwide protest movement.

the system, modernising it without managing to fundamentally change the relations of alienation and exploitation. Throughout Europe, discussions took place about how political actions could be raised to a new level. The main question was how to develop a sustainable practice based on people's experiences and theoretical insights and, to this end, how to develop structures safe from surveillance and infiltration by intelligence agencies and police.

The first clandestine structures to emerge from this movement were created in 1966–1967 as part of the campaign against the military draft, to help US soldiers desert and escape to Sweden and elsewhere instead of being sent to Vietnam. These developed into an international network, including contacts inside the military bases and with Black Panther groups that were particularly active in Frankfurt and Berlin. All that ran parallel to further discussions and considerations of how to build clandestine structures and organise the resistance.

Ingrid was part of these discussions as the movement's mobilisations in West Berlin and West Germany began to subside. During the same period, there were numerous interconnected "working groups" and "grassroots organisations" in the neighbourhoods, in which Ingrid was politically involved, as well as "factory groups" with which she had contact. Within all these groups, there were people who wanted to do more: to follow through with what had been started, to go on the offensive again, to find ways of securing their freedom of movement and their ability to act.

In early 1970, a group emerged that decided to do precisely that—to intervene politically with targeted attacks from within a clandestine structure and, thus, provide some oxygen to the liberation movements in the Third World, as well as opening up a real perspective for a revolutionary Left in the capitalist centres. Ingrid was part of this group.

In the midst of these preparations, Andreas Baader was arrested. The group estimated that his prolonged imprisonment would jeopardise the organisational process that had just begun. They also thought that liberating a prisoner as their first act would have a political impact, conveying the possibilities as well as the need for a clandestine organisation. That's how they came up with the idea of trying to free him. Despite hasty improvisation, they succeeded on 14 May 1970. The action was followed by military training at an Al Fatah camp in Jordan and a further period of preparation, leading to the creation of the Red Army Faction.

Ingrid was arrested on 8 October 1970, when a safe house in Berlin's Knesebeckstrasse was raided after a tip-off. She was caught in a police trap with four others. The following year, she was charged in connection with Andreas Baader's prison break and sentenced to six years. Three years later, she was also charged with participating in a bank robbery and with being a "member of a criminal organisation" and sentenced to a further seven years. Between 1975 and 1977, three actions aimed at liberating her and other prisoners from the RAF failed. She remained in prison for the rest of her life.

The Period of the *Letters*

The group of five people arrested together in West Berlin are the first prisoners from the RAF. Before then, militants had been imprisoned for months at a time while awaiting their trial. Within the Left, prison was perceived as merely a temporary evil. Nobody had a realistic picture of prison.

Autumn 1970 marks a shift in perspective. Brigitte Asdonk and Monica Berberich, two of the women arrested after the raid on the safe house, are sent from Berlin to different prisons in West Germany and remain there until sent back to Berlin for the start of the bank robbery trial in October 1972. The other two women, Irene Goergens and Ingrid, remain in West Berlin but are moved back and forth between Lehrter Strasse Prison for women and Moabit Prison for male prisoners on remand, held there in a special unit known as "the tower". They are transferred seven times in three years and, during their time in the "tower", they are completely isolated from other prisoners.

The following months see more RAF members arrested, dispersed across prisons throughout the country, and held in isolation. The number of political prisoners increases, including militants with other backgrounds. The Socialist Patients' Collective in Heidelberg is smashed in the summer of 1971. The RAF attacks in May 1972, on the US headquarters in Frankfurt and Heidelberg, prompt the largest manhunt in post-war Germany. Ten RAF members are arrested, including those with whom Ingrid had started: Gudrun Ensslin, Ulrike Meinhof, Andreas Baader.

The first attempt to start a hunger strike against their total isolation fails, because most prisoners hear nothing about it or hear about it too late. But the need to change the situation remains and becomes more urgent as they learn more about individual conditions. These are the most extreme for Ulrike Meinhof, who is held in a "silent wing", a completely separate and acoustically isolated section of Cologne Prison.

In January 1973, Andreas Baader uses the publicity around the trial in West Berlin, where he is called as a witness, to announce a collective hunger strike against the prison conditions. This time it works: all prisoners are informed by news broadcasts and are able to join in simultaneously. The hunger strike lasts for four weeks; it doesn't succeed in lifting the isolation, but Ulrike is taken out of the "silent wing"—after eight months.

The second collective hunger strike follows in May 1973, with the same demands. Lawyers, relatives and solidarity groups support the prisoners. The hunger strike lasts until the end of June. The prison conditions don't change, but the two hunger strikes have woken everybody up, much research is done on isolation as a scientifically developed method, and it becomes clear that experiments researching its effects on people have been going on for decades. It is not a coincidence, stupidity or paranoia but a deliberate programme of destruction.[2]

The hunger strikes provide the prisoners with the direct experience of how they can act together despite separation and isolation. For each one of them, communication is seen as essential, as is access to the same information and an opportunity for open discussion. The upcoming trials have to be prepared too. With the help of the lawyers' offices, the *info* is organised.[3]

A productive and lively period begins. A lot is being written, and there's a huge sense of the need and desire to break through individualisation and fight for a collective process again.

In September 1973, Ingrid and Irene Goergens are transferred again from the Moabit "tower" to Lehrter Strasse Prison for women. Political

---

2   From the first day of their incarceration, the political prisoners were isolated from everyone else in order to break down their collective identity and encourage them to repent. Most were held in cells surrounded by empty cells, in completely unoccupied wings or in high-security wings. Their contacts were limited, mainly to family members and lawyers. During each clandestine action on the outside, they were deprived of their radios, newspapers and all contact. In later years, these conditions were relaxed, allowing them to meet or associate in two- to four-person groups in high-security wings. However, during the Stammheim trial in 1975, medical experts appointed by the court were of the opinion that effective social interaction was only possible in groups of at least ten to fifteen people, which never happened for members of the RAF. See also page 2–3 footnote 1 on isolation in prison in the Introduction.

3   See p. II footnote 6 on the *info* in the Introduction.

prisoners are kept apart from each other, but total isolation is not possible in this small and crowded prison. Ingrid and others hear through other prisoners that Katharina Hammerschmidt is still not being treated, even though she can hardly speak; her throat is severely swollen. All possible steps are taken to get her a medical examination by external doctors. When she is finally released in November, an inoperable cancer is diagnosed. According to the doctors, she has only a few months to live, but she doesn't give up, and she lives for another year and a half.

The prisoners know that another hunger strike is inevitable. The first two hunger strikes scratched the surface of the isolation but didn't achieve any fundamental changes. The discussion about it in the *info* gets a boost when the media cover the hunger strike by prisoners from the Provisional IRA in England, which started in November 1973. They are demanding to be transferred to Northern Ireland, where "Special Category" status was granted in 1972, thus allowing political prisoners to be held together, known as association.[4] Despite brutal force feeding, the Price sisters and their comrades continue their hunger strike for many months. It ends only in June 1974, when Michael Gaughan dies, and they receive a promise that they will be transferred. During the months leading up to autumn 1974, the prisoners from the RAF come to the decision to orient themselves around this example. They understand that the conditions of struggle have changed but not the nature of the confrontation itself. Also, for each and every one of them it constitutes a new decision in favour of this struggle, clearly, openly and honestly. They know that the State will not budge unless the prisoners are willing to take it to the limit and not allow themselves to be broken up.

On 13 September, Ulrike Meinhof announces the third collective hunger strike during the trial in West Berlin, where she is charged in connection with Andreas Baader's prison break. Different prison administrations react differently, some start force feeding at an early stage, while others—for example, Berlin—only observe. When, by the end of October, Ingrid has trouble seeing and can walk in the courtyard only if held up by other prisoners, the women are transferred to the hospital wing of the men's prison in Moabit. Ulrike too, from the

---

4   In Northern Ireland, at the detention centre of Long Kesh, political prisoners were initially kept in large groups, enabling unlimited social interaction.

"tower". They are now two or three in adjoining cells—Ingrid with Anne Reiche and Monika Berberich. In the evening, when there is less noise, they can shout a few sentences from window to window. Ingrid hears Ulrike's voice again, for the first time in four years.

When the radio announces on 9 November that Holger Meins has died, the eight women spontaneously call a thirst strike but end it on the third day, because it would escalate the situation for everyone too quickly. There are large demonstrations. A West Berlin judge is shot by the 2nd of June Movement. Ulrike is transferred back to Stammheim Prison.

At the start of 1975, the authorities indicate that the demand for the end of isolation and for equal treatment will definitely not be granted, but that it might be possible to bring some prisoners together in groups, while maintaining security measures. There is, however, no definite promise. On 1 February, the prisoners start a thirst strike to force a clear decision. The women in Berlin are thrown onto a stretcher once a day, strapped down so completely that they cannot even move their head. Then a litre of porridge is pumped into their stomach through a nasal tube. They remain strapped down until it is certain that they cannot throw up the porridge. A few days later, the RAF asks the prisoners in a letter to the press to end the hunger and thirst strike, because their goal cannot be achieved in this way. After five months, the hunger strike is ended.

Ingrid and the other women are still in the hospital wing in Moabit when the 2nd of June Movement abducts the West Berlin chair of the Christian Democratic Party, Peter Lorenz, demanding the release of five prisoners, including Ina Siepmann and Verena Becker, who had participated in the hunger strike. It is shortly before the West Berlin elections, and Lorenz is the candidate opposing SPD-Mayor Schütz, which makes it difficult for the Schmidt government in Bonn to maintain its hard line. A week later, the five prisoners are flown to South Yemen, and Lorenz is released. Ina and Verena had been allowed to say goodbye to the women in Moabit, who were then sent back to Lehrter Strasse Prison. There they learn that the two prison chaplains and a Catholic social worker had been sacked. During mass, the Protestant vicar had offered a prayer for the women on hunger strike.

A few weeks later, on 24 April, the Holger Meins Commando occupies the German Embassy in Stockholm and demands the release of twenty-six prisoners, including Ingrid. This time, the government immediately decides to take a firm stand, ignoring two deadlines set by the commando, and two embassy staff are shot dead. When the embassy is stormed by police shortly after midnight, there is a massive explosion, presumably triggered from outside. Ulrich Wessel dies immediately. After a second explosion, the other commando members leave the embassy with the hostages and are arrested. Despite serious injuries, Siegfried Hausner is brought to Germany and dies in the hospital unit of Stammheim Prison.[5]

On 21 May, the trial against the so-called "ringleaders" of the RAF starts in Stuttgart. After the death of Holger Meins, only Ulrike Meinhof, Gudrun Ensslin, Jan Raspe and Andreas Baader still face charges in this trial. The trial hearings do not take place at the Stuttgart High Court but in a bunker of sorts that was built within the prison compound. During these weeks the pressure on lawyers is escalating: chosen defence lawyers are excluded, some are arrested and their legal offices are searched.[6]

In addition, from January 1975, letters and information material can no longer be circulated amongst the prisoners, following the enactment and immediate implementation of special legislation prohibiting individual defendants from having multiple lawyers. Isolation is to be the rule, the collective discussion process is to be cut off. The *info* had been targeted by the State Security agencies from the very beginning, as a tool against the isolation—it had to be eliminated.

---

5   Siegfried was in no condition to be transported. Seriously burnt and badly injured from being beaten with rifle butts, he was flown to a hospital cell in Stammheim Prison on 28 April, despite the protests of the Swedish doctors. He was denied all contact. He tried many times to convey that he had not triggered the explosion. No longer able to speak, he scribbled on pieces of paper for his lawyer, who received these only after Siegfried's death. In the trial against the four surviving commando members, all attempts to prove this were brushed aside.

6   The most thorough analysis of the Stammheim trial and the methods used jointly by the judiciary and State Security agencies against the RAF is the case study (with many excerpts from documents and declarations) by Dutch lawyer Pieter Herman Bakker Schut: *Stammheim. Der Prozess gegen die Rote Armee Fraktion* [Stammheim: The Trial against the Red Army Faction], (Kiel: Neuer Malik Verlag, 1986, and Cologne: Pahl-Rugenstein, 2007). The court hearings and numerous related documents can be found at the RAF archives (available online at socialhistoryportal.org/raf) and other collections at the International Institute of Social History in Amsterdam.

That summer, on 29 June 1975, Katharina Hammerschmidt dies of cancer in West Berlin. She had tried every possible treatment and fought for her life to the end.

Anne Reiche and Brigitte Mohnhaupt are convicted and transferred to the same section of Lehrter Strasse Prison as Ingrid and Irene. They can walk together in the courtyard and can see each other in the afternoon. In November, Ingrid and Brigitte are told that the Justice Department decided to have them transferred to Frankfurt. Both appeal the decision. If they must be transferred, they want to be together with the prisoners in Stammheim. This had been raised as a possibility before the end of the recent hunger strike: association, i.e., several prisoners to be brought together as a group.

The appeal is refused and, in spring 1976, Ingrid and Brigitte are flown separately to Frankfurt, where they are confronted with a "psychologically supervised process of integration", as Ingrid calls it in a letter to Gerti. Both make it clear to the prison administration that they will not participate in any such programme and will do all they can to be moved to Stammheim.

On 9 May, they hear the news that Ulrike is dead; she is said to have hanged herself. In many places, including abroad, demonstrations and protest actions occur. It is a great shock to Ingrid and Brigitte: they know Ulrike from their time together in the underground, and they saw her as recently as during the hunger strike in the prison hospital in Berlin. They cannot believe that a calm and rational person like Ulrike would suddenly take her own life, without a word. They now want to join the others in Stammheim even more, and they consider going on hunger strike. The prisoners in Stammheim also demand their transfer, and, finally, in June, they are flown to Stuttgart.

These are new living conditions for both of them—a modern high-security prison, impossible to take a step without a bunch of guards close by, outdoor walks only allowed on the fenced-in roof, albeit with a view far across the surrounding fields. The biggest change is being with Gudrun, Andreas and Jan. On non-trial days they can all meet for a few hours in the special unit built for their detention.[7]

Two weeks after the women's arrival, a joint PFLP-EO and RZ commando hijacks an Israeli plane and redirects it to Entebbe, Uganda,

---

7   See sketches of the unit, p. 225.

demanding the release of fifty-three prisoners from five countries. Amongst the six from Germany are Ingrid and Jan. Immediately, all prisoners from the RAF are banned from receiving post, newspapers and visits, and their radios are taken away. After a week, an Israeli military unit storms Entebbe airport and all commando members, three hostages, and as many as forty-five Ugandan soldiers guarding the airport are killed. The contact ban in the prisons is lifted, and Ingrid and Brigitte are moved into the special unit, where they are now closer to the others.

Beginning in July 1976, the defence calls fourteen prisoners as witnesses in the trial, asking them to say something about the structure of the RAF and how they each experienced it. For the prisoners, it touches upon the core of their political practice and thinking: collectivity is not supposed to exist in this trial, only its opposite: chiefs and soldiers, a world of domination and coercion. With their testimonies, the prisoners want to confront that narrative with their own collective experience. Getting out of the cell and into that sort of courtroom environment, it is not easy to speak freely and coherently. In addition, it is the daily practice of the court and the federal prosecution to interrupt the defendants so many times that barely a sentence can be completed and the contents can hardly be understood.

Ingrid has prepared her testimony thoroughly, she wants to speak about the prison break of 14 May 1970, about Andreas and about the early days of the RAF, the initial organisational phase. But she hardly gets through it; she is constantly interrupted. Surely no coincidence, as her testimony, in particular about the early days in the group, could have provided an authentic picture contrasting with the prosecution's crown witness. Nevertheless, the appearance of the fourteen prisoners remains a strong statement against the incessant propaganda of a "hierarchical structure".

On the days that Gudrun, Jan and Andreas are in court, Ingrid and Brigitte are alone in the high-security unit. This unit is a small section isolated from the rest of the seventh floor, with a narrow corridor in front of the cells. In the middle are a table and chairs, and against the wall some shelves with the prisoners' books, files and newspapers (in the cells only a small amount is allowed, to simplify searches). No windows; light comes from neon tubes in the ceiling. The corridor is closed off by an iron-bar gate with a door in it, in front of which sit two guards who observe the prisoners in the corridor during *Umschluss*.[8] When the door in the gate has to be opened, an additional guard arrives. The three women are not allowed to enter the cells of the two men, and vice versa. When one of the women, without thinking, enters Andreas's cell to tell him about a visit she just had, half of the seventh floor's guard detachment is standing behind her before she can finish her first sentence. But all of this is irrelevant; these are just the conditions.

The few hours together each day are a huge leap out of the numbness of isolation, just like the *info* four years earlier had perceptibly enabled the re-appropriation of a collective process, even if only a discussion in letters. Simply speaking to each other, being able to continue talking about it the next day, reflecting on the past few years, tackling questions and problems together. Much is being read and worked on—the restructuring of Western Europe had taken off after the Portuguese "Carnation Revolution" and Franco's death.[9] It is the period of "summit meetings" and coordinated political, military and economic pressure against all forces striving for any development in Europe other than one that would be a mere function of NATO's domestic policy. The pacification of the Left within the Mediterranean socialist parties is taken over by the German SPD.

Early in January 1977, Irmgard Möller is transferred from Lübeck to Stammheim. There is to be another trial against her, based on the testimony of the crown witness who is also responsible for the entire accusatory narrative in the Stammheim trial. For a few weeks, they are six in the high-security unit, until Brigitte Mohnhaupt is transferred to Bühl Prison in the Black Forest, before her release in February.

Following the exposure of an illegal eavesdropping operation against nuclear scientist Klaus Traube, there are increasing signs that

---

8   *Umschluss* is a term used by the prison administration to signify a situation in which two or three prisoners are allowed to be together for a few hours in one of their cells. At one point, the prisoners from the RAF in Stammheim could spend several hours a day together in the corridor of the high-security unit where they were held, a change introduced following court evidence by medical experts about the prisoners' need for social interaction. They were not, however, allowed to enter the cell of a prisoner of a different gender. See sketches of the unit, p. 225.

9   The "Carnation Revolution" of 25 April 1974 was a popular uprising led by the military, overthrowing the forty-year-old fascist regime of Antonio de Oliveira Salazar and Marcelo Caetano, and accelerating the independence of Portugal's overseas colonies. The name of the revolution derives from the fact that carnations were offered to the soldiers. 25 April is still Portugal's national holiday.

similar devices had been installed in Stammheim Prison. At a press conference in Stuttgart on 17 March 1977, the Baden-Württemberg ministers Bender and Schiess (justice and home affairs) confirm that at their instigation conversations between defence lawyers and prisoners had been bugged in 1975 and 1976. The operation was approved by the chief chancellor and carried out without the knowledge of prison staff by BND and VS agents. It was deemed necessary in order to prevent damage to the Federal Republic and possible liberation attempts, even though no evidence of either could be found. At the beginning of the trial, the prisoners in Stammheim had already said that there were indications that they were being bugged, which was dismissed as "the usual propaganda".

Late in March, the prisoners start their fourth collective hunger strike. They demand to be brought together in groups large enough to effectively enable social interaction, as recommended in 1975 by medical experts commissioned by the court.

On 7 April, the RAF's Ulrike Meinhof Commando kills Attorney General Siegfried Buback and two of his bodyguards. In its statement, the RAF holds him responsible for the deaths of Holger Meins, Siegfried Hausner and Ulrike Meinhof. The prisoners are again subjected to a contact ban, this time lasting a week. The hunger strike continues.

Later that month, the sentences in the Stuttgart trial are pronounced. Life sentences, the first ones against members of the RAF. Neither the prisoners nor their chosen lawyers are present. Two days later, the prisoners receive news from the prison director that the Stuttgart Ministry of Justice has agreed to a larger group, as the sentences have changed the situation. They end the hunger strike. Construction work starts in the larger wing that holds the smaller high-security unit. The pompous demonstration of State power, which the Stuttgart trial had put on public display over the past two years—with its special court bunker, special court, special detention and special laws—was to send its message that this was the end, that armed struggle and revolutionary politics for fundamental social change would have no chance in this country. So the trial produced the deterrent sentences but was not the end.

On 3 May, Günter Sonnenberg and Verena Becker are arrested after a shoot-out that leaves Günter seriously wounded by a bullet in the head. Both are sent to Stammheim, he to the hospital wing, she to another section of the prison.

For the International Commission of Investigation into the Death of Ulrike Meinhof, the prisoners try to examine the contradictory findings in the autopsy report. They can do so by measuring the prison towels, which are the same as those that were used to make the rope, as well as the mesh wire fixed to the cell windows, in order to compare these with the measurements in the report. Ingrid in particular can do this because of her medical knowledge. In a note of 27 May she lists and compares the different tests, all concluding that the autopsy findings are wrong.[10]

In the meantime, several prisoners in other federal states have begun hunger strikes, demanding to join the group in Stammheim. Around June, the construction work there is completed. The wall that had separated the high-security unit from the rest of the section is no longer there, and the five prisoners are able to move into cells in this area. For constant observation, there is now a glass cabin for the guards instead of the gate, and there is some natural light through glass bricks in the outer wall. Early in July, Wolfgang Beer, Werner Hoppe and Helmut Pohl are transferred from Hamburg to Stammheim. Ingrid doesn't know them, as all three were arrested after her. They have little time to get to know each other.

Other life sentences against prisoners from the RAF are announced during the following weeks: in Kaiserslautern, against Manfred Grashof and Klaus Jünschke and, in Düsseldorf, against Hanna Krabbe, Bernd Rössner, Karl-Heinz Dellwo and Lutz Taufer.

Late in July, the attempted abduction of banker Jürgen Ponto goes wrong, and he is killed by a RAF commando. In the media, the hate campaign against the prisoners is intensified; everything happening on the outside is said to have been planned and directed from within the prison cells. As in 1972, this so-called "direction from the cells" is the recurring State Security propaganda, intended to justify each new repressive measure to the public.[11]

---

10   The International Commission of Investigation into the Death of Ulrike Meinhof was created in 1976, with members including Lelio Basso, George Casalis, Simone de Beauvoir, John McGuffin, and Panayotis Kanelakis. Their final report was presented at a press conference in Paris in January 1979: International Commission of Investigation, *Report* (Paris: Maspero, 1979), with Ingrid's note on pp. 36–37.

11   Alleged "direction from the cells" (*Zellensteuerung*, or the suggestion that external actions were initiated by the prisoners inside) was used throughout 1977 to justify contact bans. In 1978, Federal Minister of Justice Hans-Jochen Vogel declared in an

There are growing signs that the group of prisoners brought together in Stammheim will not be allowed to continue existing for much longer. Only years later will it become known that the Federal Police had already intervened with the Justice Departments of the regional states against the prisoners' association.

On 5 August, provocations herald a subsequent physical assault by prison guards three days later, described in Ingrid's report of this attack.[12] The prisoners are now totally isolated and immediately start a hunger and thirst strike—they want a quick decision. Around thirty prisoners across the country join the strike. The judiciary's first reaction, on 12 August, is to transfer back the three prisoners who had come from Hamburg just a few weeks earlier. The health of all prisoners is deteriorating rapidly. At a press conference, the new attorney general, Kurt Rebmann, states that he is expecting there to be deaths.

The following night, the defence lawyers' office in Stuttgart is almost completely destroyed by a bomb. On 18 August, Ingrid is suddenly transferred back to the men's prison in Munich. As a warning against letting the prisoners die, on 25 August, the RAF attempts to attack the building of the Federal Prosecutors' Office with a home-made rocket launcher, which fails to function. In the meantime, mediation attempts by the West German section of Amnesty International fail when the Stuttgart Justice Ministry spreads false information about a conversation between Bishop Frenz and Gudrun Ensslin. According to Frenz, the situation appears to be completely intractable. The prisoners interrupt their strike on 2 September.

Three days later, on 5 September 1977, the RAF's Siegfried Hausner Commando abducts Hanns Martin Schleyer, one of the most important West German business leaders, demanding in exchange the release of eleven prisoners. Ingrid is one of them. The three bodyguards and the driver are killed during the abduction.

The government immediately decides against the exchange. To keep its hands free, it imposes a news ban and a total contact ban on more than one hundred political prisoners. The bans last six weeks. Ingrid describes in her note of October 1977 her experience of the

---

Italian television broadcast that "we didn't really assume this then and also had no proof of it". Nevertheless, "direction from the cells" continued to be used far into the 1990s to justify proceedings or cell searches.

12   See report pp. 152–60.

contact ban in Munich's Stadelheim Prison. The government is count-
ing on stalling tactics and the possible success of search operations.[13]
The commando's messages and videos, in which Schleyer addresses the
government, are systematically suppressed by the West German media.
What prevails is "the perfect silence", as *Der Spiegel* calls it.

On 13 October, the Palestinian Martyr Halimeh Commando abducts
a Lufthansa plane,[14] also demanding the release of the German prisoners, as well as two of their own comrades held in Turkish prisons. On
17 October, the Schmidt government in Bonn orders the storming of
the plane in Mogadishu. Three members of the commando are killed,
one survives. The next morning, Gudrun Ensslin and Andreas Baader
are found dead in their cells in Stammheim, Jan Raspe in the process
of dying and Irmgard Möller badly injured. The next day the RAF kills
Hanns Martin Schleyer and communicates the location where they left
him, in the boot of a car.

After the contact ban is lifted, Ingrid writes about planned visits
and wants to apply for a transfer to Frankfurt. On 12 November 1977,
she is found dead, hanging in a cell she had been moved to a few hours
earlier.

★

This Endnote has become long. It is more than fifty years since Ingrid
wrote the first letter from prison to her sister, and it has been important
for us to recall the political situation and actual conditions of that time.
Not only because a lot of it is difficult to remember after all these years
but also to be able to better understand Ingrid and the political context
in which she saw her life.

The Red Army Faction dissolved itself in 1998, after ending lethal
attacks in 1992. The prisoners had continued to fight for their association in larger groups. Their last collective hunger strike—the tenth—was
in 1989. Larger groups were never achieved. In the 1980s, even the
demand for that right had been criminalised as "propaganda for a
terrorist organisation", and legal actions brought against those relatives

---

13   On 22 September, during the search for the abductors, RAF member Knut Folkerts
     was arrested in Holland. He was threatened with death and offered 1 million DM if
     he revealed where Schleyer was being held.
14   Halimeh was the Arabic name of RZ (Revolutionary Cells) member Brigitte Kuhlmann,
     killed in Entebbe by an Israeli Special Unit.

Ingrid July 1976-June 1977

Labels in first diagram: shower; staircase; lifts and cells for visits in the northern wing; gates; guards; shelves; empty cells; Ingrid and Brigitte June-July 1976; Ulrike April 1974-May 1976; Gudrun April 1974-June 1976; staircase; food and hometrainer; Brigitte; Ingrid; Gudrun; Jan; Andreas; files, books, clothes; sentry

Labels in second diagram: Gudrun; Ingrid; sentry; shower; staircase; glass bricks; Irmgard; Wolfgang, Helmut, Werner; June-August 1977; cabin; guards; gates; cells for visits; gate; lifts at the northern wing; staircase; Andreas; Jan

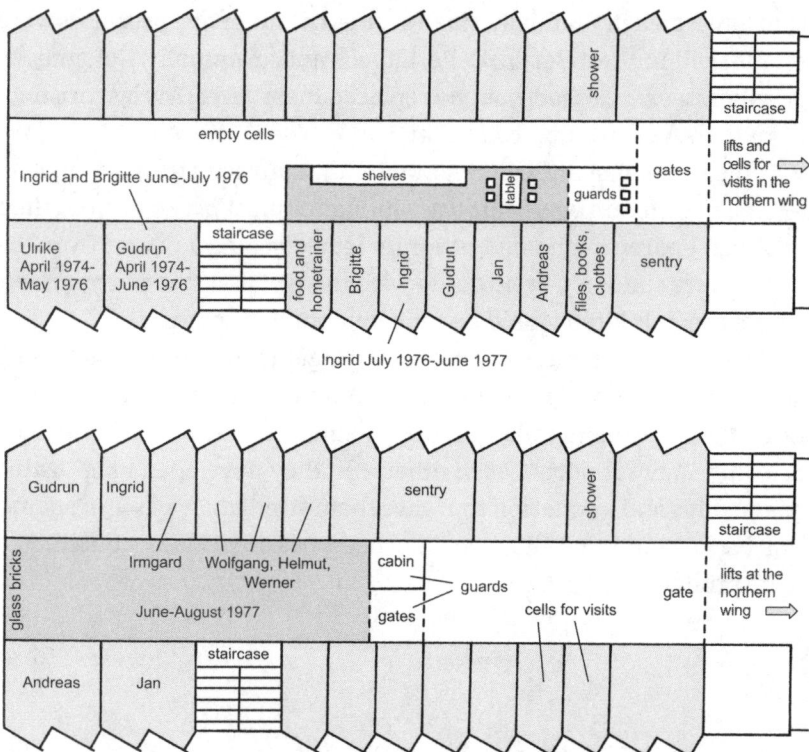

Above: The high-security unit on the top floor of Stammheim Prison's southern wing after the arrival of Ingrid Schubert and Brigitte Mohnhaupt, showing the approximate situation between June 1976 and June 1977. From early 1974, the entire top floor of the southern wing had been reserved for the upcoming trial in Stammheim. Initially, a small section within the unit was constructed to keep the men separate from the two women, Ulrike Meinhof and Gudrun Ensslin. It was occupied by Jan Raspe and Andreas Baader from early November 1974, during the hunger strike in which their co-defendant Holger Meins died. They were joined in this unit by Gudrun Ensslin one day before the arrival of Ingrid and Brigitte, who were transferred there a month after Gudrun, in July 1976. The corridor in front of the cells in this unit is the space where they could all spend time together. In December 1976, they were joined by Irmgard Möller, before Brigitte's release in February 1977.

Below: The situation at Stammheim Prison's high-security unit between June and August 1977, when (for a short while, 4 July to 12 August) Ingrid, Irmgard, Gudrun, Jan and Andreas were joined by Werner Hoppe, Helmut Pohl and Wolfgang Beer and could meet in the corridor of this unit.

Disclaimer: Both drawings are based on incomplete police reports and descriptions by former prisoners. Despite the utmost effort to reconstruct the situation of each prisoner, some details may be inaccurate.

who advocated it. Gradually, small groups of four or five prisoners were established in West Berlin, Celle, Lübeck and, eventually, Cologne. As prisoners were released, nobody replaced them there. The last prisoner from the RAF was released in 2011.

The somewhat difficult relations with family run through Ingrid's letters. In different ways, this was similar for most prisoners and their relatives—parents who had never imagined seeing a prison from the inside were suddenly confronted with the fact that this was precisely where their children would be for a long time to come.

Over the years, many of them came together in the relatives' group, acting collectively for an end to isolation detention, for the association of the prisoners in larger groups and later for their release from prison.[15] They supported each other, and they developed long-lasting friendships and a cohesion that gave them strength. It was also against this background that this book has been possible. Many contributed to its production.

---

15   The relatives' group existed for over thirty years. Over time, they met with relatives of political prisoners in France and Spain, as well as the mothers of the Plaza de Mayo in Argentina. Following the hunger strike in 1989, they fought increasingly for the release of the political prisoners. They also published the *Angehörigen-Info* (Relatives' Information Bulletin), with updates about the situation in the different prisons. See the Introduction.

Timeline

1970
14 May 1970

An armed group breaks prisoner Andreas Baader out of the Institute for Social Research in West Berlin, where he had obtained permission to work with Ulrike Meinhof on a book about adolescents in foster care. This marks the beginning of the Red Army Faction. The following year, Ingrid and others will be convicted for this action.

Summer 1970

Ingrid and others from the group receive military training at an Al Fatah camp in Jordan.

29 September 1970

In West Berlin, three banks are robbed simultaneously. Subsequently, in a separate trial in February 1973, Ingrid and others are convicted for this action.

8 October 1970

Ingrid is arrested, with Irene Goergens, Monika Berberich, Brigitte Asdonk and Horst Mahler. Ingrid and Irene remain in Berlin at Lehrter Strasse Prison for women, while Monika and Brigitte are transferred to West German prisons.

1971
February 1971

Before the start of the first trial against them, Ingrid and Irene are transferred to the "tower" at Moabit Prison, where they are completely isolated.

1 March–21 May 1971

Trial regarding the liberation of Andreas Baader. Ingrid and Irene are sentenced to six and four years respectively and are transferred back to Lehrter Strasse Prison. Horst Mahler will be convicted later.

15 July 1971

In Hamburg, Petra Schelm is shot dead by the police. Ingrid knew her well.

14 October 1971

A ladder meant to be used to free Ingrid and Irene is found near the prison wall. Both women are immediately transferred back to the "tower" in Moabit Prison.

4 December 1971

Georg von Rauch is shot dead by the police. Two months earlier, he and others had tried to free Ingrid and Irene.

1972

28 January 1972

Under the chairmanship of Chancellor Willy Brandt, the Conference of Ministers of the Interior issues a decree against "radicals" in the public service (*Radikalenerlass*). In the following years, the decree leads to the screening of 3.5 million people by the intelligence agencies and more than 1,500 professional bans (*Berufsverbote*).

2 March 1972

Thomas (Tommy) Weisbecker is shot dead by the police in Augsburg.

11–24 May 1972

The RAF is engaged in two attacks on US Army headquarters in Frankfurt and Heidelberg, as well as four attacks against Criminal Investigation Bureaus, a magistrate and the Springer press.

June–July 1972

Several RAF members and others are arrested, including Jan Raspe, Holger Meins, Andreas Baader, Gudrun Ensslin, Ulrike Meinhof and Irmgard Möller. In Berlin, Brigitte Mohnhaupt is arrested. In the following months, Verena Becker, Anne Reiche, Inge Viett and Katharina Hammerschmidt are transferred to Berlin's Lehrter Strasse Prison.

October 1972

The trial for the September 1970 bank robberies against Ingrid, Irene, Brigitte Asdonk and Monika Berberich starts in Berlin. The four women are held in the "tower" at Moabit Prison during this time.

December 1972

Ingrid and Irene are transferred back to Lehrter Strasse Prison for a brief time, because the cells in the "tower" are used for Gudrun Ensslin and Ulrike Meinhof, who have been called as witnesses in the trials.

1973

17 January 1973

Andreas Baader, also called as witness in the trial in Berlin, announces the first collective hunger strike by the prisoners from the RAF against special treatment and isolation. During this strike, lawyers hold their own hunger strike in front of the Supreme Court. For five days, 9–14 February, Andreas is denied water. The hunger strike ends on 16 February. Ulrike Meinhof is taken out of acoustic isolation in Cologne Prison's special isolation unit but is still kept in solitary confinement.

February 1973

At the end of the bank robbery trial, Ingrid is sentenced to thirteen years in total, the other prisoners to between seven and twelve years.

8 May–29 June 1973

The second collective hunger strike. Eighty political prisoners demand the abolition of isolation detention. For ten days, 24 May–4 June, Andreas Baader is denied water. Across Germany, local Committees Against Isolation Torture are established.

August 1973

Inge Viett and two other prisoners escape from Lehrter Strasse Prison.

September–October 1973

Ingrid and Irene are transferred back from the "tower" in Moabit Prison to Lehrter Strasse Prison, where they join a week-long successful resistance against the attempt by the prison authorities to weld wire mesh to all cell windows.

20 October 1973

Ina Siepmann is captured in Berlin and taken to Lehrter Strasse Prison.

30 November 1973

Katharina Hammerschmidt is released from prison; her condition is deteriorating daily: she can hardly speak, her neck is swollen, she risks suffocating from a tumour which only after her release is diagnosed as having progressed too far for surgery.

1974

January 1974

Monika Berberich and Brigitte Asdonk are transferred from Moabit Prison to Lehrter Strasse Prison.

7 June 1974

In England, the Price Sisters end their hunger strike after 205 days, during which they had demanded to be transferred to Northern Ireland. Four days after the death of Michael Gaughan, one of four other prisoners on hunger strike, their transfer to Northern Ireland is approved.

August 1974

Ina Siepmann, Anne Reiche and Verena Becker are transferred to the "tower" in Moabit Prison before the start of their trial. As is Ulrike Meinhof—she is to be charged in connection with Andreas Baader's prison break.

13 September 1974

Ulrike Meinhof announces the third collective hunger strike. Following the experiences of the first two hunger strikes and the example of the Irish prisoners in England, the prisoners decide not to end this strike until the prison conditions really change.

27 September 1974

Horst Mahler is expelled from the RAF and from the prisoners' collective.

October–November 1974

The female prisoners in Berlin are transferred one after another to the prison hospital in Moabit.

9 November 1974

Holger Meins dies while on hunger strike. Throughout Europe, people demonstrate for days on end, with fifteen thousand protesting in Berlin alone.

10 November 1974

During an attempted kidnapping, the president of the West Berlin Court of Appeal, Günter von Drenkmann, is shot dead by the 2nd of June Movement. The intention had been to hold him captive to protect the striking prisoners and to free him only when the hunger strike demands were met.

29 November 1974

In the trial regarding Andreas Baader's prison break, Ulrike Meinhof is sentenced to eight years and Horst Mahler to a total of fourteen years. Ulrike is sent back to Stuttgart's Stammheim Prison.

1975

5 February 1975

The prisoners end their collective hunger and (from 1 February) thirst strike, following a letter from the RAF requesting they do so.

27 February 1975

The 2nd of June Movement abducts Peter Lorenz, the leader of the West Berlin Christian Democratic Party. On 5 March, five prisoners are released in exchange for Lorenz and flown to South Yemen. They include Ina Siepmann and Verena Becker from West Berlin.

24 April 1975

The RAF's Holger Meins Commando occupies the German embassy in Stockholm and demands the release of twenty-six prisoners. Germany's government refuses to negotiate and agrees to a night-time attack. Ulrich Wessel is killed. Siegfried Hausner is seriously wounded, and he and four other members of the commando are arrested.

4 May 1975

Siegfried Hausner dies in Stammheim Prison.

21 May 1975

The trial against Gudrun Ensslin, Ulrike Meinhof, Andreas Baader and Jan Raspe starts in Stuttgart's Stammheim Prison.

29 June 1975

Katharina Hammerschmidt dies in Berlin.

9 September 1975

Five members of the 2nd of June Movement are arrested in Berlin. The women—Inge Viett, Juliane Plambeck and Gabriele Rollnik—are taken to Lehrter Strasse Prison.

November 1975

Ingrid and Brigitte Mohnhaupt are ordered by West Berlin's judiciary to be transferred to a prison in Frankfurt on the grounds that they had attempted to "disturb the prison order". Both apply to be transferred to Stammheim instead, to join the other prisoners there.

1976

April 1976

Brigitte Mohnhaupt and Ingrid are transferred to Preungesheim Prison in Frankfurt.

9 May 1976
Ulrike Meinhof is found dead in Stammheim Prison. Demonstrations and protests occur for days on end throughout Germany and abroad.
June 1976
Ingrid and Brigitte are transferred to Stammheim. At first, they are held in the cell where Ulrike had died.
27 June 1976
A joint RZ and PFLP-EO commando hijacks an Air France plane and reroutes it to Entebbe, Uganda, demanding the release of fifty-three prisoners from Israel, Kenya, France, Switzerland and West Germany, including Ingrid. An Israeli military unit storms the airport on 4 July. The commando, three hostages and as many as forty-five Ugandan soldiers guarding the airport are killed. During these eight days, the prisoners in Stammheim are denied newspapers, radio and visits but are allowed to take their exercise together in the caged area on the prison roof.
7 July 1976
Monika Berberich and three women from the 2nd of June Movement escape from Lehrter Strasse Prison. Two weeks later, Monika is recognised and recaptured. She is sent to the "tower" in Moabit Prison, where she will remain until her release in March 1988. Immediately after the escape, Brigitte Asdonk and Anne Reiche are transferred to Lübeck and held in a high-security unit. Irene Goergens is now the only political prisoner in Lehrter Strasse Prison. She remains there until her release in May 1977.
July–August 1976
At the Stammheim trial, the defence calls fourteen prisoners from the RAF to testify about the collective structure of the group.
December 1976
Irmgard Möller is transferred from Lübeck to Stammheim, where a new trial against her is being prepared.

1977

8 February 1977
Brigitte Mohnhaupt is released from prison.
29 March 1977
The fourth collective hunger strike begins. The prisoners demand association in larger groups.

7 April 1977

In Karlsruhe, the RAF's Ulrike Meinhof Commando kills Germany's attorney general Siegfried Buback. For days, the prisoners are again without radio, newspapers and any contact with the outside world.

28 April 1977

At the Stammheim trial, Gudrun Ensslin, Andreas Baader and Jan Raspe are given life sentences.

30 April 1977

End of the hunger strike, following the assurance that the group in Stammheim Prison is to be enlarged to eight.

4 July 1977

Wolfgang Beer, Helmut Pohl and Werner Hoppe are transferred from Hamburg to Stammheim following construction to expand Stammheim's high-security unit.

30 July 1977

Jürgen Ponto, chair of the board of the Dresdner Bank, is killed by a RAF commando during an attempted kidnapping.

9 August 1977

Following an attack on the group of prisoners in Stammheim, the prisoners from the RAF start another hunger strike.

12 August 1977

Wolfgang Beer, Helmut Pohl and Werner Hoppe are returned to the prison in Hamburg.

18 August 1977

Ingrid is transferred to Stadelheim Prison for men in Munich. Only four prisoners now remain in Stammheim: Jan Raspe, Andreas Baader, Gudrun Ensslin and Irmgard Möller.

25 August 1977

In Karlsruhe, a rocket launcher aimed at the Federal Prosecutors' Office building is found.

2 September 1977

In view of the hardened situation, the prisoners end their hunger strike.

5 September 1977

The RAF's Siegfried Hausner Commando kidnaps Hanns Martin Schleyer, president of the Confederation of German Employers' Association, and demands in exchange the release of eleven prisoners from the RAF, including Ingrid. The German government rejects the demand. All political prisoners are subjected to a total contact ban (*Kontaktsperre*), which becomes enshrined in law within weeks.

13 October 1977

The Palestinian Commando Martyr Halimeh hijacks a Lufthansa plane in Mallorca and reroutes it to Mogadishu, Somalia, in support of the demands of the Siegfried Hausner Commando.

17 October 1977

At Mogadishu airport, a German GSG-9 intervention unit storms the plane and kills three of the four Palestinian commando members.

18 October 1977

In Stammheim Prison, Gudrun Ensslin and Andreas Baader are found dead in their cells, Jan Raspe is found dying, and Irmgard Möller is found severely wounded. A gynaecological examination is forced on Ingrid in the presence of several male and female prison staff and two doctors. She is moved to an isolated and cold cell with constant neon light, white tiles on all walls and a wire screen in front of the high window. The cells on either side are empty.

19 October 1977

Hanns Martin Schleyer is shot dead by the RAF.

20 October 1977

The Federal Minister of Justice Hans-Jochen Vogel lifts the contact ban. Ingrid is allowed a visit from a lawyer who demands an end to the incessant neon light in the cell. It is replaced by a blue light at night. Observation through the spyhole every fifteen minutes is changed to every thirty minutes following the intervention of the prison doctor. Ingrid receives the first visit from a relative, seeing her father for one hour. She decides to apply for a transfer to the prison in Frankfurt, to be closer to her family, and to apply for permission to study.

4 November 1977

Ingrid becomes ill with bronchitis. The prison doctor advises that she be moved to the cell where she was initially. The cell is warmer and closer to the main prison population. But she is still isolated for at least twenty-three hours each day and has to do her daily courtyard walk alone. Nonetheless, she feels able to breathe again.

11 November 1977

The evening news reports that dynamite has been found in the cell in Stammheim Prison where Ingrid had been held three months earlier.

12 November 1977

Search of her cell while she is doing her courtyard walk. A rope made of strips of bed linen is found in the toilet pedestal.

Dr Steirer, the prison director, orders Ingrid to be moved to the cell in the prison's isolation unit where she had been held earlier for six weeks during the contact ban. Her lawyer is not informed that she was being moved back to the icy cell. According to the prison records, Ingrid eats her evening meal. Observation through the spyhole every fifteen to thirty minutes.

Discovery of Ingrid's lifeless body hanging from the window at 7:10 p.m. The last check had been at 6:30 p.m.

The official post-mortem examination is carried out later that night at the Institute of Forensic Medicine in Munich, in the presence of two of Ingrid's lawyers. The prison director who had ordered that Ingrid be moved back to the isolation cell is not interviewed, despite her parents' request, nor is there any record of the director's conversation with Ingrid that afternoon.

After November 1977

Further investigations, witness statements and expert opinions were collected over the next year, which did not alter the conclusion of "suicide" reached by the prosecutors on 12 November.

In October 1978, the family was advised by their lawyer that nothing further could be done, but that they could appeal the prosecutor's conclusion. Ingrid's parents, who had seen the outcome of investigations into the death of other prisoners from the RAF, decided not to continue with an appeal that had no chance of succeeding.

Acronyms

APO	*Außerparlamentarische Opposition*: Extra-Parliamentary Opposition
BKA	*Bundeskriminalamt*: Federal Criminal Investigation Bureau, Germany's federal police
BKA-SG	BKA Security Group
BKA-TE	BKA Terrorism Department
BND	*Bundesnachrichtendienst*: Federal Intelligence Service, Germany's foreign intelligence agency
CIA	Central Intelligence Agency
DM	German Mark (1 DM = approx. 0.50 dollars/pounds sterling)
GSG-9	*Grenzschutzgruppe 9*: Border Patrol Group 9, officially part of the Federal Border Patrol, in practice Germany's anti-terrorist special operations unit.
IISH	International Institute of Social History
IISS	International Institute for Strategic Studies
INLA	Irish National Liberation Army
IRA	Irish Republican Army
ISC	Institute for the Study of Conflict
IUK	*Internationale Untersuchungskommission zum Tode Ulrike Meinhofs*; International Commission of Investigation into the Death of Ulrike Meinhof
IVK	*Internationales Komitee zur Verteidigung politischer Gefangener in Europa*: International Committee for the Defence of Political Prisoners in [Western] Europe

LKA	*Landeskriminalamt*: Regional Criminal Investigation Bureau, police operating at the provincial (*Land*) level
MAD	*Militärischer Abschirmdienst*: Military Counterintelligence Service
PFLP	Popular Front for the Liberation of Palestine
PFLP-EO	Popular Front for the Liberation of Palestine–External Operations
PLO	Palestine Liberation Organisation
RAF	*Rote Armee Fraktion*: Red Army Faction
RZ	*Revolutionäre Zellen*: Revolutionary Cells
SPD	*Sozialdemokratische Partei Deutschlands*: Social Democratic Party of Germany
UN/UNO	United Nations/United Nations Organisation
VS	*Verfassungsschutz*: Protection of the Constitution, the German internal intelligence service, operating at both federal and provincial (*Land*) level

About the Contributors

Ingrid Schubert was one of the first members of the Red Army Faction in Germany. Arrested in October 1970, she remained in prison until her death in November 1977. Ingrid was a qualified doctor with a particular interest in the provision of community-based health services.

Gerti Wilford is the sister of Ingrid Schubert, to whom most of the letters in this book were addressed. She worked throughout her career as a family therapist in the National Health Service (England).

Jo Tunnard is an editor of publications by UK government departments, charities, and other voluntary (nonprofit) sector organizations.

ABOUT PM PRESS

PM Press is an independent, radical publisher of critically necessary books for our tumultuous times. Our aim is to deliver bold political ideas and vital stories to all walks of life and arm the dreamers to demand the impossible. Founded in 2007 by a small group of people with decades of publishing, media, and organizing experience, we have sold millions of copies of our books, most often one at a time, face to face. We're old enough to know what we're doing and young enough to know what's at stake. Join us to create a better world.

PM Press
PO Box 23912
Oakland, CA 94623
www.pmpress.org

PM Press in Europe
europe@pmpress.org
www.pmpress.org.uk

FRIENDS OF PM PRESS

These are indisputably momentous times—the financial system is melting down globally and the Empire is stumbling. Now more than ever there is a vital need for radical ideas.

In the many years since its founding—and on a mere shoestring—PM Press has risen to the formidable challenge of publishing and distributing knowledge and entertainment for the struggles ahead. With hundreds of releases to date, we have published an impressive and stimulating array of literature, art, music, politics, and culture. Using every available medium, we've succeeded in connecting those hungry for ideas and information to those putting them into practice.

Friends of PM allows you to directly help impact, amplify, and revitalize the discourse and actions of radical writers, filmmakers, and artists. It provides us with a stable foundation from which we can build upon our early successes and provides a much-needed subsidy for the materials that can't necessarily pay their own way. You can help make that happen—and receive every new title automatically delivered to your door once a month—by joining as a Friend of PM Press. And, we'll throw in a free T-shirt when you sign up.

Here are your options:

- **$30 a month** Get all books and pamphlets plus a 50% discount on all webstore purchases

- **$40 a month** Get all PM Press releases (including CDs and DVDs) plus a 50% discount on all webstore purchases

- **$100 a month** Superstar—Everything plus PM merchandise, free downloads, and a 50% discount on all webstore purchases

For those who can't afford $30 or more a month, we have **Sustainer Rates** at $15, $10, and $5. Sustainers get a free PM Press T-shirt and a 50% discount on all purchases from our website.

Your Visa or Mastercard will be billed once a month, until you tell us to stop. Or until our efforts succeed in bringing the revolution around. Or the financial meltdown of Capital makes plastic redundant. Whichever comes first.

**KER
SPL
EBE
DEB**

Since 1998 Kersplebedeb has been an important source of radical literature and agit prop materials.

The project has a non-exclusive focus on anti-patriarchal and anti-imperialist politics, framed within an anticapitalist perspective. A special priority is given to writings regarding armed struggle in the metropole, the continuing struggles of political prisoners and prisoners of war, and the political economy of imperialism.

The Kersplebedeb website presents historical and contemporary writings by revolutionary thinkers from the anarchist and communist traditions.

Kersplebedeb can be contacted at:

Kersplebedeb
CP 63560
CCCP Van Horne
Montreal, Quebec
Canada
H3W 3H8

email: info@kersplebedeb.com
web: www.kersplebedeb.com
www.leftwingbooks.net

Kersplebedeb

Our Gun, Our Consciousness, and the Collective: Letters from the Discussion in Prison

Ulrike Meinhof

ISBN: 979-8-88744-132-0
$21.95   160 pages

Ulrike Meinhof was one of the founding members of the Red Army Faction. This followed her lengthy involvement in the protest movements of the 1960s, during which she had become the left's most respected journalist in the Federal Republic of Germany. Incarcerated and held in isolation after her arrest in June 1972, she died in 1976 in her prison cell, having been subjected to years of torture as well as police and media smear campaigns. For this collection, in order to show who she really was, her surviving comrades in arms have released the letters she wrote for the group's internal discussion in prison, as well as a number of texts delivered during the main Stammheim trial against members of the RAF.

With an introduction and comments by her former comrades, as well as chronological and bibliographical references, this volume includes the last texts that Meinhof had prepared for the prisoners' collective, in which she played an active part, alongside a statement that she presented at another trial, regarding the group's founding act: the prison breakout of Andreas Baader, in addition to other texts, some published here for the first time in English.

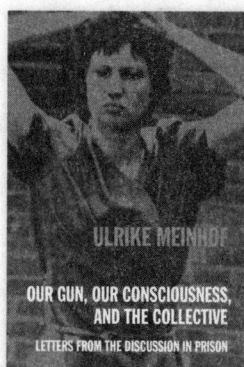

The Red Army Faction, A Documentary History— Volume 1: Projectiles for the People

Edited by J. Smith and André Moncourt
with Forewords by Russell "Maroon"
Shoats and Bill Dunne

ISBN: 978-1-60486-029-0
$34.95   736 pages

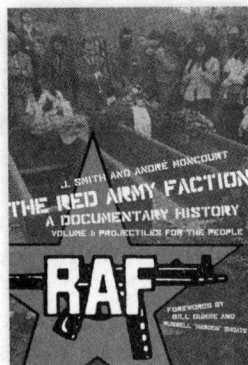

The first in a two-volume series, this is by far the most in-depth political history of the Red Army Faction ever made available in English.

Projectiles for the People starts its story in the days following World War II, showing how American imperialism worked hand in glove with the old pro-Nazi ruling class, shaping West Germany into an authoritarian anti-communist bulwark and launching pad for its aggression against Third World nations. The volume also recounts the opposition that emerged from intellectuals, communists, independent leftists, and then—explosively—the radical student movement and countercultural revolt of the 1960s.

It was from this revolt that the Red Army Faction emerged, an underground organization devoted to carrying out armed attacks within the Federal Republic of Germany, in the view of establishing a tradition of illegal, guerilla resistance to imperialism and state repression. Through its bombs and manifestos the RAF confronted the state with opposition at a level many activists today might find difficult to imagine.

For the first time ever in English, this volume presents all of the manifestos and communiqués issued by the RAF between 1970 and 1977, from Andreas Baader's prison break, through the 1972 May Offensive and the 1975 hostage-taking in Stockholm, to the desperate, and tragic, events of the "German Autumn" of 1977. The RAF's three main manifestos—*The Urban Guerilla Concept*, *Serve the People*, and *Black September*—are included, as are important interviews with *Spiegel* and *le Monde Diplomatique*, and a number of communiqués and court statements explaining their actions.

Providing the background information that readers will require to understand the context in which these events occurred, separate thematic sections deal with the 1976 murder of Ulrike Meinhof in prison, the 1977 Stammheim murders, the extensive use of psychological operations and false-flag attacks to discredit the guerilla, the state's use of sensory deprivation torture and isolation wings, and the prisoners' resistance to this, through which they inspired their own

The Red Army Faction, A Documentary History— Volume 2: Dancing with Imperialism

Edited by J. Smith and André Moncourt
with an Introduction by Ward Churchill

ISBN: 978-1-60486-030-6
$26.95   480 pages

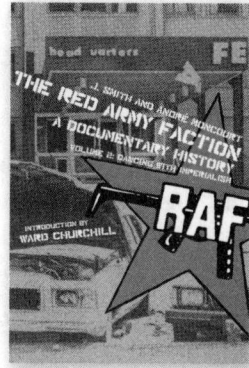

The long-awaited *Volume 2* of the first-ever English-
language study of the Red Army Faction—West Germany's most notorious
urban guerillas—covers the period immediately following the organization's
near-total decimation in 1977. This work includes the details of the guerilla's
operations, and its communiqués and texts, from 1978 up until the 1984
offensive.

This was a period of regrouping and reorientation for the RAF, with its previous
focus on freeing its prisoners replaced by an anti-NATO orientation. This was
in response to the emergence of a new radical youth movement in the Federal
Republic, the Autonomen, and an attempt to renew its ties to the radical left.
The possibilities and perils of an armed underground organization relating to the
broader movement are examined, and the RAF's approach is contrasted to the
more fluid and flexible practice of the Revolutionary Cells. At the same time, the
history of the 2nd of June Movement (2JM), an eclectic guerilla group with its
roots in West Berlin, is also evaluated, especially in light of the split that led to
some 2JM members officially disbanding the organization and rallying to the
RAF. Finally, the RAF's relationship to the East German Stasi is examined, as
is the abortive attempt by West Germany's liberal intelligentsia to defuse the
armed struggle during Gerhart Baum's tenure as Minister of the Interior.

Dancing with Imperialism will be required reading for students of the First World
guerilla, those with interest in the history of European protest movements, and
all who wish to understand the challenges of revolutionary struggle.

*"This collection is not simply a documentary of the West German revolutionary Left
at a particular point in the Cold War 1970s. It is more important for the insights it
provides into the challenges, obstacles, and opportunities of waging armed struggle
within the context of a wealthy, well-resourced, Western capitalist state. In this, the
experiences and activities of the RAF are unique in the lessons they might teach
organizers in Western capitalist milieus. In our own context, it is likely that future
conditions of radical social change, and certainly revolutionary struggles, will more
closely approximate those engaged by the RAF in 1970s West Germany than the
much more influential examples of Russia in 1917 or Spain in 1936."*
—Jeff Shantz, *Upping the Anti*

Remembering the Armed Struggle: My Time with the Red Army Faction

Margrit Schiller with a Foreword by Ann Hansen, Afterword by Osvaldo Bayer, and Appendix by J. Smith & André Moncourt

ISBN: 978-1-62963-873-7
$19.95   256 pages

Margrit Schiller was an early member of the Red Army Faction, the West German urban guerrilla group. In 1971 she was captured and charged with a murder she did not commit, and upon her release she returned to the underground, being captured again in early 1974. She would spend most of the 1970s in prison, enduring isolation conditions meant to break the human spirit, and participating hunger strikes and other acts of resistance along with other political prisoners from the RAF.

In *Remembering the Armed Struggle*, Schiller recounts the process through which she joined her generation's revolt in the 1960s, going from work with drug users to joining the antipsychiatry political organization the Socialist Patients' Collective and then the RAF. She tells of how she met and worked alongside the group's founding members, Ulrike Meinhof, Andreas Baader, Jan-Carl Raspe, Irmgard Möller, and Holger Meins; how she learned the details of the May Offensive and other actions while in her prison cell; about the struggles to defend human dignity in the most degraded of environments, and the relationships she forged with other women in prison.

Also included are a foreword by Ann Hansen, who situates the draconian prison conditions inflicted on the RAF within the context of a global counterinsurgency program that would help spawn the plague of mass incarceration we still face today, an afterword by the late Osvaldo Bayer, and an appendix by J. Smith and André Moncourt summarizing the politics and history of the RAF in the 1970s.

"Margrit Schiller's life story Remembering the Armed Struggle, *is not meant to mark a hard break with the Red Army Faction, but is more of a critical reflection in the spirit of solidarity. Even those who do not share Schiller's perspective well find it interesting to join her as she looks back on her years underground and in prison."*
—*diesseits*

"Schiller's recollections are profoundly honest and to the point. She neither glorifies the Red Army Faction nor does she repent or distance herself from her past."
—*taz*

Turning Money into Rebellion: The Unlikely Story of Denmark's Revolutionary Bank Robbers

Edited by Gabriel Kuhn

ISBN: 978-1-60486-316-1
$19.95   240 pages

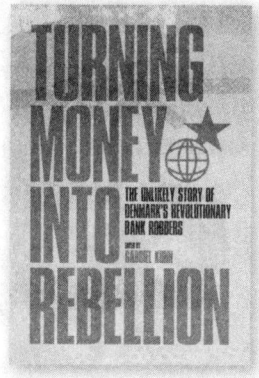

Blekingegade is a quiet Copenhagen street. It is also where, in May 1989, the police discovered an apartment that had served Denmark's most notorious twentieth-century bank robbers as a hideaway for years. The Blekingegade Group members belonged to a communist organization and lived modest lives in the Danish capital. Over a period of almost two decades, they sent millions of dollars acquired in spectacular heists to Third World liberation movements, in particular the Popular Front for the Liberation of Palestine (PFLP). In May 1991, seven of them were convicted and went to prison.

The story of the Blekingegade Group is one of the most puzzling and captivating chapters from the European anti-imperialist milieu of the 1970s and '80s. *Turning Money into Rebellion: The Unlikely Story of Denmark's Revolutionary Bank Robbers* is the first-ever account of the story in English, covering a fascinating journey from anti-war demonstrations in the late 1960s via travels to Middle Eastern capitals and African refugee camps to the group's fateful last robbery that earned them a record haul and left a police officer dead.

The book includes historical documents, illustrations, and an exclusive interview with Torkil Lauesen and Jan Weimann, two of the group's longest-standing members. It is a compelling tale of turning radical theory into action and concerns analysis and strategy as much as morality and political practice. Perhaps most importantly, it revolves around the cardinal question of revolutionary politics: What to do, and how to do it?

"This book is a fascinating and bracing account of how a group of communists in Denmark sought to aid the peoples of the Third World in their struggles against imperialism and the dire poverty that comes with it. The book contains many valuable lessons as to the practicalities of effective international solidarity, but just as importantly, it is a testament to the intellectual courage of the Blekingegade Group."
—Zak Cope, author of *Dimensions of Prejudice: Towards a Political Economy of Bigotry*

"The story of how some pro-Palestinian activists become Denmark's most successful bank robbers is more exciting than any thriller."
—Åsa Linderborg, *Aftonbladet*

Prison Round Trip

Klaus Viehmann with a Preface by Bill Dunne and an Introduction by Gabriel Kuhn

ISBN: 978-1-60486-082-5
$4.95   28 pages

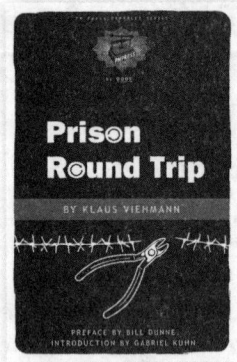

Bang. The door to your cell is shut. You have survived the arrest, you are mad that you weren't more careful, you worry that they will get others too, you wonder what will happen to your group and whether a lawyer has been called yet—of course you show none of this. The weapon, the fake papers, your own clothes, all gone. The prison garb and the shoes they've thrown at you are too big—maybe because they want to play silly games with you, maybe because they really blow "terrorists" out of proportion in their minds—and the control over your own appearance taken out of your hands. You look around, trying to get an understanding of where you'll spend the next few years of your life.

Prison Round Trip was first published in German in 2003 as "Einmal Knast und zurück." The essay's author, Klaus Viehmann, had been released from prison ten years earlier, after completing a 15-year sentence for his involvement in urban guerilla activities in Germany in the 1970s. The essay was subsequently reprinted in various forums. It is a reflection on prison life and on how to keep one's sanity and political integrity within the hostile and oppressive prison environment; "survival strategies" are its central theme.

"Einmal Knast und zurück" soon found an audience extending beyond Germany's borders. Thanks to translations by comrades and radical distribution networks, it has since been eagerly discussed amongst political prisoners from Spain to Greece. This is the first time the text is available to a wider English-speaking audience.

"Klaus's take on survival strategy tells us we can not only survive thusly but can as well continue to serve the cause of liberation—which are really the same thing. We can be captured without giving in or giving up."
—From the Preface by North American political prisoner Bill Dunne

From Hash Rebels to Urban Guerrillas: A Documentary History of the 2nd of June Movement

Edited by Roman Danyluk and Gabriel Kuhn

ISBN: 979-8-88744-061-3
$29.95   456 pages

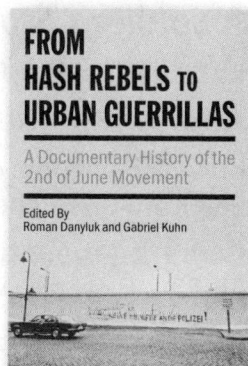

In the early 1970s, across the Americas and Western Europe, armed groups emerged out of the social movements of the late 1960s. In Germany, the Red Army Faction received most attention, but a less well-known, antiauthoritarian counterpart operated in its shadows: the 2nd of June Movement, named after the date when, in 1967, a Berlin cop killed the unarmed student Benno Ohnesorg during a demonstration. The group was composed of working-class youth who got politicized in Berlin's underground culture. They first emerged as a political collective under the name "Hash Rebels" before forming the 2nd of June Movement as a revolutionary organization. After the group's dissolution in 1980, its principles lived on in the militant network of the Revolutionary Cells and the German autonomist movement.

From Hash Rebels to Urban Guerrillas, the first book to present the 2nd of June Movement in English, documents the group's history and politics through translations of original documents and reflections by former members. This is mandatory reading for anyone interested in the politics of the era and the ongoing quest to challenge the rule of the state and capital.

"In the 1970s, the 2nd of June Movement had many fans among the left. It was the guerrilla group with the human face, denounced by the Red Army Faction as 'hippie lumpen.'"
—*taz*

"This well-structured book allows us to revisit—and rethink—the politics, practice, and consequences of the radical left-wing opposition during the 1970s in West Germany."
Geronimo, author of *Fire and Flames: A History of the German Autonomist Movement*

"Ten bank robberies, a bombing, resisting arrest, illegal possession of firearms. The defendants? Members of the criminal organization '2nd of June Movement.'"
—*Der Spiegel*

"No urban guerilla is no solution either."
—graffiti, Berlin

A Soldier's Story: Revolutionary Writings by a New Afrikan Anarchist, Third Edition

Kuwasi Balagoon, edited by Matt Meyer and Karl Kersplebedeb

ISBN: 978-1-62963-377-0
$19.95   272 pages

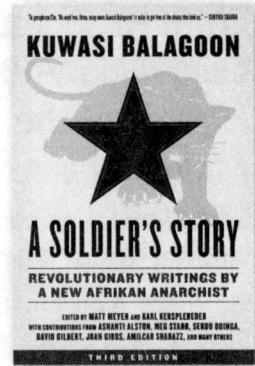

Kuwasi Balagoon was a participant in the Black Liberation struggle from the 1960s until his death in prison in 1986. A member of the Black Panther Party and defendant in the infamous Panther 21 case, Balagoon went underground with the Black Liberation Army (BLA). Captured and convicted of various crimes against the state, he spent much of the 1970s in prison, escaping twice. After each escape, he went underground and resumed BLA activity.

Balagoon was unusual for his time in several ways. He combined anarchism with Black nationalism, he broke the rules of sexual and political conformity that surrounded him, he took up arms against the white-supremacist state—all the while never shying away from developing his own criticisms of the weaknesses within the movements. His eloquent trial statements and political writings, as much as his poetry and excerpts from his prison letters, are all testimony to a sharp and iconoclastic revolutionary who was willing to make hard choices and fully accept the consequences.

Balagoon was captured for the last time in December 1981, charged with participating in an armored truck expropriation in West Nyack, New York, an action in which two police officers and a money courier were killed. Convicted and sentenced to life imprisonment, he died of an AIDS-related illness on December 13, 1986.

The first part of this book consists of contributions by those who knew or were touched by Balagoon. The second section consists of court statements and essays by Balagoon himself, including several documents that were absent from previous editions and have never been published before. The third consists of excerpts from letters Balagoon wrote from prison. A final fourth section consists of a historical essay by Akinyele Umoja and an extensive intergenerational roundtable discussion of the significance of Balagoon's life and thoughts today.

"We have to get our jewels where we can, for this is how we carry on from one generation to the next—it's revolutionary cross-pollination. To paraphrase Che, we need one, two, three, many more Kuwasi Balagoons in order to get free of the chains that bind us."
—Sanyika Shakur, author of *Stand Up, Struggle Forward*